WINSLOW HOMER

A Portrait

Other books by Jean Gould

YOUNG MARINER MELVILLE

THAT DUNBAR BOY

A GOOD FIGHT

WINSLOW HOMER

A Portrait

BY JEAN GOULD

With forty-six illustrations

DODD, MEAD & COMPANY
New York

TO

Esther Rolick

A PAINTERLY PAINTER
WITH THE STRONG CONVICTIONS
OF A HOMER,
POET AND PAINTER ALIKE

CONTENTS

ILLUSTRATIONS

WINSLOW HOMER

A Portrait

CHAPTER I

The Hermit of
Prout's Neck

1902

THE STORM HAD ABATED AT LAST. LONG ROLLING WAVES STILL pounded the Maine coastline and broke in showers of white foam against the dark, brooding rocks. A soft gray sky, streaked with low-lying strips of pink and suffused gold where it was already beginning to clear, gave promise that the end of violence was near. A fine sheet of rain dropped quietly into the water. On the cliff, from a studio house with a wide upper balcony looking out to sea, an old man of medium build, covered by oilskins from head to foot, came hurriedly out of the door and scrambled down along the deserted beach, leaping the rocky crags with an agility that bespoke a familiarity with every hazard along the way. Purposefully he hurried on, pausing now and then to suck in deep draughts of the early morning air. Under his oilskins he carried a paintbox and brushes. His palette had been set for some time.

Presently he came to a portable wooden booth with a wide pane of glass across the front of it, which he had built for use on the water's edge. His hazel eyes were alert as he scanned the sky, the sea, and the gleams of color on the rocks: this was exactly the light he wanted! He went into the booth, where he was sheltered against the spray and the gusts of wind which returned every now and then, and picking up the prepared palette, began to work on the canvas that stood on the easel. He painted with a decisive stroke, carefully, with monumental concentration; oh, the light—if he could catch it!

He had been waiting months for such a moment as this, and now that it had come, he was not going to let the effect slip through his painter's fingers. His aim was to reproduce the seascape exactly as it appeared, and nothing was to stop him. He, Winslow Homer, who had won a reputation for "naturalism" (he objected to the term, but he wished to continue painting as he had always chosen to paint), was carrying out his resolution to recapture the sea in all its moods.

He painted quickly for ten minutes, catching the light. As a rule, he would have stopped then, but today he continued steadily for more than an hour, filling in the rest of the subtle scene—the jutting rocks, piled high with that strange vegetation left by the tempest, tangled masses of seaweed mixed with the refuse of the deep. It was a pearl-gray picture in tone, one that caught the peacefulness of early morning after a storm, the awakening to calm following the great stress. It was his way of expressing, through nature, the longing of man to achieve those moments of great peace in life. He did not know whether anyone would understand this painting, but he had to keep the color muted, as he saw it. Most people never got up early enough to see this light.

Later he would hang the picture on the upper balcony of his studio and go down by the sea seventy-five feet away and look at it, scrutinizing it with his practiced eye to see 'the least thing that is out,' as he explained to John Beatty, Director of the Carnegie Institute in Pittsburgh who was a close friend of his, though they did not see each other often.

Winslow Homer saw few people at any time and for several months of the year lived entirely alone on the barren stretch of

Early Morning After a Storm at Sea

The Cleveland Museum of Art, Gift from J. H. Wade

land known as Prout's Neck, which stuck out into the ocean, weather-beaten and sturdy. In the summer his brother and sister-in-law, Charles and Mattie, came to stay in the 'big' house they had bought years before; and sometimes his younger brother, Arthur, still traveled from Texas with his family to spend some weeks at the resort. The Homers owned a good many cottages, and Winslow had looked after the rentals of these for years, to augment his income. He hated to see the 'summer people' come, however, because they took away his solitude, his ability to concentrate. So many chattering females in the summer colony!

The few natives who lived at Prout's Neck, mostly fisherfolk or farmers, were his friends, simple people who knew little of art or culture but loved the spot that was their home in spite of its ruggedness and the struggle against the mighty sea, which often enough brought them disaster. While their crochety neighbor was busy painting that sea in all its aspects, he did not discuss his profession with his friends, and they were not prying. Some of their children were occasionally permitted to watch him paint if they stood quietly, but as a rule he discouraged anyone from approaching his studio. He was known as a "character" by the summer people, but their opinion did not concern him.

He was elated when he finished his work on this particular morning. He would write Knoedler's, the gallery which exhibited his paintings in New York, as well as O'Brien, his Chicago agent, that the picture he had been promising for almost two years was nearing completion. He would write as he felt—that this was the best picture of the sea he had painted so far. It was eloquent, yet restrained and subtle. It contained the mystery of the sea, if one had the eye to perceive the riddle. The last time he had worked on it was on his birthday, the 24th of February the winter before. A whole summer had gone by, and the light he wanted had not come; now, in the fall, heaven had sent him what he had been watching for.

A slight mist stood in the air when he came out of the booth, but, he figured, by midday it should be all cleared off. He snapped the padlock on the door and started back toward his studio. If he had been the kind of man who was given to song, he would have hummed a tune as he went briskly along the coast, leaping when necessary. His leathery face, wrinkled and weather-beaten as the gnarled trees and shrubs that grew out of the crevices, was usually taciturn; a bushy mustache hid his rare smile; but often a glint of humor gleamed from his eyes though his features remained immobile.

He made his way up the path to the house through the huckle-berry bushes that had always grown there; he had planted his flower garden, in which he took great pride during the summer, at the side, choosing to let the front yard stay covered by the native shrub. Removing the ax that leaned against the door—the sign that he was out—he stood it against the jamb, a sign to the postman (the only person likely to come by, and then only if there was any mail to be delivered) that he was in and would shout, in answer to the mailman's knock, "Leave it on the step, please!" He never interrupted his work to open the door.

He went into the little house, which consisted of an attic bed-room across the top floor, now a storage place, and two rooms on the ground floor, the only ones he had used for several years. One of them was taken up almost completely by a sixteen-foot birch-bark canoe, "beached" for the winter in a room twenty-two by seventeen. The other, considerably larger, was his studio-living room. It was more like a workshop than anything else. He crossed immediately to the small, potbellied stove in the center and shook down the low fire that was glowing against the chill October winds. (This was his sole means of heat during the winter months he spent at Prout's Neck.) He would have breakfast now, when he could really enjoy it. He got down a pewter coffeepot from the shelf, filled it with water from a pail near the door, and set it on the stove lid to boil. The studio was bare of furniture save for a large table, covered with tubes of paint, brushes, and other artist's supplies; an old horsehair sofa used as a bed; and two or three chairs, placed near the stove.

A few sketches hung on the walls, as well as guns and fishing rods. On an easel near the table stood a painting of a young girl.

It was an arresting portrait, one he had painted a lifetime ago and recently put up, not to rework, but merely to gaze upon now and then. The girl was sandy-haired, with a fresh, round face, a determined mouth, and a hint of vexation as well as teasing in her eyes. She was sitting barefoot in a meadow, one hand holding up a spread of cards, fanwise, and the back of the other on her hip, suggesting impishness and impatience. Below, the legend read, "Shall I Tell Your Fortune?"

To the infrequent visitors who came to the studio he made no mention of the canvas or, if comment was made, offered the brief explanation, "An early painting." The members of his family, who occasionally came round in the summer, knew better than to ask questions. (The summer before, Charles had tried to prod him about the picture he had just completed: Winslow had the canvas and palette all prepared, but day after day passed and he had done no painting. When Charlie kept asking why he didn't do something, he always said in a good-natured tone, but firmly, "Mind your own business." And after a while his brother realized that he was waiting for a certain effect in light and weather—the one he had found this morning.) The hidden story in the painting of the young girl belonged to Winslow's personal life, and his family respected his privacy. His secret belonged to him.

When the coffee was done, he drank a cup slowly and ate a hard "heel" of bread; soon he would have to make a trip to Scarboro, four miles away, for supplies. His breakfast over, he allowed himself one pipe and set off for the cottage to the left of his, carpenter tools in hand; it was one he rented out, and he wanted to make some repairs before closing it for the winter. He unlocked the door with a rusty key and entered the living room. It was a typical summer cottage, furnished with odds and ends in the usual resort manner; but on the walls hung a dozen or more brilliant water colors he had painted on two trips to the West Indies some years before. They were among his finest work, but

The Artist at His Easel

he "threw them in" with the rental of the cottage because he didn't want to sell them. The summer guests who lived here could look on scenes of the Bahamas, dazzling sunlight and splashes of color, picturesque native Negro figures, and the deep blue Caribbean, all depicted by the master hand of a famous artist, yet he charged no more for this than for any other cottage.

He no longer had the strength to do as much building and carpentering as he had in former years when he took care of the summer places. Even the year before, in 1901, he had built a stone wall in front of this one and signed it with a large "H" near the entrance. Next to the signature he stuck a photograph of himself with the inscription, "This poor old man seen here is Winslow Homer." Now, after he had put up a shelf and repaired a floor board, he felt tired and had to rest. He took his pipe from his pocket, filled it with slow deliberate movements of his bony fingers, and went outside again to contemplate the sea. It was growing calmer all the time in the clearing air, and sunshine was beginning to sparkle in the blue-green depths.

He sat down on a large boulder near the edge of the cliff and puffed contentedly on his pipe. With Yankee practicality, he started figuring the price he would set on his latest work; he would ask $5000 for it, he decided—$4000 to go to the artist, and not a penny less. If Knoedler, or O'Brien, for whom he had painted it, could not get that much for it, he would keep the painting himself. He had waited so long for the right cast in the sky that it brought him a deep feeling of reward merely to realize he had attained it at last. He did not know how many years he had left in the world; the Homers were noted for longevity, but even if he did not live to the age of eighty-nine, as his father had, he would feel that he had accomplished his goal if he could interpret the undying mystery of the great expanse of water stretching out below the cliff by painting it over and over, in one light or another, until he died. Two years before he had spent his energies on the sunset, "working very hard every day from 4:30 to 4:40 P.M." and no more, since the light in those ten minutes or so was all he was after. He gazed out over the receding waters.

No matter what happened in the crowded areas of the earth, the ocean, like the constellations in the sky, maintained a pattern in the rotating of the tides that was changeless beneath its ever-changing aspects; despite the fury of the recent storm, the rhythm of the tides had not altered. It was linked to the moon, controlled by the satellite revolving about the sun . . . "kissing the moon," the fishermen said when the crest of a wave appeared to brush gently across the face of the mistress of the sea shining from the sky. It was as if the ocean, and those who lived by it, himself among them, were wedded to the moon, bound to a pale body that gave little warmth. As he sat musing, his life streamed before him, pictures rising out of the deep with a three-dimensional quality, as if he were viewing an exhibition in the eternal gallery of the past.

CHAPTER II

Boston Boy

1836-1853

THE FIRST PICTURE HE SAW WAS ONE OF HIS MOTHER, STANDING before a large easel, brush in hand, her handsome figure nearly covered by a neat, starched pinafore; studying the flower painting in front of her, she put her head a little on one side, a slight frown of concentration creasing her serene brow. She was so intent on reproducing, with botanical exactness, the spray of brilliant red poppies on the table beside her that she seemed scarcely to notice the small boy seated on a hassock at her feet, his elbows resting on his knees and hand cupping his chin, watching her attentively. Throughout her married life Henrietta Homer spent any leisure moments she had in painting water colors, an art she had learned in the young ladies' school she had attended in Cambridge during her teens. Unlike her classmates, she had not used her talents merely as a means toward marriage, but had pursued an artistic career in between household duties and through pregnancies, occasionally exhibiting her work in professional shows. Before Winslow was born, she had painted up almost to the end. One of the many family cousins years later took delight in telling everyone, "He got it all from his mother. She was always painting pictures. I went to see her *just* before Winslow was born, and

10

she had on a big pinafore and was standing before a large easel, painting."

However little sign she may have given, Henrietta was well aware that her second son found a fascination in watching her paint which his brother Charles, two years older, had not shown, and she was pleased. If one of the boys inherited her talent, he might have more chance, being a male, of developing it on a professional level. Not that he could ever earn his living by artistic endeavor—that would be too much to expect—but the possibility of his receiving recognition would be far greater than hers had been with her water-color painting, which was still considered little more than a ladylike accomplishment. She put her heart and soul into delineating each petal and leaf of the poppies exactly as it appeared, and her arrangements showed a true sense of design; yet if she decided to show the picture in the fall exhibition of the Boston Athenaeum, it would probably make no greater impression than the study she had submitted seven years earlier, in 1836, some months after Winslow was born.

They had been living in Boston then, in a narrow house at 25 Friend Street, but before long moved to a roomier place near Bowdoin Square. As soon as Winslow could walk, he followed his mother around—when he was not tagging after his older brother Charlie—and if she wanted him to be still, all she had to do was to start painting, and he would be indefinitely entertained, watching her quietly. By the time he was three or four, he wanted to "draw, too," a wish his parents gratified a few years later by giving him a set of crayons, which he put to immediate use by coloring the illustrations and prints in *Ballou's* or other pictorials brought into the house occasionally by his father.

Charles Savage Homer, like other members of his family, had gone into business for himself when he became of age, and by the time he was courting the "dressy" Miss Henrietta Maria Benson of Cambridge, whose family were considered "very stylish folks," he was esteemed a solid citizen who had established a brisk trade importing hardware. Good-looking, genial, he was a pleasant father who took an interest in his children but never an over-weening one; he seemed, rather, a little remote by reason of his frequent travels abroad in connection with his hardware importations. To Winslow, both parents seemed Olympian only by reason of parental authority; otherwise he thought of them as two friendly beings with feet of clay. If he looked up to his mother more, it was because he felt a deep, instinctive admiration for her talent, a subconscious identity with her ability to draw.

The peaceful quiet of the morning room, which served as Henrietta's studio because of its north light, was broken by a loud banging of the side door and a rush of feet up the half flight of "cellar" steps, and then his brother Charles stood in the doorway.

"Win . . . we need you . . . for Beetle 'n Wedge!" Charlie was out of breath, his hair awry under his round cap; one leg of his dungarees had fallen down to his ankle; the other was still rolled up.

Win's first impulse was to jump up and join his brother; ever since they had moved to Cambridge the year before—right after 'the baby,' Arthur, was born—he had loved nothing more than playing in the wide, flower-strewn meadows just outside the village; but he hated to leave his place beside his mother right now, when she was beginning to round out the red poppies, and the whole picture was taking form, coming to life like magic under the strokes of her brush.

"Come on, Win!" Charlie was on his way out already.

"Will you be painting long, Mother?" Winslow asked her hopefully.

Henrietta understood his conflict, and as a wail arose from a crib in the downstairs bedroom off the dining room, she laughed good-naturedly. "From the sound of things, I'll be painting *again!* Thanks to Charlie's shouts, I must look after the baby now. So run along and play if you like." She began rinsing the brushes quickly and emptying into a basin the small cups of water she used for different colors.

Winslow needed no further indication that she was going to stop, and he was off the hassock, running for the door, grabbing his round boy's hat from a peg on the hall tree as he went, before she had finished cleaning up.

"Coming, Charlie!" he called, sprinting after his brother, who was halfway down Main Street where the Homers lived, close to the edge of town.

As they approached the open fields he slowed down to a walk.

"I'm not going to hurry any more," he balked. "I'll have to be beetle anyway, I suppose." He was referring to the role of the mallet, or "beetle," he would have to play in the game—a human hammer!

Charlie nodded. "You're the smallest. I'll have to be the wedge; that's harder. Come on, Win!" He dashed ahead.

But Winslow refused to be goaded. He took his time, pausing to pluck a stalk of butterfly weed and pinch its red stem to see the milk ooze out. From the corner of his eye he saw Charlie reach the others—his Benson cousins—and the three now hustling him; farther down the meadow, two little girls were picking daisies. He still moved slowly through the grass, stopped again to look up at the blue sky and let the summer breeze brush against his cheeks, and finally ambled up to the trio.

"It's about time!" the boys grumbled, but he only smiled.

His cousins grabbed hold of him on either side, each one taking him by an arm and a leg and hoisting him into the air. In this spread-eagle position he braced himself to be hurled violently against Charlie, who, as the "wedge," squatted down on all fours in the grass and braced himself against the impact.

During the moment of suspension in mid-air, just before he was sent crashing against his brother, Winslow, like all "beetles," felt his muscles go stiff with tension, his eyes roll apprehensively to one side in an effort to gauge the distance between himself and Charlie—and the ground, in case his cousins should happen to lose the grip and drop him. The feeling never crystallized into actual fear because the wham! of collision took place almost immediately, but for an instant which seemed like an eternity the quiver of life force held sway and he was caught by mixed sensations of strength, joy, and terror. It was a moment that might impress itself on any boy's mind, and Winslow Homer possessed an inner capacity to record life's poignancy with the sensitivity of a dry-point etching.

When autumn came, the Homer boys attended a one-room village schoolhouse, within whose flaking clapboard walls a pretty young teacher tried in vain to keep order among pupils of all ages. At first Winslow sat with Charlie on one of the wooden benches on either side of long wooden tables placed rectangularly around the room, but he was soon moved to another table among beginning readers. In the center of the rectangle stood the teacher's desk—hardly more than a frame box set on sawhorses—providing a view of most of her charges at once. She usually placed girls at the bench behind her back as they were inclined to be more studious and quieter than boys. On the wall at one end of the room, between two windows, hung a smudgy blackboard, and at the other end the inevitable map of the United States—somewhat streaked with soot from the coal stove that heated the schoolhouse after the frost set in. Otherwise the walls were bare; the only "pictures" Winslow could see were those of the distant hills, framed by the windows.

He looked out at them very often. While he was not actually noisy, Winslow Homer was no student; learning lessons and reciting them by rote, parrot fashion with the other pupils, bored him from the beginning. Schoolwork was easy, but it did not interest him particularly. And he had his own quiet way of creating a disturbance. Like the other boys, he decorated his notebooks, and texts, when he was old enough to be given them; surreptitiously, systematically, the large *O*s would be filled in with faces, the tails of the *Y*s would be elongated with curlycues, and the *T*s would receive double crosses or other flourishes. But

Winslow's embellishments had an extra flair; the face in the *O*
might sport a mustache or a hat perched on the top of the oval;
with a few additions to the crossbar, *T* might become a full-
branched tree and *Y* a slithery snake or a winding river. As he
experimented and grew more experienced, he carried schoolbook
décor a step farther by making sketches in margins, or on the
flyleaf, where there was plenty of space to draw. The others took
to watching him instead of keeping their noses in their own books,
and more than once their craning to see what Win was doing got
him into trouble.

One spring day when he was in the fourth grade, he was gazing
out of the window while he was supposed to be 'doing his sums,'
and he saw an old farmer coming down the road pushing a
wheelbarrow. As he watched, the man stopped a moment to rest,
still holding onto the handles almost as if he was striking a pose.
Automatically Winslow's pencil ceased copying sums and started
sketching the figure outside; he slid down the bench a little to
get a clearer view, attracting the attention of the boys around him.
Ned Wyeth, a neighbor, slid along beside him, and the boy on the
other side hunched closer to see what was going on. With a few
precise, firm lines, Win was putting the final touches on the man's
legs, after which he began on the barrow. He knew nothing of
the laws of perspective, but because he had watched his mother
so often, he did what she would have done—he drew *exactly what
he saw*: an arc of the wheel, the tips of the wooden standards,
and somehow the illusion of the whole was cast. The others
crowded closer with whispered comments or suggestions—any
diversion was welcome during study time.

The teacher, who had been on the opposite side of the room
with her back to them, hearing the five-year-olds recite the ABCs
out loud, now turned around and saw the little huddle around
Winslow. She tiptoed quietly across the floor, and only a loud
"Psst!" from Charlie at the far side of the table warned the boys
of her approach and sent them sliding back to their places.

"Winslow Homer, what are you doing?" She stood above him, exasperation and disapproval on her young face.

He pushed the paper so she could see the drawing—no use hiding it now.

"Wasting paper again! Have you completed your sums?"

He shook his head.

"Can't you speak? Go and stand in the dunce corner!" It was not the first time she had caught him, and he fully expected the command, but as he stood up and started to climb over the bench, she changed her mind. "No, stay where you are. You will remain indoors during noon recess and recite your sums after you have learned them by heart." She had an idea this would be much more of a punishment.

She was right. Winslow sat down abruptly, his face clouded with disappointment, though he uttered no protest. It was an unexpected blow, a real deprivation not to be allowed to play outdoors, especially now when the skies were soft again and the ground springy enough with new grass so you could fall down and hardly feel hurt. He sighed and sought comfort in putting a title and his signature on the drawing he had made. "A Man with a Wheelbarrow," he printed, along with his full name and the date, in precise letters.

When the twelve-o'clock bells sounded in the village tower and the teacher announced crisply, "Noon recess," he watched enviously while the girls and boys ran to get their lunch pails from the table in the corner and rushed outside. Charlie whispered "Too bad" to him on the way, which made him feel some better. After they left, he walked over and picked up his lone pail.

"Couldn't I just eat my lunch outdoors, Miss Abbie?" he asked hopefully as he noticed the teacher standing in the doorway, breathing in the warm, fragrant air.

For a moment it seemed as if she wavered, but she stuck to her guns. "No indeed," she said vigorously, marching back to her desk.

Winslow sighed again and munched his bread and cheese rather mournfully. He would have to be more studious from now on, not because he considered it wrong to draw pictures instead of studying, but he didn't want to be kept indoors. He picked up his arithmetic and tried learning his sums, but the shouts and laughter from outside were too distracting. He could see the boys in formation for Snap the Whip and he longed to be part of the line. Occasionally some girl's pigtails flying from under her sunbonnet went past the window; the girls almost always played tag during recess. He held the book in front of his face and tried to concentrate, but it was almost impossible; the noon hour, which usually flew by, now seemed interminable.

For her part, the teacher appeared as annoyed as her pupil at being confined on a soft, sunny day. She sat at a nearby table, a picture of feminine irritability, looking out of the window and tapping her foot while she waited for him to learn his arithmetic lesson. A frilly white apron covered the front of her black alpaca dress and extended over her bosom in the shape of a heart; her hair was held back by a ribbon, from which a few curls escaped onto her neck. At least she was pretty, and he did not mind looking at her when she called on him to recite.

He was nowhere near ready, however, and made several mistakes, which brought an irate note from the teacher to his father, complaining that Winslow was an idle pupil who spent his time drawing instead of studying.

That night he waited until his father, wearing smoking jacket and house slippers, was comfortably settled in the wing chair by the fireplace and had finished the evening paper. Like most Boston businessmen, Mr. Homer considered perusal of the papers —in the morning at the breakfast table, and in the evening by the astral lamp in the living room—a daily ritual, and woe betide anyone who interrupted his reading. Winslow handed him the note without a word of explanation. Mr. Homer read it through twice, his bushy eyebrows raised in surprise above his bristly mustache. Then he repeated the charge out loud. "Is this true, Winslow?" he asked.

His son nodded. "But I don't feel idle when I'm drawing," he said in self-defense.

"I understand Win's point of view perfectly," Henrietta spoke up suddenly from the wing chair on the opposite side of the fireplace, where she was working on some embroidery.

"No doubt," her husband said with a dry smile. "Drawing is all very well and good as a *pastime*"—he emphasized the word—"but" —he shook his finger at Winslow—"it must not interfere with your studies. If I get one more such report as this, I shall take away your crayons for a month. Is that clear?"

"Yes, sir," Winslow said, half hoping his mother would protest, but she kept still; in matters of discipline her husband's word was law. If his father's edict seemed harsh, Winslow offered no objection; he was well aware that he had got off easy and that most parents of the time would have been far less understanding of his predilection for drawing.

Indeed, his father relented shortly afterward, and on his next buying trip abroad he sent a special present for Winslow from London.

"Package for you, Win," Charlie announced on the day it arrived, and Arthur, who was begnining to enter into things, wanted the privilege of opening it, but the string was too knotted, and in the end their mother had to cut it while the three boys looked on expectantly. Inside was a complete set of lithographs by Julian—line drawings of heads, ears, noses, eyes, faces, trees, houses—and underneath all of these, lithographs of animals by Victor Adam. A real treasure house of "representations"! Winslow's hazel eyes shone; his thin, delicate nostrils quivered with anticipation. His brothers, who had displayed a mild interest in the animal pictures, tried to persuade him to come to the neighborhood kite-launching across the Common, but for once he preferred to stay indoors. He was eager to try his draftsman's hand at making "copies"—to find out exactly how human limbs were drawn and how he could have done better with the hands of the man with the wheelbarrow.

As soon as the summer arrived, all the boys in the neighborhood, including the Homers and their Benson cousins, went barefoot in the fields and woods, waded in the streams, and nearly every day shouldered their fish poles for a hike to Fresh Pond, where the perch and small bass darted in and out of the sunlit water. The boys would plop down on the mossy bank or a rotting log from some fallen tree that hung just above the surface, bait their hooks, and laze for hours, occasionally dangling their feet as well as lines in the water. They spoke little in order not to scare the fish and sometimes dozed in the heat, hatbrims pulled over their eyes, while the dragonflies droned past their ears and the chipmunks chattered in the trees. Sometimes a whole morning or afternoon passed sleepily by without so much as a nibble, but nobody seemed to mind.

Winslow loved fishing above all other recreation. He would get up very early in the morning, sometimes before sunrise, to dig for earthworms in the garden and have a clay potful by the time his brothers and the rest of the household were ready for breakfast. Once in a while his father would allow Charlie and Win to take the hurricane lamp and look for "night crawlers" in the evening after a thundershower. The lure of fishing was to last all of his life. His uncle, James Homer, owned a barque which he sailed between New England and the West Indies, providing a colorful background for adventure stories, and once or twice he took the boys fishing in deep water, an experience Winslow cherished for years and which was one of the influences that eventually led him to the sea. (The family history had a salty flavor that intrigued him, from his ancestor Captain John Homer, master and part owner of a trading ship which he plied between Boston and London in the latter half of the seventeenth century,

to Uncle Jim and Grandfather John Benson, now a retired Down-
east storekeeper, but whom Winslow liked to think of as a
"pirate," since he began his career as a merchant in the West
Indies trade.)

The next year the Homers moved to a larger, more comfortable
house in Garden Street, Cambridge, right across from the Common and close to the Washington Elm, which the boys sped past
heedlessly on their way to the Washington Grammar School on
Brattle Street near Harvard Square. The new school was one of
the advantages in moving, Mr. Homer felt; the boys would
receive a more thorough education in this fairly large brick
building, where each grade had its own classroom and each pupil
a separate desk and bench. If possible, he wanted all the boys to
go through Harvard when they had completed the twelve grades
at Washington. Arthur, who was just beginning, would be exposed to a more scholarly training from the start; Charlie, already
a competent student, would be in the upper grades where he
would soon be thinking about college; and here perhaps Winslow
(only two years younger than Charlie and five years older than
Arthur, but still the "middle" child) would settle down to some
real 'learning' and forget his continual drawing—talented though
he was, his father had to admit.

By this time, with the exception of one or two crayon "copies"
he made of his mother's pictures, he always sketched from life—
whatever he saw that struck him—and his subjects reflected the
interests of an eleven-year-old boy, yet his handling of them was
remarkably mature. One afternoon shortly before they moved,
the boys had initiated Arthur into their favorite game; held in a
viselike grip by Charlie and George Benson, he was the hapless
"beetle"; Winslow had expected to be the "wedge", but at the last
minute Ned Wyeth had come up, begging to play, so Win relin-
quished his place to their neighbor. As he sat on the side lines
watching he whipped out the paper and pencil he had recently
taken to carrying around in his pocket.

"Stay that way!" he shouted, beginning to draw. He knew they

Beetle 'n Wedge

couldn't hold the pose for long, so he sketched rapidly; he wanted especially to draw Arthur, poised in mid-air above Ned.

"Come on, Win!" George protested, but Charlie shut him up before he could go any farther by asking, "Tired already, George?"

"*I'm* tired," Arthur put in.

"Just one second longer," Win urged. He had almost finished the foursome. With a few last scratches of his pencil he shaded their faces to denote the sunlit pasture they were playing in. "Go ahead!" he called, and Arthur was brought down, wham! on the backside of Ned Wyeth, who never budged, so they raised Arthur for another blow, and Winslow was able to record a few more details, though he did not ask them to hold still again. He sketched in a few blades of grass, some meadow flowers, and the distant hills while the others went on playing. At the bottom of the page he drew a "Key to the Picture": four tiny cartoons of boys, separated, but in the several positions as they appeared in the drawing above—Arthur, arms and legs apart, suspended by himself in mid-air, Charles and George in their respective stances on either side, but not holding Arthur, and Ned, squatting in the grass. Each cartoon was labeled with the name underneath. (Years later he found the drawing and presented it to Charlie, adding to title, "The Youth of C.S.H., Jr.")

When he showed his mother his latest attempt, she was pleasantly surprised at its graphic quality: little Arthur, his eyes rolling to one side, was quite obviously apprehensive; Charlie's face was hidden by the brim of his hat, but one could see that he and George were both straining to hold Arthur aloft. She did not fully grasp the mastery of weight and movement that the drawing implied for an eleven-year-old artist, but she realized that "Win's talent" was exceptional. She had taken a few lessons in painting after her marriage; perhaps Winslow should be given the opportunity to study art, but that could come later. In the meantime she praised his work and encouraged him to keep on—outside of school hours. His father was still adamant on the subject of studies.

Theoretically Mr. Homer was perhaps correct in his belief that exposure to greater learning and the 'modern methods' of teaching would develop a more scholarly attitude in his second son, but practically it made little change in Win's preference for anything resembling art work. He 'excelled' at making maps, according to his teachers, who in turn made the most of his ability to aid them in presenting geography and history to the class; but he was inclined to neglect other subjects for the sake of drawing. While he was not actually a poor student, he was not as diligent in mathematics and general book learning as his father felt he should be if he was to make his mark in the world.

The value Mr. Homer placed on "opportunities" for his sons was based on ambitions of his own. His hardware business was prospering. The firm of Homer, Gray & Company at 13 Dock Square in Boston, which he had headed at the time of his marriage, had become, through a series of changes in partners and expansion of imports, a name company—"Charles Savage Homer" —in Merchants Row. When he moved the family to Garden Street, he bought new furniture, and Mrs. Homer was able to engage a part-time girl in addition to the 'hired help' who did the heavy work. They did not entertain lavishly but set a good table, at least the equal of their Benson and Homer relatives.

The taste of prosperity, however, led to a desire for more. Stories began to come back from the West in 1849—fabulous tales of prospectors who had become rich overnight in the discovery of gold. Mr. Homer would read excerpts aloud from the paper, and gradually the idea grew on him; if others became wealthy in land investment, so might he. He had caught the gold fever. He began to talk to a few people and before long had formed the Fremont Mining Company. Winslow and the other boys listened to talk of staking claims, routes of travel—through the Isthmus of Panama or around Cape Horn—and one day the delivery wagon came pounding up to the door with two handsome brassbound trunks that their father had bought for his journey. The shiny strips gave promise of riches in the boys' eyes, and the three of them watched with admiration while Mr. Homer opened and packed the trunks. He had already loaded a sailing vessel with mining machinery and sent it around Cape Horn, heading for the Pacific coast. He had decided to take the shorter route himself— across the country to the Isthmus of Panama, and through the canal to California. He had turned his business over to a former partner to raise the cash necessary for the venture and was ready to set out in a few days. It was a tremendous risk but, he was confident, one that would prove worth while. Henrietta, pre-occupied with a new experiment in her work—landscapes—did not think to question his judgment, which she had always trusted. Winslow listened to the mention of far-off places with something like awe, yet he did not express himself like Arthur, who declared enthusiastically that some day he would go West to get rich, too —"just like Papa." There was an air of glamorous adventure in the house for days before and after Mr. Homer left.

It was weeks before they heard from him, but that was to be expected; mail was slow in getting through—often the trains were held up by bandits, who ransacked the mail bags as well as passengers' purses, and many a letter was lost along the way.

Then came upsetting news: when he arrived in California, Mr. Homer wrote at last, he found that his company's claim had been "jumped" by somebody else who got there before him, and so far he had not been able to regain control of the property, although he was trying to do so by every means he knew, and he felt sure he would succeed eventually. More weeks and months went by, and the meager word was always the same—he was still trying to establish his claim and assume control; rumor had it that the false owners had struck gold on the property, and he was not going to give up so easily. But the months lengthened into a whole year, and still he did not return.

In the house on Garden Street, Henrietta and the boys were as confident as Mr. Homer at first. The Benson family, though large, had always been "well-fixed," and neither Henrietta nor her brothers and sisters (of whom there were nine) had ever had to worry about money; and after her marriage, although she had the New England habit of thriftiness, Henrietta did not concern herself with financial affairs. That was her husband's province. However, as the weeks went by, the bank account Mr. Homer had put in her name began to dwindle, and she wondered how long she and the boys would be able to hold out.

For a while they kept up the pretense, even among themselves, that Papa would be successful. But when their mother let the household help go because she could no longer afford the little they cost in wages or food, the boys stopped pretending. As another year set in without their father, they did what they could to help their mother; she had very little time for painting, and no money for materials, but somehow she managed to do a little work in water color even during the most trying times. And when she stood in front of the easel, her face always looked cheerful and serene, though often when she went about the marketing or household tasks, Winslow noticed that it was pinched with worry.

For two long years the seesaw of hope and discouragement bore them up and down. On several occasions it seemed as though Mr. Homer was on the verge of victory, but by the next letter, action on his case had bogged down again, and more delays set in. Winslow's fourteenth birthday passed with little to mark it except a severe late-February snowstorm. The drifts were piled as high as the windows when the boys woke up that morning, and they had to "shovel out," making a narrow path through the white wall of snow from the porch to the street; it was impossible to go farther, and their mother agreed that they could not reach school, so Win's birthday brought an unexpected vacation. He spent the time, after the household chores were done, in making a careful copy of one of his mother's recent land-scapes—a peaceful scene of a bridge leading to an old mill across a country stream.

He still drew pictures during school hours, but he was so quiet that he never got caught any more. Because he was absorbed in what he was doing, he kept to himself a good deal, and the friendly girl who sat next to him received little response to her whispered comments, although he was pleasant enough about loaning his eraser or showing her how to color maps. She considered him "a nice boy, studious, quiet, sedate." Every once in a while, however, he would surprise her with some quizzical remark, made with a perfectly sober face, and it was usually not until after school that she realized how funny the quip had been.

At last Mr. Homer could not hold out any longer, he wrote, and would soon be coming home—news welcomed by the boys and their mother. That he had not been successful didn't seem to matter—the important thing was that he would be home again! But when he arrived, they could not help noticing how worn and shabby he looked as he got out of the stagecoach, carrying only a tattered gripsack tied with a string. There was no sign of the brassbound trunks. Like the mining machinery, they had been sold to defray expenses. Everything had gone down the drain. He would have to start all over again.

Philosophically, he still held that "nothing ventured, nothing gained," and proceeded to borrow a small amount of capital from the relatives on both sides of the family in order to set up a modest hardware business once more. Profits were slow in coming, and then a good portion went into paying off the debt. They were able to keep the house on Garden Street only by cutting corners at every turn. There was no more talk of college education for the boys, although they knew it was a dream their father hated to relinquish.

Charlie and Win joined with a group of Cambridge boys and

girls, including Benson cousins of both sexes, who went on clambakes and hayrides in the summer, attended apple "bees" and
cornhuskings in the autumn, and in the winter skated on Fresh
Pond or piled into sleighs for a ride across icy country roads.
The family finances were too low for weekly "allowances" outside of school expenses, and even those were closely watched.
Every penny counted.

Charlie showed some aptitude for science and, by the time he
received his diploma from high school, was proficient enough to
warrant a try at Harvard; his parents were willing to make a few
more sacrifices to give him higher education if he could manage
to "wiggle through." His reports gave promise that he would.

Mr. Homer had some hopes that his second son would follow
suit. But Win had little liking for academic knowledge. He
wanted to draw.

CHAPTER III

The Grindstone
At Bufford's

1854-1859

MR. HOMER MADE IT QUITE CLEAR THAT WINSLOW WOULD HAVE TO go to work if he did not want to strive for a degree from Harvard. It was unfortunate that there was not more of a future in painting, because the boy had undeniable talent and was happiest when he was drawing. But the family income couldn't support an artist. Win completed his secondary schooling six months after his eighteenth birthday, and his father immediately started casting around for jobs that would be appropriate for his son. He knew several merchants in the clothing industry, and there was always room for one more clerk in a gent's furnishing store; Win's neat, dapper appearance would be an asset to some fashionable shop in Boston.

"As a clerk in a high-class clothing store he should do very well, if he is alert and on his toes," his father told his mother, speaking as if Winslow wasn't anywhere in sight one evening when they were all sitting around the dining-room table after dinner.

"I'm sure Winslow would work hard, whatever he did," was his mother's only comment.

"What do you say, Win?" his father asked him finally.

"If you think I'm suited to it," Winslow said slyly, in an offhand way, which brought little explosive bursts of laughter from Charlie and Arthur, but Mr. Homer failed to catch the joke or let it pass.

"I'll speak to some of my friends in the morning," he promised.

Winslow offered no protest, although he did not care for the prospect of becoming a clerk in a gent's furnishing store. However, his father had impressed them all with the hard fact that they must earn a decent living, and the boy accepted it realistically, as a matter of necessity on his father's part as much as his own. There was an unspoken understanding between the boys and their parents, a bond of reasonableness that tied them closely together, and Win was willing to work at any job if necessary, because he felt secure in the knowledge that his father wouldn't expect it of him except in need.

Fortunately there were no vacancies to be filled in any of the stores at which Mr. Homer had business acquaintances. It was the slack season; perhaps there would be openings in September, when men started buying fall suits, winter overcoats, and fur caps before the snows set in. Winslow was more than content to wait. He wanted to get in some fishing during the summer if possible.

One morning a week or so later his father saw an ad as he was scanning the "Help Wanted" columns in the paper. "Listen to this!" He put down his coffee cup and read aloud: "Boy wanted; apply to Bufford, Lithographer; must have a taste for drawing; no other wanted." He beamed at the family around the breakfast table. "There's a chance for Win!"

Henrietta and the boys nodded; it did seem made to order.

John Bufford was a friend of his, Mr. Homer went on, and a member of the volunteer fire company. The fire department in Cambridge was conducted by public-spirited "gentlemen,"

who had elected Mr. Homer as foreman. It would be a simple
matter to arrange an interview for Winslow. "Get your drawings
together, my boy!" He clapped his son on the shoulder.

Winslow had kept all of his drawings in a neat pile and dated
—from the first crayon reproductions he had made in 1847 to
his recent sketches in 1854. His mother helped him select the
most impressive of the lot, and his father arranged to take him
to see Bufford at the latter's "earliest convenience." As they set
out to catch the omnibus to Boston a few mornings later, his
mother smoothed his tie, and Charlie called, "Good luck, Win!"

The meeting took place in Mr. Bufford's private cubicle of an
office in the front of the establishment, so that Winslow couldn't
see much of the large shop in back. The proprietor was a pomp-
ous-looking man with a brusque manner in doing business. He
needed only a look at the work in front of him and accepted
Winslow on trial for two weeks, during which time he gave
the young artist a number of routine assignments and supervised his drawing. With his native ability, Win 'suited' and was
apprenticed to Bufford's for slightly more than two years—or
until he 'should come of age.' As a rule, apprentices paid $300
for the privilege of learning the craft of lithography, but in view
of his talent, Win's bonus was reduced to $100, which Mr. Homer
considered a handsome favor on Bufford's part. Apprentices received five dollars a week after one year, and the hours at the
shop were from 8 A.M. to 6 P.M. a standard workday. The Homers
felt that their son had been launched in a good profession, one
that had possibilities for advancement.

The picture of Bufford's, the largest lithographic house in the
country, employing over a hundred men at the time Winslow
began his apprenticeship, rose sharply in his mind, so that he
could almost smell the acrid odors of the lithographer's trade.
In the huge room rows of men sat on tall stools at high desks,
bent over their drafting. The place was a beehive of activity,
turning out a broad variety of lithographs, from cards, posters,
and illustrations for sheet music covers to engraved reproductions

of daguerrotypes or of the new methods for portraits, photography, which was the latest invention in the printing field.

Win's first assignment was an illustration for the cover on the sheet music of the popular ballad, "Minnie Clyde," which was all the rage among romantically minded young men and sentimental young ladies who gathered around the spinet for an evening of songs. He drew a moonfaced girl, curls framing her forehead, and ribbons and bows decorating the gathered neckline of her dress across her full (and, he tried to imply, heaving) bosom. His two fellow apprentices, Joseph Foxcroft Cole and Joseph E. Baker, boys about his age, who started when he did and also had artistic learnings, ribbed him about his knowledge of women's fashion and figure. He told them with a remote smile that he had lots of girl cousins—and he also had eyes.

Mr. Bufford worked closely with the boys during the first few weeks, giving special attention to Winslow, whose skillfulness he recognized as unusually promising. He kept all three busy with new assignments, for fresh orders kept coming in, and the house had a reputation for promptness as well as quality. Artists were not allowed to sign their work, since it was the establishment that received the commissions and therefore had a right to be credited for the caliber of the art work involved, in the opinion of the proprietor. With his sharp eye he saw that 'the Homer boy's workmanship' was far superior to the other apprentices' and even exceeded that done by older craftsmen; the more he could do, the better for business, to Bufford's way of thinking, and he began loading him down with most of the pictorial designs that required exacting labor and creativity.

Winslow's natural ability allowed him to complete them all and still have time for quick sketches of his fellow artists in between—pictures he drew for his own amusement, tossing them on the floor carelessly when he finished; sometimes Cole or Baker would pick them up and find a thumbnail portrait of themselves or a slight caricature of the proprietor, with his gold watch chain across his paunchy front, holding the watch in one hand,

and shaking the forefinger of the other at some poor beggar of
an artist who happened to be five minutes late. Long as the
hours were, Bufford expected everyone to be on time and to give
him full measure. Moreover, he was quick to find fault, and if
a drawing was not exactly what he wanted, the artist would hear
about it, even Winslow, whom he considered his star apprentice.

His tongue-lashing could be fierce, and the other two boys
often winced at his words or grew red with anger if he shouted
that a drawing was "all wrong" after they had worked at it several
hours. His tirades never bothered Winslow, however; or at any
rate, he showed no emotion if Bufford didn't approve a piece of
work. His expression hardly changed, his hazel eyes remained
cool and somewhat aloof as he listened to the reasons for rejection, and then he would say in a flat voice, "I'll do it over, Mr.
Bufford," as though the matter was really of no importance.
The other two admired his manner and wished they might be as
poised and unconcerned in such moments.

There was an air about Winslow Homer, the others felt—an
indefinable quality that set him apart. For one thing, although
he was rather short, and delicately built, he had a good figure
and an aristocratic bearing, due, in part, to the fact that he made
a point of holding himself very straight. He noticed right away
that the older men were roundshouldered from bending over
their desks, so he worked standing up half the time in order
not to become stooped. He wore his clothes well and managed
to lend style to a threadbare jacket that was a hand-me-down of
Charlie's altered to fit him. From the top of his well-shaped
head, with its shock of wavy brown hair, down to his small but
agile feet there was a gentility mingled with a sturdiness of spirit
about Winslow Homer that caused Joseph Baker to pronounce
him "a luxurious chap, fine as silk."

The three young hopefuls had adjoining desks at Bufford's, so
they saw a good deal of each other during the long work week.
Cole was interested in becoming a sculptor (an ambition he was
to realize) and Baker had artistic aspirations of some sort.

Winslow had definite ideas of his own, but he said little during the first few months. He was unusually self-sufficient, and there were moments when Baker and Cole felt he "didn't seem to care for anybody," but it was simply because he led an inner life more than an outer one; he was preoccupied rather than unfriendly. His mind was busy with his profession and his dreams for the future. Although he considered the general output at Bufford's, including his own, mere hack work, he was gaining experience in drawing every day and he made the most of it. When he had an assignment he thought worth while and felt he had done it justice, he smuggled his initials onto the "stones" because he didn't want his work to be anonymous. For the present he at least would know what "W. H." stood for, and some day the world would know.

In the meantime he stood through the interminable hours at Bufford's and turned out reams of drawings. It was a treadmill existence. He and his father would catch the omnibus to Boston early every morning and meet every evening to ride back to Cambridge together, sitting on one of the back benches of the open horsecar to capture all the breeze they could. At night he was too tired to do anything more than spend an hour or so on the porch talking to Charlie, and then he went to bed because he had to get up early for the trip to Boston. Not that he minded. The daily ride back and forth furnished the only fresh air he got, except a scant half hour during lunch time, when the three apprentices strolled in the streets near Bufford's, staying out till the last minute to avoid going back into the stifling shop, where the heat, combined with the strong smell of ink and lithographic acid, was suffocating. For Win, who had loved the out-of-doors from the earliest days in Cambridge, it was a hardship to be shut up in a shop almost all day, and he sorely missed the fresh air of the open fields, the spicy fragrance of the woods, and the wonderful water smell that rose from the smallest pond or stream when he sat on the bank with his bamboo pole. He had done precious little fishing since he started his apprenticeship!

Around the middle of the summer he decided, suddenly, after an especially sticky day, that he must do something to remedy the situation. He went to bed right after supper, without even talking things over with Charlie. At three o'clock in the morning his brother heard him moving around softly in the bedroom they shared.

"Win?" Charlie asked, raising himself on one elbow. "Anything wrong?"

"Nope," came the answer out of the semi-darkness. "I'm just going fishing."

Charlie sat up, not sure he had heard correctly. "*Where*—in the washtub?"

Winslow ignored his tone. "I'm hiking out to Fresh Pond. Want to come along?"

If it had been two hours later, Charlie might have been tempted; now he yawned. "No, thanks. I think you must be out of your mind to set out at this hour, but that's your privilege." He lay back on the pillow again and turned over, already half asleep.

Win smiled to himself and slipped out of the room.

By the time he had covered the two and a half miles to Fresh Pond, the first streaks of light and color were beginning to glow in the eastern sky; the "night birds" twittered drowsily and were silent again until the colors grew stronger—layers of lime and lavender and rose that brightened into golden yellow as the sun came up in the center. Win, stretched out on the bank with his fishing pole, watched the wavy reflections in the water as his cork bobber floated in rainbow circles on the surface. He breathed in the soft, sweet air of dawn as if he had just been released from a dungeon, and, indeed, he felt that Bufford's was a prison, in which he was forced to work at slave labor.

He knew his father had had his best interests at heart when he arranged the apprenticeship at Bufford's; it must have appeared to him the perfect solution to the problem of a son who seemed fitted for nothing except the drawing board. He could not have known that Winslow would feel chained to the stone almost from the start: he could not draw what he wanted nor the way he wanted—assignments must all be done according to Bufford's specifications and within too short a time for careful work. Even then, it was often not his own, but reproductions of other artists' work that Winslow had to turn out, sentimental trash, and he hated it. He realized only now, as he lay on the mossy green bank, how much he loathed the evil-smelling shop and its overbearing master to whom he was bound by commercial law. His fellow workers were decent enough, Win thought, but the job itself was deadening, degrading; until this morning he had felt only half alive during the two months he had been at Bufford's.

There was nothing he could do about it, however; he would have to serve his term. After that—he could not plan further, for a sharp tug on his line broke off his thoughts abruptly, and he was busy for the next half an hour landing three good-sized perch. They were really biting this morning . . . before he knew it, the rim of the sun had risen above the color. He would have to hurry if he was to be at Bufford's by eight o'clock! He strung his line with his catch and started back down the road to Cambridge at a dogtrot.

There was no time for his mother to fry the fish for breakfast. His father had already left for the city. Win changed his clothes quickly, gulped down a cup of coffee, and dashed out of the house. If he could just catch the omnibus that was rounding the corner of the Common at the fastest clip the horses could make with the load of passengers they were pulling. . . . A number of people were waiting to get on. With an extra sprint he reached the spot as the last ones were crowding up to the door; he put one foot on the steps, hoping to hook a ride standing up. But before he could shoulder a space for himself, some man at least ten years older, and twice as broad, pushed him off the step with a walking stick; the driver cracked his whip, the horses started up, and the omnibus rolled away.

He had to wait for the next one and was late getting to the shop. When he walked in—outwardly calm and impassive—Mr. Bufford was standing by Winslow's desk, inevitable watch in hand. He had been consulting the other two boys. He was fuming.

"Homer!" His voice trembled with controlled anger. "Where have you been?"

"Fishing," Winslow answered honestly, trying to make it sound as casual as possible.

"Fishing!" The word came out like an explosion in the shop. The artists looked up from their drawing boards and the printers turned from their stones. "Fishing? On my time?" The proprietor nearly dropped his watch as he held it up accusingly, directly under Win's nose. "Don't you realize how late you are?"

Winslow nodded. "I'm sorry, Mr. Bufford. I would have been on time except that I missed the omnibus."

"No apprentice of mine can expect to go fishing and walk in any time he chooses," growled the proprietor. "See that it doesn't happen again, or I shall have to take steps with your father." He snapped the gold lid closed and slipped the watch into the pocket of his checkered vest.

"I won't be late again, Mr. Bufford," was all Winslow would promise, as the proprietor, with a final glare, turned and went back into his cubicle.

As soon as his back was turned, the other two apprentices closed in on Winslow. "What happened? Did you really go fishing?"

"Certainly I did." He eyed them coolly. "And I intend to go often," he added quietly, with a hint of the stubborn determination mixed with ironic humor that came to characterize his actions. Now that he had found a means of escape from the lithographic grindstone at Bufford's, even if only for a few hours before work, he was going to enjoy it to the full. For the rest of the summer he rose before daylight several times a week to make the trek out to Fresh Pond and back before breakfast. When he was through fishing, he shoved his pole under some bushes, leaving it there for the next time. He said nothing to his family about the altercation with his employer, except to complain to Charlie that the man was a slave driver, but he saw to it that he was not more than a minute or two behind the others in getting to his desk, and usually he was there first.

In those early hours, while he waited for a bite and watched the subtle beauty of the sunrise slowly unfold until it became a burst of splendor, he had time to think further of the future and what he was going to do as his lifework. Clearly he was not cut out for the lithographer's trade, and drawing was not enough to give him the deep satisfaction he longed to feel—the serenity his mother derived from her water-color studies of flowers (which surpassed her attempts at oil painting). But he would like to go much farther than his mother had gone in her particular field. Outside rather casual encouragement in the form of crayons and the Julian figure prints, his parents had not given him any tools to develop his talent. His mother, for all her sympathy, had kept her artist's materials sacrosanct; the boys, including Winslow, were not allowed to touch them. They were scarce and expensive, not to be wasted. Winslow did not resent her attitude, if he thought about it at all; he admired and revered his mother. He wanted to show the same devotion toward painting that she did, but he wanted to go beyond it, to include his whole life interest. He was sure of his ability.

He said as much unexpectedly one day during lunch hour, when the three apprentices were looking at a picture in a gallery near their shop. It was a large canvas by Edouard Frère, an interior kitchen scene with a number of figures—a "genre picture," according to Cole, who had taken a few lessons.

Winslow, after looking it over very carefully, selecting details he liked and those he did not, remarked, somewhat to his own surprise, "I'm going to paint."

The others looked interested. It was the first time he had declared himself.

"What kind of work will you do?" Baker asked.

Win pointed to the Frère. "Something like that—only a damned sight better." He said it without conceit, but with such assurance that his companions accepted his statement without question.

And somehow the mere voicing of his dream served to set him on his course, to make him feel more mature. He spoke out in no uncertain terms when he came to a conclusion. In November the three apprentices took to ducking into picture galleries during their lunch hour to escape the sleet and cold, going from the work of one artist to another until they were more confused than enlightened.

"If a man wants to be an artist, he should never look at pictures," Winslow said, wrapping his muffler around his neck as they hurried back to Bufford's after visiting the fall exhibit at the Athenaeum. His tone was half-ironic, but the others were inclined to agree with him at the moment; and from then on he did not go with them most of the time. He had ideas of his own and preferred to walk, shivering, through the Boston streets, observing the city scenes, the amusing little incidents that took place, and the character lines etched in the faces of passers-by. He was storing up "material" for the day when he would be able to do his own work.

With the winter season came a rush of orders for greeting cards, calling cards, "whist" decks, and framing prints suitable for Christmas gifts. Winslow was assigned to do most of the latter, and, although he was copying the works of other artists, he managed to endow his duplications with a certain individuality. One of the extra printers hired for the rush season was a French engraver named Damereau, who complimented Winslow on his drawings.

"Your work has *verité*—truth," he said. "Have you tried to draw on the block?" He was referring to the material for wood engraving, the process generally used for illustrations by publishing companies like Ballou's, for whom he did a good deal of work.

Winslow had a sudden intuition that he had found a chink in

the wall set against his freedom by the lithographer's stone. He said eagerly, "No, but I'd like to learn how to do it." His fine, thin nostrils quivered with anticipation. "Could you show me?"

Damereau, a Parisian, whose white teeth shone from a dashing Vandyke beard, smiled up at the young apprentice. "It is my lifework; by now I should know something—even if I am not the artist," he added. "Would you like to come to my studio some night after the shop closes? Then we will have time."

Winslow needed no second invitation. Before the week was up he made arrangements to stay in town instead of meeting his father after work. It was already dark when he and Damereau came out of Bufford's and walked toward the Ballou Publishing House Building on Winter Street. The gaslights threw fitful shadows across the snow that had been falling all day, and they had to walk carefully to keep from stumbling into drifts. When they reached the Ballou Building and climbed the stairs to Damereau's studio, they found an icy room, bare of furniture except for a workbench and table, strewn with engraver's tools, a few chairs, a cot, and a stove; in one corner was a copper sink, with a hand pump. Damereau lit a sputtering gas jet above it and touched the match to the fire he had laid in the stove.

"Stand over here with me, and you will soon be warm," he said to Winslow. "But don't take your coat off just yet!"

In a surprisingly short time the little stove was glowing, and when they were thawed out, the engraver proceeded to keep his promise. Picking up one of several different-sized blocks on the table, he told Win to run his fingers over the smooth surface.

"Like silk, *non?*" he asked.

Winslow nodded, running his forefinger along the edge of the block.

It was cut of boxwood, Damereau told him, because of the fine grain; it had been polished to brilliance and then coated with white to make it pleasant to work on. The artist had to put his drawing on in reverse—perhaps the most difficult task in the whole technique. Damereau would show him later just how it

was done. Once the drawing was on, the block was turned over
to the engraver, who pared away the white surface with his sharp
cutting tool so that the lines of the drawing stood out in relief.
He went to the table and picked up another block, which he had
recently finished, and Winslow could see that he was a master;
the lines were clean and distinct. When these were inked and
printed, Damereau went on, they reproduced the picture as
the artist had drawn it originally.

He gave Winslow a few practical pointers about drawing directly on the block so that his lines would be suited to cutting
and none of his talent—or very little of it—would be lost in the
process. Some of the artists at *Ballou's* didn't put the drawings
on the block themselves but let a staff man do it, and in that way
more of the "personality" of the artist was missing in the final
product. The original was, in a sense, always destroyed bit by
bit in the different stages of the process; a fine-line drawing was
metamorphosed into a block print; but if the artist himself drew
the lines on the block, and the engraver was a man who knew
his craft, the "feeling" of the original had a much better chance
of being preserved, Damereau said.

It was simple to grasp the idea of engraving, but Winslow
thought his first attempts at drawing on the square of boxwood
were quite awkward. Damereau assured him, however, that
he showed much greater skill than most beginners and that he
would improve with practice. He offered instruction from his
mechanical knowledge. "You must put the lines on *this* way,
and then the engraving is much sharper."

Winslow accepted his suggestions, and in the months that
followed he went to the engraver's studio as often as he could.
He felt as if he had discovered a secret passage out of the prison;
he said nothing to the other apprentices about the plans for escape
he was laying carefully but went about as before—casual, friendly,
slightly preoccupied. He grew a tiny mustache, so slim that
Charlie, who was already sporting waxed ends, made family
jokes about "Win's dirty face" and the boys at work asked if he

had drawn the lines on with charcoal. He informed them all with a good-natured smile that he expected to grow a Vandyke beard as well, if it took till he was ninety. His mustache grew apace, but the beard appeared in little patches on his cheeks and chin, and there it stayed, a strange-looking affair indeed. But he didn't let the stares he received from Baker and Cole bother him in the least.

"My beard is in house lots, isn't it?" he asked complacently, patting the sparse unshaven squares.

His colleagues, laughing, forgot to make fun of it, and they never forgot his droll remark.

He was full of quaint, unexpected quips, a dry humor that poked slyly through his drawings, adding flavor and dash to the most commonplace subjects. Damereau taught him how to prepare drawings for engravings in tone, using pencil and wash instead of pen. He was steadily perfecting his technique, and the engraver encouraged him. When the rush season was over, Winslow had started going to the studio in the Ballou Building during his lunch hour, and he felt right at home in the bare workshoplike room. By spring he knew that he could compete with other free-lance artists, if not surpass them.

But the drudgery at Bufford's went on. In the summer he found relief again by snatching a few hours in early morning to go fishing before work. And, since he was used to the routine, he was able to go out more in the evenings, usually with Charlie and a group of the young people they had known at school. Although he enjoyed the company of girls at parties, he was not interested in any particular one, and he was extremely reserved with them —partly because he had had no sisters and was not used to seeing girls around. One of his cousins, Florence Tryon, was growing up into an exceptionally pretty young lady, and he liked to dance with her at family gatherings; sometimes he confided in her, but that was the extent of his companionship with the opposite sex. His reticence, however, was due mostly to the fact that he was undemonstrative by nature. None of the family, except Arthur, who as the youngest had been somewhat of a pet, was inclined to show affection, much as they might feel it. As dearly as he loved his mother, Winslow could not imagine himself giving her a bear hug the way Arthur did occasionally, even while she was standing at the easel, 'not to be disturbed.'

Winslow was entertained by the sight of a bevy of pretty girls, with their flounces and furebelows, their hoop skirts and French heels, their gay and giddy laughter, but closer contact did not interest him. He was an observer rather than a participant and chose to remain so, at least for the present. He could laugh with everyone else at the cornhusking festival in the fall when one of their old schoolmates uncovered a red ear and ran after the nearest girl to claim the prize of a kiss; but he thought that if he himself would shuck a red ear, he would slip it into the barrel before anybody noticed.

First and foremost, he was concerned with becoming a painter; until he reached his primary goal, he was not going to be distracted by falling in and out of love every other day. He was only six months over twenty; he had plenty of time. Meanwhile, since he had begun the second year at Bufford's, he had been receiving the small stipend handed out by the master every week; and of the little he earned, Winslow was salting away a small sum, planning carefully his next big move.

In all the strong-minded Homer-Benson clan, there was no one so determined as he, mild though he seemed on the surface. On Thanksgiving Day there was a huge family gathering at Grandfather Benson's in Belmont, the next suburb out from Cambridge. The big farmhouse was full to overflowing with three generations of family; besides the lengthened board for the elders and grown children, there was a large round table full of little children. In the evening, after the immense dinner, they always held a family dance, with one of the Benson aunts playing the harpsichord, and everybody, young and old, dancing with whatever steps they happened to know or prefer. Thanksgiving was one of Winslow's favorite holidays, but this year he was hardly aware of the gay goings-on.

Bufford had just told him of a big assignment he was going to get—portraits of the entire Massachusetts State Senate, forty-two of them, to be drawn from photographs for one large print. It was one of the major commissions the lithographing house had ever received, and he was turning it over to Winslow as soon as the photographs came in. Winslow realized that he must be capable indeed or Mr. Bufford would never entrust such an important piece of work to him, an apprentice, in preference to the older, more experienced men in the shop. Now that he had definite proof of his value, he was more anxious than ever to try his wings as a free-lance artist.

When his cousin Flossie suggested that they join in the square dance Charlie was trying to organize, he did so, but he paid no more attention to Charlie's calls for steps than Grandfather Benson, who, with a gold-headed walking stick was doing his rheumatic best to dance a minuet with a nine-year-old granddaughter. Winslow usually entered into the spirit of fun, especially when Charlie was the instigator, but the zest was overshadowed by his greater zeal to get started on his career. Flossie finally led him to the settee in the center hall where they could talk and asked him what the trouble was.

He shrugged, rubbing his patchy beard. "The same old question." He mimicked a painter daubing at a canvas with an imaginary brush. "When?" He was never one to waste time on unnecessary words. He could express himself better by other means.

His cousin smiled at his gestures. "Win, don't you ever think of anything else?"

"Not much; perhaps a few things." He smiled. "But this comes first."

The portraits were completed on the dot and then the assignments returned to regulation designs. As the winter wore on, Winslow grew more impatient with the work. Toward the middle of February it suddenly dawned on him that, although his term of apprenticeship would ordinarily go on for another several months, his contract read "or until he shall come of age," and he was going to be twenty-one in a week! He was not quite as well prepared financially as he had hoped to be, but he would have to take the risk. Damereau would help him, he was sure. . . .

On the twenty-fourth of February he came down to breakfast with his mind made up. After he had received a birthday kiss from his mother, congratulations from his father, and several jokes from Charlie and sixteen-year-old Arthur on "Win's being a man," he patted his Vandyke, which was filling in respectably, and announced, "I'm giving notice at Bufford's today." He spoke quietly, almost casually, but with such resolution as to leave no doubt that he would carry out his intention.

His mother was not surprised; she had known for a long time how discontented he was, and more than once in recent months she had seen the gleam of candelight coming from under the boys' bedroom door until after midnight while Charlie and Win were talking things over in low tones.

His father wanted to know what he intended to do when he left the lithographic house.

"I'm going to be a free-lance artist." His voice made it sound matter-of-fact, but inside Winslow felt as if he had delivered his own emancipation proclamation. His father, beyond a few practical questions, had nothing further to ask.

It was a blow to Mr. Bufford to learn that his star apprentice was leaving, yet he knew that he could not expect so talented a young man to stay; besides, he could make money by taking on a new apprentice at the full fee and saving the salary he would have had to pay Homer. Winslow's fellow workers were genuinely sorry to hear the news; they would miss him. As a memento of the months they had been together, Joseph Baker sketched his portrait before he left. It gave Winslow something of a start to see himself as his colleague saw him: a sensitive young man, with soft wavy hair, a neat mustache, and small, pointed beard, whose clear, thoughtful eyes stared back at him with a rather owlish

Drawing of the Young Homer by J. E. Baker

expression. Baker had done well by the Vandyke, but Winslow wondered whether he was as placid in appearance as his fellow artist had portrayed him.

At lunch time the other two accompanied him to the Ballou Building, where he rented a studio, and Damereau welcomed him to the fraternity of free-lance artists and engravers.

"I feel you will soon be published," the Frenchman said confidently.

When he rode out to Cambridge with his father that night, Winslow felt as if he had been released from bondage. He knew he would have to work hard in order to make a go of it, but he would be on his own; he could do as he chose—as much or as little as he liked; he could choose his own subjects, draw what he wanted to draw; and, when the time came, he could paint, what and when he wanted to paint. He said nothing of this to his father; his face remained mild and impassive, but a great exultation beat in his heart as they cut through the snow going up the walk to their house. His twenty-first birthday was the most memorable of his life: he had not only 'become a man'—he smiled —but a free one!

It was June before his first drawing appeared in *Ballou's Pictorial,* and in the meantime he perfected his method of drawing on the block and he practiced on-the-spot sketching of outdoor as well as indoor scenes, to get a sense of light and movement, a feeling of nature and of action into his drawings. He roamed the streets of Boston, making rapid first drafts; then he would go to the studio and work them over; his lines were bold and precise, his eye true. Now the visual training he had unconsciously absorbed in watching his mother bring out the natural design of flowers with her devotion to exact line of leaf and petal came to the fore, so that his scenes were authentic, "true to life." He worked very hard, but he loved his labor, and he had no master bending over him, telling him what to do. His was no longer a treadmill existence but a supremely individualistic life. When the spring balminess arrived in April, he could spend a whole morning fishing if he felt like it; on the other hand, he could stay up half the night if he wanted to complete a drawing that was pretty well in shape.

His first appearance in *Ballou's Pictorial Drawing Room Companion* was no great departure from the hack work he had been turning out at Bufford's; it was a portrait drawn from a photograph, published in the June sixth issue of the magazine, but it was a beginning, and the editors asked for further contributions. There were certain specifications set forth by the publishers, who prided themselves on the fact that their publications could be "placed in the hands of the wife, the daughter, the son, or any within the sacred circle of home, in perfect confidence that their effect will only prove salutary." There could be no "indelicate allusions," no reference to politics, and no crime stories; very little humor found its way into the pages of the magazine.

Fortunately the restrictions did not affect Winslow's self-expression, because the subjects he selected fell within the prescribed realm. The following week, on June 13, 1857, his first truly creative work, a scene he had sketched on the corner of Washington and Sumner streets one day when he was out with his pencil and pad, attracted by the lively hustle and bustle, was printed in a prominent position with a flattering notice. His father read it aloud while the family was sitting around the table after dinner: "The local view upon this page, drawn expressly for us by Mr. Winslow Homer, a promising young artist of this city, is exceedingly faithful in architectural detail and spirited in character, and represents one of the busiest and most brilliant spots in all Boston."

Mr. Homer held the magazine at arm's length. "That's the Washington-Sumner corner, all right, Win! I never can get across that street without waiting half an hour!" His reaction was typical of *Ballou's* readers, who were delighted with the familiar scene depicted with humor and vitality. Winslow had included the signs of a famous apothecary (Geo. Tompkins), Geo. Turnbull's

Dry Goods Emporium, a jewelry store, and other shops frequented by proper Bostonians, and recognition of the spots added to the charm of his work. Damereau cut most of his drawings, put his name on the block along with Winslow's, and encouraged him to submit more.

Once he had been published, it was easy. He did a whole series of Boston scenes for *Ballou's:* "The Fountain on Boston Common"; "A Boston Watering Cart" (here the horses were pulling the street sprinkler over hot, dusty cobblestones on an August afternoon and one could almost feel the heat); "South Market Street," with its vegetable stalls and milling shoppers; "Immigrants on Arrival at Constitution Wharf" in which the young artist showed a remarkable insight into the emotional conflicts of people arriving in a new land as settlers; "Boston Evening Street Scene at the Corner of Court and Brattle Sts."; and other sights that struck his fancy as he went from one neighborhood to another in the sprawling city. When Charlie graduated from Harvard, Win drew "Class Day at Harvard University" as he watched the ceremonies, and *Ballou's* published it on July 3.

Shortly after he began the series, a new magazine, *Harper's Weekly* ("A Journal of Civilization"), had appeared on the stands, causing a sensation because of its broad policy and the high caliber of its contributors. Cole and Baker, bubbling with excitement, brought an early issue into Winslow's studio; here was a publication by a famous house, opening its doors to illustrators, including in its columns political cartoons and humorous drawings. As Winslow leafed through the pages, he noticed several famous names among the authors—Dickens, Bulwer-Lytton, W. D. Howells—but he did not know the illustrators or artists as well. Looking over their work, he saw no reason why his could not compete and promptly submitted some of the Harvard drawings he had made while wandering about the Yard, attending a football match, and observing the freshman hazing that went on every year. The new magazine accepted the first four drawings he sent in and published them on August 1, under the title "College Life in New England—Freshman and Sophomore," in a two-page double spread!

From then on *Harper's* took everything he sent in and usually gave him a full page, while *Ballou's* rarely granted him more than half. Both publications were eager for his work, and he was kept busy all the time, drawing for one or the other.

It was an interesting life for the young artist, if not a very remunerative one. Although payment from *Harper's* was better than *Ballou's*, Winslow barely managed to make his studio rent and artists' supplies. There was rarely enough for little extras or clothes. When fall came, he decided he needed a new suit, but he had no money to buy the sort he would like. Among the Boston street characters he had come to know by sight was one Monsieur Paunceloup, a conceited and pompous Frenchman, who used to strut along fashionable Washington Street with his top hat and cane and considered himself quite a man about town. Winslow caught him in a typical moment, walking down the street in a high-style suit with a flowered waistcoat, his chest thrown out and his big, waxed mustaches waving rhythmically up and down. It was a delicious likeness, and Damereau wanted Winslow to transfer it to the block, but the young artist had other ideas.

He took the drawing to the custom tailor who made Paunceloup's clothes. The man was delighted with it, particularly for display purposes in his show window.

"What do you want for it?" he asked.

"A suit of clothes," Winslow said.

The deal was made.

He continued to draw the Boston setting—pretty women in stylish crinolines, and men in elegant top hats; but after the first of the year he began to include the country around Cambridge— the scenes with which he had grown up. Winter pastimes, skating on Fresh Pond, sleighing on country roads provided subjects for drawings, and, when the weather grew warmer, riding,

picknicking, and bathing, until the girls complained that Win
was always sketching on excursions. He would only laugh and
go on outlining a hoop skirt lifted by the breeze on the seashore
to display a slim ankle.

In the fall he made the most of the cornhusking, and now
when a young man who uncovered a red ear went after his kiss
from the girl beside him, Winslow put it down on paper. There
were at least forty people in the barn at the husking, and he
included them all in different attitudes, laughing, shouting,
shucking, kissing, in true festival spirit. This year when he accompanied the family to Grandfather Benson's for Thanksgiving,
he took along his drawing pad and pencil; and the next week
Harper's published a 'Thanksgiving Day" spread: "The Dinner"
and "The Dance," showing much the same happy family scene he
had been moping in two years before. How much more content
he was now, even though he was only beginning to do what he
hoped to accomplish. He still did not like to think about the
years at Bufford's.

By spring he began taking trips to nearby towns for new subjects—sometimes on assignment. He did a full-page drawing of
"A Cadet Hop at West Point" for *Harper's* in June; the engraving
was one of grace and movement, evoked by the swirling skirts of
the dancing partners of the young cadets. In August he went to
Newport for the bathing and came back with a series entitled
"August in the Country—the Seashore." A characteristic touch
was a copy of *Harper's Weekly* lying on the sand and artist's
sketches scattered around. It was his way of inconspicuously in-
jecting himself into his work, and he enjoyed a sly poke at himself. The next week he was sent to Cape Cod, to cover an old-
time religious camp meeting for *Ballou's;* when the orgy of
sobbing, praying, chanting sinners proved too raucous, he left
the tent and in one scene depicted himself—slim, short, and
trim in his city suit—standing outside, calmly sketching the
emotional meeting.

The assignment was one of his last for *Ballou's.* They had

decided to give up the *Pictorial Companion* (and other illustrated publications) because the competition from *Harper's* was too great. As there were no other illustrated papers in Boston, and *Harper's* was accepting all his work with requests for more, Winslow made one of his sudden unwavering decisions: he would move to New York, art center of the country. When he told his family of his intentions, they agreed that it would be a wise move although his parents would miss him as they missed Charlie, who had accepted a post as a chemist at the Pacific Cotton Mills in Lawrence. However, Win was twenty-three, a young man with a mind of his own, and certainly the opportunities for artists were greater in New York than Boston.

His mother was confident that he would be successful and pleased at his determination to become a painter; her way of telling him so was to admonish him to get busy so that they could "show" paintings in the same exhibits. His father, as usual, offered practical advice, and Arthur, who had chosen to go into business instead of college, made remarks about the bohemian artists' life in the big city. Charlie, when he received the news, wrote that he would soon visit his brother.

Before Christmas, Win had packed his belongings and boarded the coach for New York. He had the feeling that he was merely going on a trip: New England would always be home.

CHAPTER IV

Front-Line Artist

1859-1866

NEW YORK CITY IN 1859 WAS BEGINNING TO PUSH NORTH TOWARD the open areas where the new Central Park had recently been laid out. Elegant mansions were still being built on lower Fifth Avenue, but some of the nearby older places had been turned into boardinghouses, and in one of these, run by Mrs. Alexander Cushman, at 128 East Sixteenth Street, Winslow found a comfortable but very small room. Mrs. Cushman informed him, however, that the other 'painter-feller' who boarded there, Alfred C. Howland, rented a studio to work in, and perhaps Mr. Homer could do the same. He took her advice and the next day rented a studio in Nassau Street for almost nothing. He was set up, at least for the time being.

His fellow boarders, some five or six 'young gentlemen' about his age, seemed to be as interested in advancing their careers as he in his, particularly Alfred Howland and his brother Henry (a beginning lawyer who would become Judge) and Charles H. Voorhees, the three with whom he was most friendly. With them he went about the city, seeing the sights, visiting the few art galleries there were at the time. More than the pictures, Win loved the smell of the paint and remembered it long afterward, when he had forgotten most of the paintings. The one memorable canvas in those first weeks in New York was William Page's "Venus Rising from the Sea" at the Dusseldorf Gallery; it had a richness, an arresting beauty of flesh tones and color he had not seen before. In Boston people had turned away their heads after one quick look at Page's "Venus," but in New York it was widely discussed, and Winslow Homer studied it long, entranced. The odor of pigment was a fragrance to him and made him pine to work with palette and brush instead of pencil and wash.

Harper's however, kept him busy with drawing assignments, and he needed the money. Yet when they made him an offer to join the staff at an attractive salary, he turned it down. True, he occasionally accepted assignments which he considered hack work, but he did so only to ease the financial strain of the moment, and the choice was his to make. He was not going to let himself be led into artistic bondage a second time. Some fifteen years later, when he was being interviewed by the art critic George W. Sheldon, he still felt so strongly on this score that he was impelled to say, "I declined it"—the job of staff artist—"because I had had a taste of freedom. The slavery at Bufford's was too fresh in my recollection to let me care to bind myself again. From the time that I took my nose off that lithographic stone, I have had no master, and never shall have any."

He enjoyed doing the double-page Christmas drawing for the magazine, showing the contrast of the holiday celebration between the rich and poor. After he had sketched the lavish but genteel merrymaking on lower Fifth Avenue, not far from his boardinghouse, he went up to Fifty-ninth Street and jostled with the Irish squatters and their goats, whose shacks were soon to be shunted off the empty lots bordering the new park. He was sampling the city in all its wide variations of mood and tone; he was young and impressionable—and he had the gift of recording those impressions with startling clarity, insight, and humor.

Although he was already one of *Harper's* leading artists, he decided to attend a drawing school in Brooklyn to increase his facility, so that he would have more time to explore the exciting spheres of oil and water color. The Academy of Design was only three blocks away, on Thirteenth Street, and he enrolled there also, in the night school, for a course given by Professor Cummings. The Academy was supposed to be one of the two best art schools in the country, boasting a fine collection of casts; but as it turned out, Cummings' class had nothing to offer except supervision in copying the plaster arms, legs, hands, feet, and all the rest, a dreary occupation indeed. Winslow, bored with the limitations of the course, soon dropped it for experiment and study on his own.

Shortly after the first of the year he and his boardinghouse companions were taking a respite from Mrs. Cushman's customary corned beef and cabbage on a Saturday night, pooling their funds to have dinner at St. Nicholas' Roadhouse; they had just arrived and were about to go through the swinging doors when the horses of a departing sleigh shied at an oncoming cutter and there was an upset! The young lady in the sleigh went head over heels into a snowbank, skirts flying, ruffled petticoats and pantaloons exposed; her companion flew out in the other direction, and the coachman careened off his box in a third. A small dog rushed up and began to bark furiously. In the midst of the excitement, while the other onlookers were helping to put the passengers back on their feet, and the overturned sleigh back on its runners, Win was outlining a sketch of the lightning impression he had received in the moment of the upset; he would fill in the details—not too many—the next day at his studio. He wished that he had had a longer look, but he could hardly ask his "models" to pose or to take the spill a second time!

The next afternoon, as he was coming out of the tobacconist's shop on fashionable Twenty-third Street across from Madison Square Park, there was a great commotion just ahead of him as a heavy bank of snow slid off the awning of the store on the corner. Some woman was knocked off her feet, catapulted toward the curb into the path of a small pushcart which over-

The Sleighing Season—The Upset

The Cooper Union Museum

turned; men's top hats were sent flying, and passers-by generally were powdered with snow; mingled with the cries of women and the curses of the men were the giggles of a gawky youth, gaping at the upturned skirts. It was an amusing scene, and Win got it down in a flash before he hurried away to his studio.

On January 14 *Harper's* carried two wood engravings—"The Sleighing Season—The Upset" and "A Snowslide in the City"— by the young artist from Boston. He was proving a first-rate on-the-spot reporter, and for the most part the publishers gave him free rein as to subject matter and handling. He drew the New York setting as he had the Boston—little, everyday events lifted out of the commonplace by the artist's eye for poetry of movement, for the frailty of human nature, and for gentle humor. He did not love the city as he did the country, nor did he feel the deep attachment to it; but he had an immense curiosity about life and people, and he knew that this was the best way for him to learn his chosen profession—to work in it, and to earn a reputation for himself, so that when he began to paint, the name of Winslow Homer would not be strange; he would not be an unknown.

The nearest approach to the country was Central Park, toward which he gravitated instinctively. When the winter freeze brought in the skating season, he and his "pals" were among the first to try the ice. Whole families were out, bundled in woolens and furs; gay-colored scarfs blew back on the wind, and mittens flashed brightly as couples crossed arms and skated in pairs. Moppets playing tag darted in and out among the skaters, and their shrieks mingled with the shouts of youths in an improvised game of hockey. After a few turns around the Gentlemen's Pond, as this was called, the young men crossed the park to the Ladies' Pond. Here they had to be content with watching, since the rules read that "no gentlemen are allowed to skate unless they are accompanied by ladies." The scene resembled a ballet, with the swirl of ladies' skirts and the high fashion of men's top hats and canes; Win did not waste time wishing for a girl—he was too busy sketching the sprightly and charming picture.

He returned several times by himself, and the drawing, which appeared in *Harper's*, "Skating on the Ladies' Skating Pond in the Central Park, New York," was one of his most successful to date. It spurred him to try his luck in a different medium; he did a small picture of the same scene in water color and was intrepid enough to enter it in the running for the National Academy's spring show. His first offering to the austere Academy was accepted almost immediately, and if he was surprised, he did not show it, but he was deeply pleased and excited. His work was going to be on exhibit at last; he wrote the news to his family laconically, but he hoped his mother would be proud of his accomplishment.

The park was perhaps the most intriguing novelty of the day, attracting crowds to witness its development in the spring plantings, the spadework for recreation buildings and playgrounds. Winslow made the most of its appeal, and in one of his engravings, published in September, readers of *Harper's* could recognize the slopes in "The Drive in Central Park," where seedlings had recently been set out; he also included a derrick as a realistic note.

Around Thanksgiving he repeated the kind of double spread he had done for the magazine at Christmas time the year before; it was entitled "Thanksgiving Day, 1860—The Two Great Classes of Society—Those who have more dinners than appetites, and those who have more appetites than dinners." Eight panels depicted the wide gap between the feasts of the wealthy and the famine of the poor, some of whom had not even a crust of bread to celebrate the holiday. He covered the city, making notes which he developed in his studio.

It was a nuisance to have to go down to Nassau Street every day in order to work. He had become acquainted with a number of artists who had studio-living quarters in the New York University Building on Washington Square, and when one of them, Eastman Johnson, told him of a vacancy there, he was more than ready to leave Mrs. Cushman's. Alfred Howland had sailed for

France in June, and boardinghouse life was dull at best. Winslow felt at ease with other young artists like himself, struggling to get a foothold, and at this point, preferred their company to any other. He went to inspect the room, and although it was not large, and was located at the top of a long flight of steep stairs, in the tower of the gloomy building, he saw that there was a fine view from the single window and a door opened out onto a flat roof. He rented the place and moved in early in 1861.

He had hardly got his belongings settled when *Harper's*, convinced of his ability as a reporter, commissioned him to go to Washington to cover Lincoln's inauguration. When the president-elect passed through New York on his way to be sworn in, Winslow had drawn him as he addressed a crowd of well-wishers from the balcony of the Astor House, and it seemed fitting that the young artist should carry through at the inaugural ceremonies. This was Winslow Homer's first view of the nation's capital, and he was delighted to have the opportunity for sight-seeing, although he did not have time for a great deal.

On March 16 the cover of *Harper's* featured a full-page drawing of "The Inaugural Procession at Washington, Passing the Gate of the Capitol Grounds." The scene showed Lincoln in an open carriage, flanked by cavalrymen, and statesmen on horseback on both sides. Crowds lined the street, and tall hats waved at the grave, youngish face of the incoming President as he looked to Winslow Homer—a man assuming the tremendous responsibility of settling the slave question by peaceable means if possible; a kindly, homely man, with a short-cropped beard hiding the lower half of his deeply lined face. On an inside page of the same issue, in a close-up of Lincoln and Buchanan entering the Senate chamber before the inauguration, Winslow had portrayed Lincoln as serious, strong almost to the point of stubbornness, his great eyes unyielding in their expression, his bony hands awkwardly holding the papers of his inaugural address. It may not have been a good portrait, but it was an interesting one, and the assignment gave Winslow the impetus to act on his determination to be more than an illustrator.

As soon as he returned to New York, he looked up a genre and landscape painter by the name of Frederic Rondel, who gave lessons in his studio in the Dodsworth Building, near Grace Church. Roswell Shurtleff (usually called "Russell") the landscape painter who lived in the studio below Winslow, and who was already a friend, had recommended Rondel as being right for beginners. While he was not a great painter, he had just been elected an Associate of the National Academy, which indicated that he had some reputation; yet he was not enough of a master to expect his pupils to be his disciples.

There were several other students taking lessons in the big untidy studio in the Dodsworth Building, and Rondel, a Frenchman who, like Damereau, had immigrated to Boston, where he had lived before coming to New York, was showing them how to handle a brush when Winslow joined the group. From the large canvas on the outsize easel he saw that Rondel had an honest approach toward his work in spite of the fact that he painted in the current sentimental style, which omitted or glossed over all realistic detail. He was satisfied that this Frenchman could help him as Damereau had—with practical instruction. For four Saturdays in one month he walked over to the Dodsworth Building, where he learned the rudiments of painting—how to hold the brush in different ways for different strokes; how to set his palette, using the primary colors with white, and raw sienna— a formula he hardly changed throughout his career; how to adjust an easel, how to stretch a canvas. He had watched his mother— and recently his fellow artists, like Russell Shurtleff and Homer Martin—but he had never performed the simplest procedure of painting. His observation stood him in good stead, however; after four or five lessons with Rondel he was ready to start out on his own.

He could not buy his equipment or supplies just yet, because he had used up his small reserve to furnish his studio—if it could be called furnished. A cot, a stove, a battered wardrobe, a few

chairs, a wobbly three-legged stool, and a model stand he had
inherited from the artist who was there before him, which was
of little use as yet, except as additional seating space. However,
the place was his own, all he needed, and no barnier than the
studios of the other eight or ten artists in the building; the loca-
tion in the tower suited his taste to a T, although Charlie, who
came to visit about the time he moved, complained of the long
climb up the steep stairway after mounting two or three flights
of the floors below.

"It's like a stepladder," Charles grumbled as he greeted his
brother. "And what have you got after you get up here?" He
glanced around disparagingly.

"A view"—Win extended his open palm toward the sky and
rooftops beyond the green of Washington Square glimpsed
through the pane of glass—"and a place to paint." He smiled
fondly at his older brother.

Charles offered no more objections. He could see that Win
was content with his surroundings and with his new friends.
The young men in the University Building led a kind of community life of carefree poverty, pooling their resources for an
occasional party, exchanging ideas, loaning each other artists'
supplies, tobacco, or coffee, as the case might be. Evenings they
gathered in one studio or another, and their genial laughter,
singing, and storytelling dispelled the gloom of the dark, clammy
stone structure.

Winslow's tower room was a popular place from the beginning.
On a single night while Charlie was there, a dozen or more artists
and friends dropped in, and most of them stayed. A drawing for
Harper's had to be finished by midnight, but Win invited everybody to come in and meet 'brother Charlie,' all the while keeping
on with his work, under the glare of the gaslight. At one point the
room was blue with tobacco smoke, and the hubbub was so great
that Win, sitting on the model stand working away in the midst
of it all, had to shout, "Here, one of you boys, fill my pipe for
me! I'm too busy to stop." Shurtleff obliged, and Winslow,

with a nod of thanks, clenched the stem in his teeth, scarcely interrupting his labors while the studio chatter rose and bubbled around him.

This was the artist's life, and Win felt completely comfortable in it—that much was clear to Charlie. He was proud of his brother's success in drawing and encouraged him to continue his efforts in painting. He offered to pay for the lessons, but Win had cut him off almost harshly, in heated tones. "No charity, please! If I can't earn my own way, I'll quit the business."

Charlie smiled. It was like Win to refer to his chosen profession in mundane terms in order not to reveal his reverence for it or the depth of his longing to be a good painter; he also disliked any sign of 'arty' tendencies and went out of his way to disenchant rather than glamorize the world of art and artists. His poetic expression of life in his work would never be completely divorced from his Yankee practicality, his strict ideas about earning a decent living, instilled in both boys by their father.

It was summer before he bought his painter's tools—"a tin box containing brushes, colors, oils, and various equipments," including a palette and easel. In the meantime war had been declared, and from his tower window above the "Parade Grounds" of Washington Square, Winslow could look down on the drill sergeant, barking orders at the raw recruits who had volunteered or were persuaded to enlist at the outbreak of war. The marching of trained soldiers could be heard at all hours of the day and night as companies passed through the city on their way to embarkation points downtown at the Battery. There was an immediate demand for news and pictorial reporters at the front, and *Harper's*, like other publications, assigned its artists and writers to various companies to serve throughout a campaign.

Winslow Homer, one of their big names among the artists, was expected to take such a post, but he preferred to remain independent as long as he could, doing one commission at a time on short trips, so that he could come back into New York to put the drawings on the block himself. He had discovered more and more, as Damereau had pointed out in the beginning, that if the lines were transferred by a staff artist, the drawing lost about half the quality of the original, the distinctive flavor which made it the work of a true artist instead of a hack.

His first assignment came on a mild spring day in the middle of May, when the 79th Regiment of the New York State Militia —the colorful Highlanders—paraded through the streets in their kilty outfits, hat streamers flying and bagpipes playing; the full-page drawing of "The 79th" appeared in the May 25, 1861, issue of *Harper's*, but by then Winslow was somewhere on the Potomac, just about to return to New York from his second assignment. On May 24, at the dark hour of 2:00 A.M., he had sketched, under the flare of a torchlight, "The Advance Guard of the Grand Army of the U.S., Crossing the Long Bridge over the Potomac." The endless line of soldiers on horseback stretched as far as the eye could see in the dim light, winding around the curve of the bridge and beyond, pushing ahead slowly but steadily through the darkness toward a fate unknown. It was an impressive yet ominous sight; in it for the first time Winslow sensed the portents of the desperate struggle that would ensue, a feeling he conveyed in swift, sure strokes as he stood by the parapet of the bridge. Back in his studio, he completed his notes, drew the lines on the block, and the engraving was published on the eighth of June.

By then he had locked up his studio and gone up to New England. His parents had recently moved out to Belmont, near the Benson relatives, and he wanted to see the new place; moreover, he needed a vacation and, with the opening blast of summer heat, fresh air. He never realized how much he missed the country until the warm weather came and the city grew stifling—to him, unbearable. He was carrying out his determination to run his life exactly as he wished insofar as was humanly possible. He enjoyed being with his family again, talking shop with his mother about his career, as much as he ever discussed it with anyone; he showed her the supplies he had bought, but he did not ask for instruction or advice in the technique of painting. He felt too deeply on the subject to speak about it. He did some initial experimenting on his own, going off by himself to paint out of doors. He set his palette as Rondel had shown him—white, yellow ochre, red ochre, permanent blue, and raw sienna—and started in. His first attempts pleased him only because they represented the fact that he had begun to paint at last. He showed them to no one except his mother. She understood his problems, discussed them with him like a colleague. She posed as the central figure in a landscape he essayed at Marshfield among the dunes.

To Charlie, who came for a few days of fishing while Win was there, he confided that he had made a beginning and hoped that within a year or so he would see some signs of success. He dropped the information parenthetically one morning as he was preparing a new gut leader and asked Charlie to hand him the hunting knife, mentioning that he had bought a palette knife among other things. Charlie asked for particulars and received enough to let him know that Winslow was moving toward his goal.

At his uncle's house he found his attractive cousins and their friends busy making havelocks for the men at the front; and the sight of a roomful of pretty young ladies, chattering almost as fast as they sewed, but intent on doing their part in the war effort, inspired him to sketch them at their work. Florence teased him for always thinking about 'business,' and the others giggled at the thought of being in a picture, but he admonished them to be still and went on sketching. *Harper's* was delighted with the unusual (and charming) aspect of preparedness and published it as a full cover drawing on June 29, under the title, "The War—Making Havelocks for the Volunteers."

In October he received his first assignment to the front, as a "special artist" for *Harper's,* who supplied him with a letter which read, "The bearer, Mr. Winslow Homer, is a special artist

attached to *Harper's Weekly,* and is at present detailed for duty
with the Army of the Potomac. Commanding generals and other
persons in authority will confer a favor by granting to Mr. Homer
such facilities as the interests of the service will permit for the
discharge of his duties as our artist-correspondent." Hardly
knowing what to expect, he set off with his usual realistic outlook
combined with his artist's sensitivity. He found the Army under
McClellan in camp outside Washington, in process of being re-
organized after its defeat at Bull Run; and for the next few
weeks, attached to the military staff of Colonel Francis C. Barlow,
he received a thorough taste of army camp life, living with the
soldiers, sharing their hardships and their jokes, their routine
duties and nightly recreation, making friends with men of every
stripe, from officers to orderlies, from army teamsters to Zouaves,
always sketching, sketching. Although he asked for no favors
because of his profession, Colonel Barlow, who took an immediate
liking to him, was extremely co-operative and did all he could
to "facilitate" (and later to promote) the young artist's work.
Winslow, embarrassed at times by the extra attention, occasionally
poked fun at himself on his job; once he drew a portrait of the
artist, sitting on a cannon barrel sketching furiously, and labeled
it "Our Special"; at another time he drew himself, a dapper little
figure, doing—in contrast—full-length likenesses of two giants
from the western regiment. The soldiers, reputedly six feet seven
in height, dwarfed him completely.

Army camp life in the war, he found, had little glory and less
excitement; tent inspection, drilling, rifle practice, three mess
calls, with trips to the sutler's tent in between, for those who
could afford his delicacies of herring and hard cider, pie and
cheese—such activity made up the day. At night the men might
gather around a bivouac fire, or huddle inside a hut, playing
cards or outdoing each other with tall tales of love and adventure.
Soldiers always seemed to be hungry and thirsty and were con-
tinually arguing or quarreling. On the other hand, there were
moments of sheer fun, of quiet humor, of drama touched with

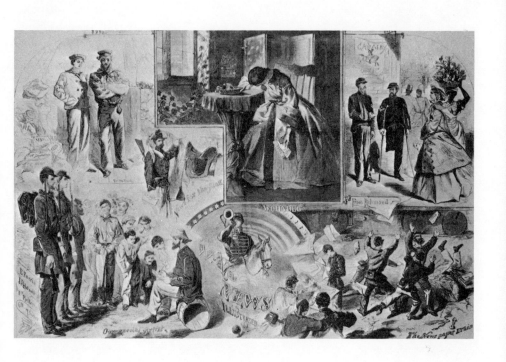

News from the War

The Cooper Union Museum

Civil War Sketches

The Cooper Union Museum

pathos—and all of it was grist to the artist's mill of Winslow Homer. Unlike his colleagues, he made no attempt to gloss over the primitiveness of army life or to draw paradelike pictures of the men in drill formation; he presented the human side of military training, as he saw and felt it.

On one of the first evenings, as they were sitting around the bivouac fire, gazing with bored fascination at the leaping flames, having exhausted the meager supply of news from the fighting line, a Negro wagoner began strumming on a banjo, and somebody called to the cook, who was a jolly fellow, "Give us a dance, Sam!" He jumped up to oblige, performing a shuffle in perfect rhythm, moving in a circle around the fire, his hands spread out, his wooly head dark above the red glow. Winslow caught the scene as it occurred, missing none of its picturesque quality— the quaint, dancing figure, the lights and shadows cast by the fire on the faces of the men and the surrounding tents, the dim glow of cloudy moonlight in the background.

He had not seen Negroes at close range before, and he found them of great interest artistically, with their large eyes, high cheekbones, and dusky skin. He liked their friendliness and good-natured laughter and for his subjects often went around to the mess tent where several of them assisted the cook. He made a sketch of "our jolly cook," with his tasseled cap over one ear, breaking into a dance unexpectedly in the middle of the morning. He drew the wagoners at their chores; and later, when he came on four of them, snoozing on the ground by the sunny side of the tent, he could not resist getting the picture down on paper. The men came to know him, greeted him with welcoming grins, and were usually ready to pose if he asked them.

The Zouaves also provided a certain dash and entertainment to offset the drabness of camp life. They were an amusing lot, with their swaggering red-and-blue uniforms which made them look like the tribe of Algerian warriors from whom they took their name rather than the New York City firemen from whose ranks they had been recruited. Watching the regiment's intricate drill and perfect precision was like seeing a circus parade, and its members put on a show even when they were relaxing. They were hearty fellows and, after a few days, hailed Winslow as he approached their quarters by calling out, "Here comes 'our Special,'" or, "How's 'our Special' today?" He would smile good-naturedly and start wielding his pencil. He drew the Zouaves frequently on this and subsequent trips to the front with the Potomac Army.

As winter came on, camp life grew rougher and the soldiers harder to restrain. Winslow found himself sketching with freezing fingers, for it was impossible to stay near a fire all the time. The men were constantly in trouble for infractions of rules, and he drew them being punished for intoxication or gambling, as well as in moments of melancholy or homesickness, which occasionally overtook even the toughest. Every payday saw a run on the sutler's tent as the men squandered their silver in gorging themselves; and at Christmas time most of them dived into the holiday boxes from home like starving beggars, falling on the packages of food, plum puddings and homemade crullers, the knitted socks, and tins of tobacco. Books and biblical tracts were tossed aside without so much as a glance. Amused, Winslow drew the raucous picture, but the men hardly noticed him. In his own box from home he was surprised to find a copy of Chevreul's *Laws of Color*, sent by his brother Charlie—a gift he put to immediate use and treasured all his life.

He returned to New York before the end of the year with a portfolio full of sketches; since he had not covered specific events of battle, but everyday occurrences of army life, he had not sent any of his drawings on paper in to New York to be but half delineated on wood by some staff artist. As usual, he preferred to work his notes into full illustrations and put them on the block with the precision and skill for which he was gaining a reputation. *Harper's* published as a full cover picture in the first issue of the new year (January 4, 1862) his "Xmas Boxes in Camp, Christmas, 1861." The editors were impressed with his realistic yet percep-

OUR JOLLY COOK.

Campagne Sketches, *Our Jolly Cook*

tive portrayal of the Civil War soldier, presented as no other artist had shown him. They hinted that a second job offer might be forthcoming, but he forestalled it by saying that he had plans for work in a different field. He had no desire to be a staff artist, no matter how much security it might mean.

He did have plans—to use some of the scenes he had done at the front as a basis for paintings. With Chevreul's *Laws* as a guide, he set about learning to mix colors, to work in oils. This time he was not simply experimenting, as he had been the summer before in Belmont; he was in dead earnest about placing his pictures on exhibit, and he concentrated on teaching himself the technique. Art dealers in the neighborhood, who knew his wood engravings, promised to display any pictures that 'qualified'—or those which, in their opinion, would have enough appeal to be sold. But before he felt confident enough to offer them anything for exhibit, he received another assignment to the front, this time to the scene of action. The offensive against the Confederate capital at Richmond was finally being launched, and he was to cover the operation. *Harper's* agreed to pay him "twenty-five" a drawing—or so he understood.

He was in Washington by the first of April and went to the Provost Marshall's office where he obtained his military pass to the battle lines. He was again attached to McClellan's Army of the Potomac, scheduled to embark at Alexandria. When he reported for duty, he found himself once more under the command of Barlow, who had been promoted to Brevet Major General of the 2d Corps. The officer had requested Winslow Homer, he learned, in preference to other reporters, and welcomed him back like a friend.

"Glad to have you aboard, Homer," he said, shaking hands.

His greeting could be taken literally, since they were about to depart aboard an army transport en route to the Peninsula. Winslow sketched the troops embarking and then hustled on deck as the gangplank was being raised. The transport was crowded with soldiers, some apprehensive, some happy to be moving into

Civil War Sketches

action after the long delay. Tension ran high during the brief voyage, and when they reached Yorktown, they found McClellan besieging the city instead of moving his offensive on Richmond. The 2d Corps joined the siege, and for the next six weeks or so Winslow was constantly on the alert, recording the scene as soldiers on both sides carried out their tasks of reconnoitering, skirmishing, charging, pursuing. The action was "minor," but it was constant, and the sketches had to be reported at once—part of the dispatches from the front. The engravings could not be signed, but the magazine gave him a credit line, "Sketched by Mr. Winslow Homer," or, "Our special artist, Winslow Homer." The staff artist who transferred the drawings was by no means as skillful or as careful as he, but this could not be helped. He was outraged, however, when *Harper's* reduced the size of his drawings, put four on a page, and paid him twenty-five dollars for the packet. Mild-mannered though he was, unfairness of this sort brought a flare-up of indignation, and he made no bones about issuing a complaint.

By the beginning of May the Rebels, pinched by the siege, yet unwilling to surrender, opened operations for a full-scale move toward Richmond. It was a warm, dark night with a threat of thunder in the Virginia skies that had been hot with sunlight all day; Winslow was sketching some of the soldiers as they lounged or played cards beneath the rough pine-bough shelters that had been hastily thrown up, when suddenly the alert came: the Rebs were reconnoitering again. He joined the line of advance guard, and, as they crept up on the Confederate earthworks, he sought to outline the dark figures faintly illuminated by stray beams from covered lanterns they carried. It was an eerie sight and a suspenseful moment; at any second a volley of fire might ring out. He had to draw quickly, without getting close enough for detail, on penalty of discovery by the enemy. Yet he managed to convey a sense of drama in the scene which was not lost, even in transfer by someone else. *Harper's* printed it on the cover—full-page once more—of the May 17 issue, as well as other action picture reports.

*Rebels Outside Their Works at Yorktown
Reconnoitring with Dark Lanterns*

Events occurred rapidly. Following "Rebels Outside their Works at Yorktown, Reconnoitring with Dark Lanterns," Winslow, in the thick of things, sent in "The Union Cavalry and Artillery, Starting in Pursuit of the Rebels up the Yorktown Pike," which he drew as the gray uniforms moved out of the city, and the race toward Richmond began. Some of the encounters were bloody, marked by face-to-face bayonet fighting.

Sketches of the bayonet charge, a cavalry charge, a scene at the rear, in which he caught the terror and sadness on the faces of the wounded as the surgeon went to work with his knife, Winslow kept until he got back to New York around the first of June. These he worked up with care to bring out the harsh realism of war in contrast to the pageantry of the battle scenes painted by other artists. In "The Army of the Potomac—Our Outlying Picket in the Woods," he showed the soldiers on their bellies, edging along the ground, their rifles poised for fire. "The Cavalry Charge" emphasized the wild brutality of horses' hoofs trampling fallen soldiers. "A Bayonet Charge," which he had drawn at such close range he could hear the clash of sabers and see the thrust of steel as the men assailed each other's hearts, brought out the voilence of war. *Harper's* acclaimed it "one of the most spirited pictures ever published in this country."

On its appearance the publishers made Winslow a generous offer to join the staff permanently as a featured artist; the salary would be more than he had earned from his free-lance work at any time. He was tempted to accept at once, but he did not give them a definite answer. He stopped in Russell Shurtleff's studio on his way up to the tower the day he received the offer.

"What did you tell them?" Shurtleff asked when he heard the news.

Winslow shrugged his shoulders and shook his head to indicate that he had not made up his mind. He picked up a drawing pencil and idly sketched Russell's round German head with its thatch of reddish hair. "I want to be dead sure first that I can't paint," he said.

Civil War Sketch, Cavalry Officer's Boots

The Cooper Union Museum

Russell nodded; he understood.

Up in his own studio, Winslow sent word to his family; whether he accepted or not, he wanted them to know he had received the offer. It represented a measure of success in drawing at least and was proof that he could earn a good living if he liked. Though he would not countenance the idea of financial help from Charlie or anyone else in the family, their approval and recognition of his talent was important to him. He might live in a garret, but he did not have to starve.

Within the next few weeks he painted steadily. He had made color notes on some of the sketches he did at the front, and these he carried out on canvas, recording faithfully the hard, bright hues of Union blue and Confederate gray—and, in a later picture, the glaring red and gold of the Zouaves' outfit. He bought a lay figure from an artists' supply shop and managed to get hold of uniforms in which he dressed his dummy impartially as a Northern or Southern soldier.

"My model takes either side," he said to Russell, who came up to watch him at work on his first picture. It was to be called "Sharpshooter on Picket Duty" and depicted the hawk-eyed lookout Winslow had come upon during the siege; he was perched in a tree top, partly camouflaged by the thickness of the pines, aiming his rifle at a distant Reb. To reproduce the effect of sunlight on the green boughs, Winslow took his canvas onto the rooftop, which served as an outdoor studio, protected by a stone parapet all around. He set up his easel and posed the jointed figure to resemble, as closely as he could make it, the live form he had sketched near Yorktown. Masses of light and shadow had always fascinated him, and one of the effects he was striving to achieve in painting was the purity—and glory—of natural sunshine. The muted tones of the "Hudson River" school of painters, who rarely ventured more than a sickly yellow, seemed to him 'dead as a doornail.' There were few pines in Washington Square, but he could see the rays of the July sun falling through the topmost branches of the trees beyond the tower, and this was all he

Civil War Sketches, Army Maneuvers, Marching Infantry Column

The Cooper Union Museum

needed.

Russell came up and sat with him for hours every day while he worked on the canvas, which was small for an 'oil,' sixteen by twenty. They discussed at some length how much Winslow could ask for the work, considering it was his first offered for exhibit. On the other hand, he had gained a reputation for his drawings, which should count for something. *Harper's* paid him sixty dollars for a full-page drawing on the wood, and the painting should be worth that much at least.

"I'll set the price at sixty," he decided finally. "And not a penny less," he added firmly. Shurtleff agreed that the figure was perfectly fair and that Winslow should stick to it. The two, like other young artists, kept up each other's courage by such an exchange; the practical problems of being a creative artist were shared by all of them and formed a common bond which held them together in spite of their differences on theories of art or techniques of painting.

When he completed the painting, Winslow copied it on the block for *Harper's*. "That way I'll be sure of my sixty dollars," he remarked to Russell dryly. Inside he was quivering with hope and expectation, content with himself for having produced such a work: it had character, 'story' interest, and a quality all its own—*his* way of putting on color. He would never again be as well satisfied with a picture, or with himself as a painter, as he was at this moment. *Harper's* published "The Sharpshooter" on November 15, with the line, "From *a painting* by Winslow Homer, Esq.," and just reading the credit brought him a feeling of happiness.

Before he had quite finished the first canvas, he had started a second, which showed a private in the Potomac Army, standing on an upended wooden crate, holding a log over his shoulder; near him was a guard, his back to the viewer, who evidently paced up and down, bearing a rifle. The legend read, "Punished For Intoxication," and represented a familiar scene in the Army camp. Although he later considered the picture 'about as beauti-

ful and interesting as the button on a barn door,' Winslow thought
now that it was nearly as good as the "Sharpshooter," and he took
them both to the art dealer, who placed them on exhibit—for sale.

The die was cast. All he had to do was wait. He went home
and wrote Charlie that unless the two pictures were sold, he
would forget about painting and accept *Harper's* offer of a steady
job.

To Charles, Winslow's decision was alarming because he knew
his brother would carry it through. Charles believed in his
ability and felt quite sure the pictures would sell eventually—but
would Win be able to wait? His own salary as a chemist at the
cotton mills was not large, but he expected it to increase, and on
the strength of this he made a secret trip to New York to buy his
brother's paintings, with the proviso that under no circumstances
should his name be revealed. If Win found out, the consequences
might be serious.

"Don't worry," the dealer told him. "We often have anonymous
buyers." He winked.

Charles left the shop (which was near Washington Square)
and hurried back to Lawrence before he ran into anyone from
the N.Y.U. Building—especially his brother.

Winslow himself refused to go near the art gallery, because he
didn't want to hover over his paintings, no matter how much he
might enjoy seeing them on exhibit. For several weeks he kept
busy with drawings, and the November Twenty-ninth issue of
Harper's carried a full-page engraving of "Thanksgiving in
Camp," a scene outside the sutler's lean-to, with its canopy of
pine boughs, on which hung signs of "Pies," "Herring," "Cider";
lounging soldiers, some laughing at a bit of horseplay, others
moody, were eating and drinking; a jug, tossed aside as soon as
it was empty, rolled along the ground. When Winslow brought
the drawing into the office, *Harper's* editor asked him whether he
had made up his mind about the job.

"'Not yet," he said shortly. He did make up his mind to see if
the dealer had received any inquiries about his work, and when

he heard that both of his canvases had been sold to a single party, he was astonished and elated; his poker face, however, remained calm.

"Who bought them?" he asked.

"I'm sorry, Mr. Homer—the purchaser asked to remain incognito," the clerk answered, and would give him no particulars.

"I see." Winslow did not press him—the paintings had sold!

With his first check from a dealer he bought more supplies, to go on painting: a roll of canvas, some new brushes, tubes of paint. From the art store he went to the Jefferson Market place, to spend some of his earnings on cheeses, crackers, and a keg of beer for a celebration. When he appeared in the doorway of Russell's studio laden with the purchases, his friend guessed his good fortune before he could say a word.

"You've sold a picture!" he exclaimed, putting down his brush and relieving Winslow of a few bundles. "Which one—'The Sharpshooter'?" He felt a special interest in the first oil.

"Two," Winslow corrected him. "Both pictures went to an anonymous buyer."

That night he and Russell, along with Oliver Lay, Homer Martin, and Eastman Johnson, rounded up all the models they knew, a dancer or two, invited the other artists in the building, and held a party in the tower. When the beer ran out, all that could be found was half a jug of moldy wine in Johnson's studio, but it did not seem to matter. Spirits were high in any case. Winslow, usually quiet even in the thick of things, sang in a loud unmusical voice when a chorus of war songs started up as one of the painters began strumming a patriotic tune on his guitar. The high-pitched laughter of the girls rang in the tower, and applause for a fandango performed by one of the dancers resounded through the empty corridors of the gloomy building. It was late when the evening ended, but nobody knew, or cared, what the hour was. Winslow kissed all the girls good night in turn—or, in congratulation, was kissed by them, to which he had no objection. Most of them were pretty, and he liked to be with pretty girls on occasion, to dance with them and kiss them. Once or twice, since coming to New York, he had fancied himself in love, but the feeling had not lasted longer than a week or two. His love for painting came first and was so demanding that he did not have time for any other sort of mistress. And with the encouragement he had just received, he was about to become more deeply involved than ever, more closely bound to the realization of a dream.

He could not devote himself full time to painting right away, because he was sent on short trips to the front again. *Harper's* wanted him to continue on a free-lance basis, and military assignments were in the category of patriotic duty, not to be turned down. The opening week of 1863 found him with the Potomac forces again, recording the action close to enemy trenches, which were in the process of completion.

He stayed in camp another week or so, and one cold night he sketched the "Winter Scene Inside of a Hut"; at least forty men were huddled in cramped quarters, trying to keep warm from the heat of a blaze in the rude fireplace at one end of the hut. All kinds of activity occupied the soldiers: several groups of two, three, or four were playing cards; a storyteller in the center of the floor was holding a circle of listeners spellbound; a few were trying to read or write letters home by the dim light; several arguments were going on, some with mild fisticuffs. At the back, eight or ten hardy souls, stretched out on the floor, slept soundly through it all. Winslow developed the drawing on his return to New York, and it was published on January 24, one of the most graphic reports he had made.

During the rest of the winter he was able to put in more time on his painting, and in April he entered two companion works in the spring exhibition of the National Academy, both dealing with the intimate, informal aspect of army life he had portrayed in his drawings; in one, "Home, Sweet Home," he touched on a moment of nostalgia he had witnessed as McClellan's regimental band began to play the familiar air unexpectedly, and two soldiers, listening, were overtaken by a wave of homesickness. The picture was so appealing that it was sold on the opening day of the exhibit; and George William Curtis, *Harper's* art critic, wrote, "It is a little work of real feeling. . . . There is no strained effect in it, no sentimentality, but a hearty, homely actuality." The other canvas, entirely different in mood, was humorously entitled "The Last Goose at Yorktown" and showed a couple of scalawags about to sneak off with the lone remaining delicacy in the sutler's tent. It was bought a week or so after "Home, Sweet Home," and Winslow felt more than justified in continuing his career as a painter.

He did far fewer drawings for *Harper's* in 1863 than in any year since he had come to New York, and even less the following year, although he was sent to cover Grant's advance through the woods in Virginia, where he sketched the scenes of battle. By 1865 he was devoting most of his time to painting the Civil War soldier instead of sketching him. Interest in the subject ran high, since nearly every family had someone in the service, and those who could afford it were eager to own a permanent artistic record. In order to establish himself financially as well as professionally, Winslow made the most of the universal appeal of the Civil War soldier and produced more than twenty paintings of him, nearly all based on sketches he had made during his assignments at the front. Three highly successful pictures were those of the Negroes in camp, particularly one called "The Bright Side," showing the four teamsters he had seen snoozing in the sun outside the cook's tent. The Zouaves, too, provided material for one of his best canvases, "Pitching Quoits," perhaps the most colorful of the war paintings; the men in their swaggering uniforms, gracefully tossing the rings, intent on their game (a favorite recreation during long hours at the fire station back in New York), were an exotic sight on the banks of the Potomac, and Winslow's painting was alive with the zesty richness of it.

The National Academy quickly recognized his ability. With

Civil War Sketch, Wounded Soldier Given a Drink
from a Canteen

The Cooper Union Museum

the spring exhibition of 1864, exactly a year after his debut, Winslow Homer was elected an Associate, no small achievement for a young artist of twenty-eight; and only one year later he became a full-fledged member of the august Academy. He went to Belmont to tell the family the wonderful news. His mother was immensely proud of his success; that her son was an Academician at twenty-nine was more than she had hoped for, but both she and his father warned him that it might still be difficult to earn a living as a painter. Charlie, visiting their parents at the same time, found it hard not to make a slip about his share in Winslow's initial success. However, he thought it wiser not to mention his anonymous purchase; Win had written him about it in all innocence, as the single factor in his decision not to take a steady job, and Charlie saw no need for lessening his brother's elation by enlightening him as to the identity of the "patron" who had bought his first paintings.

Toward the close of the long struggle, when General Lee's Confederate soldiers began the retreat that ended in surrender at Appomattox, Winslow went one last time to the scene of action. He was at the railroad station at City Point, where Lincoln, with his young son, Tad, waited beside General Grant, and he made a little drawing of the three in that momentous hour.

During that final trip he saw the full misery of war, the pathos and dejection of the defeated forces, and out of his experience came his finest painting to date, "Prisoners From the Front," which he did not complete until the war was over, in 1866. Three weary, wretched Confederate soldiers—one an officer—in tattered uniforms, part of a captured unit, were brought before Major General Barlow, who looked over the prisoners with a practiced, yet sympathetic eye. They were pitiful, trying to be defiant in the face of defeat, yet ashamed of their torn, mud-spattered uniforms. The Union officer, assured, immaculate, yet obviously moved, kept himself aloof and efficient only with effort. Winslow, sketching hurriedly, was deeply impressed with the underlying

Civil War Sketch, a Negro Teamster

The Cooper Union Museum

feeling that accompanied Barlow's inspection of the prisoners; of the mixed emotions of the old man in the captive ranks, who stood staunchly beside his Confederate officer; and of the drama that was being played out in the moment of victory.

The creative power in his painter's fingers was able to present the scene with its potential fully realized, and when the picture was shown for the first time, at the exhibition of the Academy in 1866, it was hailed by critics and public alike—the sensation of the show. The name of Winslow Homer was famous in a single night—it became known across the country as soon as the reviews appeared. Henry T. Tuckerman wrote that "Prisoners From the Front" . . . "attracted more attention, and . . . won more praise than any genre picture by a native hand that has appeared of late years." Clarence Cook said in a later review, "No picture in America in our day has made so deep an appeal to the feelings of the people. . . . Though painted in the heat of war, and when the bitterest feelings were aroused on both sides, the influence of this picture was strong on the side of brotherly feeling."

The painting was bought, shortly after the exhibition closed, by no less a person than John Taylor Johnston, the well-known New York collector, who was to become the first president of the Metropolitan Museum. Winslow himself was somewhat surprised at the widespread success of his painting; he had not been as well satisfied with it as he had with "Sharpshooter"; when he read the notices, he could hardly believe they were written about his work.

Yet he did not allow himself to be overcome by success, nor would he continue to paint war pictures, as he could easily have done; he had other areas to explore in the world of art. But first he was going to travel the earth.

CHAPTER V

First Trip Abroad

1866-1868

HE MADE PLANS TO GO TO PARIS WITH SOME OF HIS 'PALS.' THE
Universal Exposition was opening in 1867 and was going to include a small section exhibiting American art—a mark of recognition by European circles for the cultural achievements of the
country as well as for the artists who were asked to contribute.
The fame of "Prisoners From the Front" had brought Winslow
an invitation to show the canvas along with one or two others in
the American section; he chose only one—"The Bright Side"—as
a contrasting piece, and the two were shipped abroad with the
paintings of the other Americans who had been invited to show.

His friend Eugene Benson was one of these, and as the time
to leave drew near, they conferred about the possibility of holding
a joint sale of their work to help cover expenses; as usual, Win's
finances, in spite of his successes, would scarcely allow him an
occasional trip to Belmont, let alone a sojourn in Europe. He had
continued the drawings for *Harper's*, including "Home From the
War," showing the joyous yet tearful reunion of soldiers with their
families near the close of the war, and two postwar engravings;
one, entitled "The Veteran in a New Field," pictured an ex-
soldier harvesting the wheat—Winslow's way of implying that

swords were already beaten into plowshares; the other he sketched during a weekend in Newport, when he saw an amputee veteran riding in an open carriage. It was one of a series, "Our Watering Places," and was called "The Empty Sleeve at Newport." Printed in August 1865, this was one of the last drawings with reference to the war. He had to pay his own expenses on these jaunts since he worked on a free-lance basis, and most of the time he did little more than break even.

He might have been ahead, except that he spent a good deal of money on clothes after he moved to the tower studio—the result of his having to wear Charlie's outgrown suits and jackets in the lean years while he was growing up. He had even gained a reputation as a natty dresser among the artists in the N.Y.U. Building, who often ribbed him about his smart checks, his cutaways, high collars, and bowler hats; his mustache now extended way out on either side in true handle-bar style, and he kept the ends neatly waxed (he had shaved off the Vandyke after the war); when he went out, he looked disgraceful, like a real dandy, the others told him, but he was impervious to their jokes. His independence held in all areas, and he was certainly not going to affect shabbiness when he enjoyed being well-dressed.

He and Benson secured the Leeds & Miner gallery for an exhibition during the last two weeks of November, and Winslow selected nineteen paintings as his portion of the sale, which opened on the seventeenth. Between them, the young artists raised enough for their passage to Europe, with a fair amount left over for their keep in Paris, if they did not stay too long.

Early in December the group of newly recognized painters sailed for France; some of them had crossed the Atlantic several times and made nothing of the voyage except to complain of its length. Winslow, save for the taste of 'the salt' he had received on his Uncle Jim's barque, had never been on the high seas before and found the experience a source of wonder, sounding a chord deep within him, an exultant note, even when the wintry gales sent towering waves crashing across the deck and the reeling passengers clung to the ropes, or huddled in their cabins, seasick. He was stirred by the power, the majesty of the ocean, the infinite reaches of sky and water; and he had the curious sensation that he had been here an age ago, perhaps in another life. He knew the water until now from inland lake and stream, or from resort beaches along the shore, yet this voyage did not seem strange to him. Nobody had to give him advice on getting his 'sea legs'; he knew instinctively what to do. He was awed by the wild splendor of a storm-tossed sea, and moved by the beguiling beauty of a calm one. Yet it never seemed alien to him. He spent hours on deck, sometimes at night, watching the phosphorescent lights that shot up as the ship's prow cut through the dark waves.

He said nothing of this to his companions, and he did almost no sketching during the weeks of passage. He kept his emotions to himself, as usual; if his fellow artists noticed any difference in his amiable, placid disposition, it was merely that he seemed quieter than ever.

In Paris it was another story. Winslow found the famous city of lights gay and diverting, with its boulevards and bistros, its dance halls and theaters, its bookstalls and sidewalk artists along the Seine. At the Long Gallery in the Louvre he was less interested in the old masters than in the young students; instead of copying the famous paintings themselves, he sketched the scene at the gallery, crowded with aspiring artists seated on stools or camp chairs, earnestly copying the great works. On his arrival he looked up a friend from Belmont, Albert Kelsey; he had a studio in Montmartre and suggested that Winslow share the place with him for as long as he wanted to stay in Paris; his money would stretch farther, and he would be right in the midst of the 'bohemian' life of the city. Winslow, looking around his friend's barren atelier (which, except for an antique cabinet or two, some velvet hangings, and a broken zither strung from a crossbeam in the cracked ceiling, closely resembled his quarters in Washington Square), was happy to accept the offer. The two made the rounds during the next few weeks, visiting the art galleries and sight-seeing by day, frequenting the dance halls and cabarets at night. Winslow's drawing of "Gargoyles of Notre Dame" included a portrait of Albert, who was standing at the railing, gazing out over the rooftops of Paris. (A similar drawing, which he called "View of Paris," showed a cat clinging desperately to the tip end of a gargoyle and a man trying to coax it back to safety; the city, spread in all directions below, seemed almost incidental.)

They went to the Casino and stood with the crowd, mostly men, at the edge of the dance floor, watching a pair of expert waltzers, whirling so fast that the girl's feet scarcely touched the floor and her skirt flew up, revealing her legs above the knee. At the Jardin Mabille several couples were dancing the wicked cancan, the men wearing silk toppers, and the girls kicking their gartered legs high, at the same time swishing their upturned skirts back and forth, fanwise. This was heady fare for two bachelors from Belmont, Massachusetts, and Winslow caught the full flavor of it when he drew the gay scene during one of their nightly sprees. At the Mabille he noticed a rose that had fallen to the floor from a dancer's dress, providing an added touch of abandon for his picture. He was not at all sure that *Harper's* would publish such drawings, but he meant to submit them, shocking or no. (The magazine eventually printed both scenes, but felt called upon to censure such licentious practices with a word of pious warning. "We shall not venture to look into the abyss on the brink of which these frenzied men and women are dancing, and this too curious crowd of spectators is treading," the editorial comment finished. "This is work for the severe and steady eye of the preacher and moralist.")

When the exposition opened, Winslow went with his colleagues to check on the display of paintings in the American section. It was small, and the canvases seemed too crowded to permit much evaluation of individual worth, but there they were, at any rate, for all the world to see. The French critic, Paul Mantz, of the *Gazette des Beaux-Arts*, observed in writing of the two Winslow Homer pictures, "This is firm, precise painting, in the manner of

Gargoyles of Notre Dame

Collection Mr. James M. Thomson

Gérôme, but with less dryness." Winslow, who knew little of
Gérôme's style and cared less, was much more pleased by the
comment in the *London Art Journal*, which said, "These works are
real; the artist paints what he has seen and known."

"At least there's a kernel of truth in the *Journal*," he remarked,
passing it along to the artist next to him. About eight or ten of
them were sitting in one of the cafés on the exposition grounds,
sipping absinthe, reading the reviews and speculating on the jury
awards to come. Some were discussing the work of the French
painters in the exposition and the "wild" show staged independ-
ently outside the fairgrounds by Manet and Courbet, two of the
most flagrant revolutionaries. Winslow listened to the shoptalk,
but he said very little. He was no more interested in learning
from his French contemporaries than from the old masters. His
Yankee stubbornness would not allow him to accept ideas or
techniques of other painters any more than he would accept
financial help from anyone. He had to do things in his own way,
in his own time. The one section that made a definite impression
on him was the Japanese, displaying the delicate prints for which
they were famous. The selectivity and sense of design struck a
kindred note in him; this was what he had been trying to do in
the wood engravings. The Japanese art exhibit was the only one
to which he returned several times, but he mentioned it to no one.

When the international jury finally made its awards, four members voted to give Winslow Homer a medal, but their number
was not enough; the dean of American panorama painters, Frederick E. Church, won the prize for his huge canvas of Niagara
Falls. Winslow received their decision philosophically; he had
not expected to win any medals in the first place. But to himself
he made a secret vow.

By the beginning of May, when the horse-chestnut trees shook
out their chandelier blossoms over the Champs Elysées, Winslow
was ready to shake the dust of the city from his shoes. He had
painted only a few pictures, among them one of a pretty flower
girl at the fair, carrying a brimming basket of nosegays for sale.

Now, as the weather grew warmer, he felt the need to get out into the open countryside, to paint the flowers of the field, the French landscape, the *paysan* tilling the soil. Several of his traveling companions were taking lessons from French painters; it was considered the thing to do when an artist came to France. Winslow preferred to go into the country and paint by himself.

He chose to go into Picardy, where he stayed among the farmers, depicting the rural life in France as he had in America; a young peasant woman, chasing geese down a road bordered by poplars, might take his eye, or the field workers, hoeing between the long green rows; the tile-roofed farmhouses, whose doorways and fences were spilling over with masses of pink roses; the buxom milkmaids, the bearded farmers, the sunburned boys who helped with the haying. His French was practically nonexistent, and the few words he had picked up in Paris he pronounced with a crisp New England accent, but, as usual, he managed to make himself understood by means of a few gestures or, if necessary, a little sketch. People liked his simple, unaffected silence and trusted him because of his direct, honest dealings.

He was staying at the village tavern in Cernay-la-Ville, not far from Paris, making his way back to the city in easy stages, when he ran short of cash. He knew that painters like Courbet and Daubigny had paid many a bill here with a picture, with which the innkeeper happily covered his cracked walls. In a pantomime of brush strokes Winslow offered to do the same before he left, and the host, nodding, pointed to a door panel sadly in need of varnish. Winslow went to work, and soon a haymaking scene covered the defects. He signed it in the lower right-hand corner; and several years later, Alden Weir, stopping at the same *auberge,* reported that the painting was in good condition.

Back in the gay metropolis before the end of August, Winslow half considered going home, but he hated the idea of leaving just when his work began to show the results of his weeks in the country. Casting around for a source of income, he remembered a painting he had done in Belmont, among his first attempts in the romantic setting of Waverly Oaks, near his parents' home. The canvas had not pleased him particularly since it was not well-defined; but it possessed a dreamy, shadowy, imaginative quality that appealed to his friends from Mrs. Cushman's, who often dropped in at the tower studio. On an impulse he wrote to Charles Voorhees, "Perhaps you remember the picture of mine 'Waverly Oaks.' I lent it to Henry Howland. If you are inclined you can do me a great favor without incurring any loss by sending me $100 for it. Including the frame for which I gave $55. If my request bores you in the least, take no notice of it. I am working hard, and have improved much, and when I come home can make money, but I wish if possible to stay here a little longer." He put the letter in the post at once, before he had a chance to change his mind.

Charles jumped at the opportunity to own "Waverly Oaks," and when the money came, Winslow and Albert Kelsey went on several excursions, for painting and pleasure alike; on one of these they fell in with the latest fad of having a photograph taken to commemorate the occasion. The print was blurred, the pose stiff, but it was a souvenir of the comradeship the two had enjoyed during Winslow's stay in Paris, a feeling which prompted his friend to inscribe the picture, "Damon and Pythias." They frequented the cafés in St. Germain-des-Prés, where the artists gathered and might dawdle a whole afternoon over a glass of *eau sucré* if their purses allowed nothing more.

The broad circle of painters in Paris represented, if possible, a more carefree lot than the band of talented tenants in the University Building in New York. Here was a set of "merry fellows" who always seemed to be singing, smoking, fencing, drinking, besides painting industriously, and arguing endlessly over techniques. Eating, if incidental, was hearty and lusty. In Kelsey's studio one Sunday morning four of them came barging in carrying supplies for a late breakfast—six sausages, three long loaves, and a bottle of wine—and they had an impromptu feast, for which the ringleader took up a collection, fifteen sous apiece. They used no plates or knives; sausage links were snapped apart by fingers and the crisp French bread "broken" in "Biblical style," somebody said. (A few of them had attended High Mass at Notre Dame.) The crisp French bread, topped by spicy sausage, washed down with the red wine, was exotic breakfast food for Yankee palates, but Winslow enjoyed it all with quiet amusement, particularly when he thought how horrified his parents would be if they could have seen him at this moment. The Homers kept 'the Sabbath' with New England strictness, going to church morning and evening; no one lifted a finger in 'trade' or daily labor. If his father, especially, had walked into the atelier and found him, after the pipe-smoking and stories that followed breakfast, painting industriously while two of the artists who were musicians posed for him with violin and cello, he would have let loose a tongue-lashing on the indecency of laboring on Sunday. His mother, he felt quite sure, would have shown more understanding, born of her own urge to paint on many a sober Sunday.

He called the small oil started that day "Musical Amateurs," and though he worked on it from memory when he returned to New York, it was never quite completed; the hands holding the instruments were awkward, clumsily fingering the strings. Perhaps he should have spent more time copying the casts at the Academy, but it was too late now—he was a full-fledged Academician; and, anyway, he would rather learn by himself, through trial and error. . . .

He stayed in Paris as long as he dared on the money Voorhees had sent, but by the last week in October his funds were so low that Albert had to pay for his return passage. Winslow was extremely grateful for his friend's kindness, but he could not express his feelings in so many words. Eugene Benson and some of the others had gone home earlier; two were remaining in France longer to study art at the staid Salon; Winslow was going back alone. Albert saw him off, and they shook hands warmly, but beyond promising to write at once, Winslow said nothing by way of gratitude or sentiment. It was not in his nature to display emotion, however much he might feel it. (Later, after his return, he wrote, offering Albert the choice of any painting he liked among 'the Winslow Homers to date.')

From the moment the liner put out to sea, and he felt the roll of the great ocean beneath her bow, Winslow found himself again exhilarated by the rhymthic rise and fall of the waves, fascinated by the mysterious power, the surging strength of the sea. It was as if he had made an amazing discovery of a larger self, linked in some unfathomable way to the vast outer spaces of the universe, of which he had had no real knowledge before and now had little more than an inkling. He stood on deck, gazing out across the rail with rapt eyes—to all appearances a neat, well-dressed, well-groomed Yankee businessman, mildly enjoying the scene; but inwardly his painter's soul was stirred to the depths of his being, and he responded with a wild pounding of his pulses to the inscrutable poetry of the sea.

After a few days he settled into the voyage and at once had the urge to draw the scene around him. He made a number of sketches of life on board—the passengers on their 'daily constitutional' around the deck; the ship's officers; the crew, 'singing out at the ropes.' During the second week they ran alongside a school of porpoises, or 'snub-nosed dolphins,' the captain called them, leaping, racing, and generally disporting themselves off the port bow. Many of the passengers rushed to the rails to get a good view of the hilarious sight, and Winslow was able to create a drawing full of interest—the crowd of passengers lining the rails, the ship listing to port, and several officers on the bridge, one of them looking through a marine glass at the romping mammals of the briny deep. He called the picture "Homeward Bound" and meant to offer it to *Harper's* as soon as the liner docked.

If not especially fruitful—he was bringing back only sixteen canvases—his stay in France had been delightful, a fact he realized more fully when he told some of his cronies about it. A few days in New York pointed up the difference between the flavor of life at home and abroad; and when he ran into his old friends from Bufford's, Cole and Baker, in the art shop on Astor Place, it gave him quite a worldly air to announce that he had just come back from Paris. The pair had come to New York to study and were eager to see his work, especially what he had done in the gay city.

"You must have some that is most—ah, interesting, *non?*" Joseph Baker imitated Damereau, lifting an eyebrow and twirling his mustache.

Winslow nodded, smiling. He invited them to come back to the studio with him, where he showed them a number of studies he had made of the dancing girls at the Mabille; he was preparing to make a composite of them for the drawing for *Harper's.* He would have preferred to start on new paintings, but he had to rebuild his finances before he could even buy supplies. The cancan was a revelation to the visitors, who exclaimed at some length over such risqué dancing and asked for further details.

Instead of enlightening them, Winslow took out other studies, one of a room in the Louvre where antique marbles were exhibited and in reproducing them on paper, he had included the imperfections of the statues, a touch that Foxcroft Cole thought was naïve if not unnecessary.

"Don't you think you're carrying realism too far?" he asked.

"Certainly not!" Winslow said crisply. "Why, I wouldn't dream of leaving out those defects. I have to put down what I see, or," he amended, "what I select out of all I see, and *as* I see it."

His finality ended the discussion; his tone left no doubt that he was a man who knew what he was doing, and why, even when he was experimenting. He showed them next the unfinished painting, "Musical Amateurs," relating the incident in the Montmartre studio; he asked if the two would pose for him, provided he could get hold of the proper instruments. They agreed, but he never got around to having them come in, for more than one consideration . . . He had too many other things he wanted to accomplish.

At the close of the Universal Exposition his paintings were sent

to Brussels and Antwerp, where international art exhibits had
been arranged, following the fair. His pictures were well received
in both cities, but he was gaining an "undesirable" reputation, to
his way of thinking, as a genre painter of Civil War pictures, and
he did not want to be a 'genre painter' of any sort. Any 'type'
implied limitations, and his horizons had broadened during his
stay abroad to the point where he would tolerate limitations even
less than he had before. He had had a taste of the sea, the strong
flavor of which made him thirst to explore its mysteries; and he
had seen in the work of other painters from other countries two
elements he wished to develop in his own—the Japanese art of
selective design, and the French handling of color and light. On
the latter he had had his own ideas for some time, and he in no
degree wished to imitate; but he meant to make use of some of the
hints he had gleaned.

In the meantime he would have to insure a steady income for
himself by illustrating. *Harper's* published the Parisian dance-hall
scenes right away, in spite of the pious attitude expressed in the
magazine's editorial comment; they appeared on November 23,
while "Homeward Bound" and "Art Students and Copyists in the
Louvre Gallery" did not come out until the third week in December, to his amusement: even a family journal like *Harper's* was
not above snapping up a feature which bordered on the sensa-
tional.

He was busy most of the winter with engravings, so occupied
that he had no time for painting, and when the National Academy
sent the notice for entries in the spring show, he contributed three
canvases he had done in France (one of which was entitled
"Picardie") and, at the Academy's insistence, "Prisoners From the
Front." The international acclaim of his final war picture had
further increased its fame, and the Academy felt that the American public should have a chance to view the work again, even
though it had been exhibited only two years before. Winslow was
reluctant to have this phase of his career emphasized more than
it had been already, but in the end he agreed.

A Parisian Ball—Dancing at the Mabille, Paris

His parents came from Belmont for the opening, and Charlie came from Lawrence, bringing with him his beautiful bride, the former Martha French of West Townsend, whom he had recently married. (Arthur, true to his word, had gone out to Texas to seek his fortune.) Thirteen years younger than Charles, Mattie, as she was already called by everyone in the family, was highly intelligent, spirited, and utterly charming. Winslow, who was apt to be wary of 'outsiders' until he became well acquainted with them, took an instant liking to his sister-in-law. She was more like his mother than any other woman he had ever met, and he could see that there was a rapport between them that was most unusual to find among 'in-laws.' Mrs. Homer, never having had a daughter, would probably have welcomed any girl into the family; and Mattie, although much younger than 'the boys,' showed such a keen interest in art and such understanding of the artist that she was a source of constant delight, not to say comfort, to his mother.

Henrietta was immensely proud of Winslow's work, but she was not above being critical and spoke her mind if there was something in it she did not like. She also now asked for his advice occasionally but, for the most part, stuck to her water-color paintings of flowers, which, she knew well enough, were her forte. (In a few years she and Winslow would be exhibiting in the same shows.) There was indeed a friendly rivalry between mother and son, which he was inclined to foster rather than resent. It served as a spur to both of them. Winslow much preferred his mother the way she was to the adoring or doting parent she could so easily have become.

His father, always practical, regarded his son's success with grave reservations. To him, Win was still trying to earn a decent living with his pictures, no matter how good they might be. After one visit to the tower studio, he refused to climb the steep steps and stayed in the hotel room while Winslow boiled water on his little stove and served tea to the rest of the family. Mr. Homer's remarks about the bare attic rooms, which he thought hardly fitting for a famous painter, represented his gruff concern for his talented son, as Winslow well knew, but he made no move to coax his father to join them.

Mattie and Charlie invited him to come to visit them in Lawrence where they had bought a home. It was small, but they would always have room for him.

"Make it soon," Mattie said as he saw them off at the station. She was perceptive enough to realize that the bond between the two brothers was very close, if not outwardly sentimental. Both had the family stock-in-trade Yankee crispness and the same dry sense of humor. They even looked alike, but Charles was heavier and more handsome than Winslow, whose bony features and slight figure kept him from being a good-looking man by the accepted standards.

Winslow promised that he would be glad to visit them, and when the exhibit closed, he went to Lawrence for a few days before moving on to Belmont to spend some time with his parents. While he was there, he visited Charlie's office in the Pacific Cotton Mills and, as usual, found grist for his own in the sight of the factory workers coming to take their places at the looms—a whole army of them, crossing the bridge over the canal which supplied the water power to the huge mills. Their feet seemed to drag even as the bell urged them to hurry. This was the first of a number of drawings he was to do on the same theme, several of them at smaller mills in the country. He felt an immediate sympathy for those who had to shut themselves indoors all day, bent over monotonous routine toil. He always remembered Buford's when he saw the factory workers, and his heart went out to them. He called the picture "New England Factory Life—Bell Time."

Charles and Mattie were not quite settled in their house. Boxes and barrels were still waiting to be unpacked, and Win offered to help. At the bottom of one crate he unpacked he found what seemed to be a framed painting, wrapped in a quilt for protection. He uncovered it and let out an exclamation—the painting was

"Sharpshooter on Picket Duty!" Charlie, busy with another box, had his back to him.

"What's the matter, Win?" he asked.

"Where the devil did you get this?" Win demanded, staring at the "Sharpshooter" as if he had seen a ghost.

"What?" Charlie turned around. "Oh." He hesitated; for the moment he had forgotten that Winslow never knew who his first patron was. As long as he had discovered the painting, Charlie thought he might as well confess what he had done—especially since things had turned out so well.

To his surprise, Winslow was livid with anger at the thought that he had been hoodwinked. In one of his rare outbursts, he swore like the troopers he had camped with in the Army. Mattie, coming from the next room to see what the commotion was, covered her ears.

"But, Win," Charlie protested, "as long as you've been successful, I don't understand why you are so upset."

Winslow, remembering the happy celebration in the studio, could not tell his brother exactly why he was so irate. He felt as if he had been duped, cheated, some way. Uttering a few more choice oaths, he stalked out of the room, packed his grip, and left the house, slamming the door with a loud bang.

It was weeks before he spoke to Charlie—or wrote so much as a line, though they were in the habit of exchanging letters every few days. His ire, once aroused to white heat, did not cool quickly.

CHAPTER VI

Favor and 'Fortune'

1868-1875

HE WENT STRAIGHT TO BELMONT, WHERE HE BEGAN TO PAINT furiously. The summer before he sailed for France, he had done several drawings and two paintings of his cousin Florence and her friends trying out the game of croquet, the latest sport for women. Charlie and he had played one game with the girls; and as he stood, leaning on his mallet, waiting his turn, he thought of the charming subject this would make for a painting— the girls, bright-colored hoopskirts against the green, like balloons or peacock fans trailed across the lawn. When the game was over, he had asked them all to pose for him, Charlie down with one knee on the grass, measuring a shot, the girls over him, watching intently. Later he did another version, of the ladies alone, and when the croquet scenes were shown in the spring of 1866, the *Nation's* critic wrote: "As regards costume alone, these pictures ought to be taken care of, that our descendants may see how the incredible female dress of the present day actually did look, when worn by active young women."

Now he did some further studies, noting the change in women's dress. Hoopskirts had been discarded, in keeping with the greater freedom that came to the feminine sex as a result of participation in the war effort, as nurses on the battlefield or in hospitals; her costume, while still long and frilly, of several layers and ruffles, caught up in the back by a great bow, was not as cumbersome as the crinolines had been. He made a drawing from the studies, which was later published in *Literature, Science and the Arts,* along with a piece on the recent trend among gentlewomen to get out into the fresh air, taking part in sports, like croquet, surf bathing, and horseback riding (sidesaddle, of course). Winslow encouraged his cousins and their friends in their athletic activities. He liked the decorative note and the companionship of young women on jaunts to the seashore or the mountains and in his particular style portrayed the modern American girl who emerged from the Civil War—comely, vivacious, spirited, but withal possessed of a certain innocence and modesty that added to her charm.

He suggested that a group of them go riding in the White Mountains—he would ask some of his Boston artist friends, and his cousin Florence could ask some of her "chums," girls in their late twenties who had not yet married. (He had said nothing to his parents about the rift with Charlie, except to explain his appearance in Belmont sooner than he was expected by mentioning that something his brother had done 'got his hide up.' As a rule, the two took a trip somewhere together during the summer, fishing in nearby lakes or mountain streams, and Mattie had intimated that Charlie's marriage must not change their custom. Win, however, was still burning up at the thought of Charlie's 'trick.')

Florence agreed to round up a bevy of girls. "But I suspect," she added, "that your real motive is to make sure you have models."

"Certainly it is," he admitted, smiling.

He rode into Boston with his father to shop for supplies and to see how many of his friends were in town—Cole and Baker, and Louis Prang, the lithographer, who had published a portfolio of Winslow's war drawings, entitled "Campagne Sketches";

The Croquet Match

Collection Mrs. Edwin S. Webster

some were printed as sets of small cards and had sold very well. Albion Bicknell, another painter friend, might be in town. When Winslow finished his shopping, which took longer than he expected because of certain distractions on the way to the art store, he stopped in at Bicknell's studio.

His friend was pleasantly surprised to see him; Winslow did not often drop in like this, unannounced. "What have you been up to?" he asked, removing a pile of drawing paper from the only chair in the room.

For answer, Winslow reached in his coat pocket and pulled out a handful of ribbons, in every color of the rainbow, in silk and satin and velvet, in all sorts of sizes and lengths. "I've been shopping," he remarked airily.

Bicknell stared. "What on earth do you want of so many ribbons?"

Winslow smiled, shaking his head slightly. "I have no use for them, believe me. But," he explained with the merest twinkle, "whenever I see a pretty face behind the counter at the Emporium or anywhere, I stop and buy a few ribbons." He shrugged his shoulders and his friend laughed heartily.

The excursion to the White Mountains was a complete success; two of the New York painters—John Fitch and Homer Martin— joined the party, and Winslow, in addition to several canvases of fair feminine riders on the bridle path, did a painting of himself and his friends, three in a row at their easels, "Artists Sketching" on a bare mountainside near the top of Mt. Washington. He was in his element, painting out of doors, putting into practice some of the hints he had picked up in France. In the cool, clear white light of the mountains he felt serenely happy, his anger toward Charlie vanished, and he sought to put into his painting something of his mood. After all, if it had not been for Charlie's kind act, he would not be in the White Mountains at this moment, painting away as he pleased. No doubt *Harper's* would have given him a short vacation each year, but at the magazine's convenience, and he would have had precious little time for painting outside of that. Subjects for drawings would have been handed to him summarily, and, whether they appealed to him or not, he would have had to produce a picture. (Occasionally, in the next few years, *Harper's* commissioned him to cover the courts, jury duty; New York Charities; "Station-House Lodgers," the unemployed, sleeping at police headquarters; and a scene in Chinatown, "Baxter Street Clubhouse"; and, with the exception of the last, where he captured the occult, sinister atmosphere of an oriental gambling and opium den, these were among the least inspired or successful of his drawings.) As a free-lance artist, he could not only choose his own subjects but could make use of them for oils and water colors as well as drawings. One of the preliminary sketches that he did now for a painting on the summit of Mt. Washington was later used as an engraving for *Harper's* and *Harper's Bazaar.* He drew the colorful scene in this "coolest spot in New England"—men and women vacationists (most of them from his party), happy at having reached the top, some on horseback, some walking about with the horses tethered nearby. The girls, exclaiming over the "view," held silk parasols daintily over their heads against the bright sunshine (even while riding), and a few stalwarts who had climbed up carried alpenstocks.

The paintings were higher in key, brighter, more faithful in reproducing outdoor light than any he had done before going to France, and he was pleased with the results. Other paintings of that summer, done on the beach at Long Branch, where he went to get away from the heat after his return to New York, possessed the same lightness of mood and color. He wrote Charlie that he had completed a number of new works and that his brother should stop to take a look at them the next time he was in the city. (From that time on he always notified Charlie when he completed a painting or a group which he thought was important.) He made no mention of his recent hotheadedness; the break between them was sealed and never opened again.

Nevertheless, he determined to make sure that his brother would not feel called upon to help him out a second time, secretly or otherwise. Independence, especially in terms of financial assistance from the family, was almost an obsession with him. He did not want any patronage from them because he had chosen an artistic profession instead of business; he insisted that painting was as much a "business" as anything else and probably entailed more work in the long run than any job. It just happened to be work that he liked. And some day, when his technique was perfected, and his paintings more widely understood by the critics, who, except for "Prisoners From the Front," condemned his realism, he could command a decent price for them, he hoped. Frederick E. Church and some of the "Hudson River" school of painters were getting as much as $15,000 a canvas. He could never bring himself to paint the way they did, but he would also be satisfied with less remuneration. "All I want is to earn as much as a department-store clerk," he said once. His attitude was half-humorous, but with an undercurrent of dead seriousness.

In the meantime, in order to reach the point where he could paint exclusively, he did innumerable drawings, branching out with contributions to a number of magazines besides *Harper's* —publications like *Appleton's Journal, Hearth and Home, Our Young Folks,* and *Galaxy* were delighted to include his work. From May through September he illustrated a novel in *Galaxy*— five drawings of increasing drama and action. (His studio friends said they would not have to read the book after seeing the illustrations, which began with a mild scene for the line, "She turned her face to the window," and showed a young woman on a sofa, leaning back, toying with the edge of a lace curtain. Three drawings later the climax was reached in the picture for the exciting but grammatically correct cry for help, "Orrin, make haste, I am perishing!" from the heroine, seen hanging onto a log in deep water under a bridge, reeds and lily pads around her. The denouement was depicted in the setting for the impassioned protest, "I cannot! It would be a sin! A fearful sin!" showing the heroine kneeling on the floor, hands covering her face, with a man standing over her, his expression one of anxiety and distress.) This was hack work, but it was rather amusing, paid well, and he did not do enough to make it a bore. Occasionally he illustrated books of verse by New England poets—Whittier, Longfellow, Lowell, and Lucy Larcom—and the result was a fusion of the arts, in which the drawings translated the words into another medium without altering the cadence or meaning of the poetry; more than any other artist, he was able to preserve the full New England flavor of the lines in the ones he put on the block. He also illustrated the works of Tennyson and Bryant and one year turned out pictures for several children's books.

For the most part, however, Winslow preferred to contract for individual drawings as a means of building or augmenting his income, and over the next five or six years, until 1874, he did literally hundreds of them for as many as five different magazines. During this period he also painted, both in water color and oil, but he was so busy with the drawings that he did not have time to do all he wished—that would come later. And in the course of his self-imposed concentration on the form that would bring him the greatest financial return, he became a master of wood engraving.

As he increased the volume of his work, his skill increased, yet he never lost sight of the fact (as several of his fellow artists did) that wood engraving was basically a line medium and called for the kind of strong, careful drawing he had always been able to execute. Bold outlines, effective contrasts of light and dark, clarity, and objectivity were essential to successful engraving, and in these he excelled. Some of his contemporaries sought to reproduce every sort of medium—oils, water colors, even an etching—on the wood, and the result was more of an exercise in technique than an artistic achievement. Winslow stuck to the traditional technique in line drawing, using some tone at first, and then more and more. When he transferred a painting to an engraving, as he did in "The Summit of Mount Washington," he did not try to make it look like an oil painting in print, with every brush stroke reproduced; instead he *drew* the picture on the block, always with the credit, "From a picture (or painting) by Winslow Homer," so that it was a translation but not a reproduction of the scene in the canvas.

With the use of greater tone his wood engravings might be termed water colors in black and white, so much like pictures had they become, but they were not; they were engravings of the highest order—entities in their own right. His illustrations, as he went on, were rarely reportorial, covering an event, and not often of "topical" interest, printed with a correlating text, like the piece on dancing in Paris or women in outdoor sports. They could stand alone. Under his fingers wood engraving became an art form in itself. Not that he set out consciously to raise the standards so high. He was, however, a perfectionist, and in the process of perfecting his technique through the countless drawings that were published, he produced works of enduring value and charm. Moreover, he found himself considered an expert if not an authority in the field.

The name of Winslow Homer in New York art circles was growing synonymous with fine line drawing on wood, a fact he viewed with mixed feelings. By 1871 or 1872, when he walked into *Harper's* offices with a portfolio of sketches under his arm, he was always ushered into the office of the art editor, Charles Parsons, with great respect from James E. Kelly, the editor's young assistant, who worshiped Homer from afar. (Winslow, correct in his cutaway, striped trousers, and black tie, perhaps wearing a carnation in his lapel, looked more like a publisher himself than a painter, but he was so preoccupied with the "business" in hand that he was hardly aware of the young man's presence.)

Parsons always received him with "marked consideration"; he would go over the sketches with close scrutiny, making suggestions wherever they were necessary, yet never insisting on changes or additions. Winslow, who in turn respected his editor's judgment, would usually accept his ideas with a nod and a word or two: "I see," "Yes, you're right," or, "Very good." Then he would take a desk in the outer office and complete his drawings on the block, while the young artists gathered around to watch him—James Kelly, who wished to become a painter or sculptor, and two staff artists, Abbey and Reinhart, who were beginning to make a name for themselves but hoped to pick up valuable tips by watching him work. He had no serious objection, as long as they were quiet. He did not like to have anyone in the profession—outside of a few close friends—watch him paint, but that was much more intimate; drawing on the block required concentration and skill, but it was strictly business. He would not have tolerated meddlers, but he did not mind observers, especially young men with a desire to learn. It surprised him that anyone should expect to glean from him, but the knowledge that he excelled in one medium brought a certain satisfaction. In all others he felt he had much to learn—or to teach himself. There was not enough time for everything he wanted to do.

In the midst of all this, or through it all, and perhaps a cause in part of his tremendous output of drawings—he fell in love.

As the picture of the only girl he had ever really loved rose before him, he bit down on his pipestem and sucked in hard, the smoke bursting from his lips in explosive puffs. He saw her not as she appeared in the painting on the easel in the studio but as she looked at the height of the struggle between them—her brown eyes flashing, her delicate rosebud mouth, which had so captivated him, curled in a mocking leer. She was not beautiful, or even as pretty as the girls behind the ribbon counters. She had a piquant face, a pert, saucy look that could easily become petulant; her retroussé nose was too short for beauty, her cheeks too full; but with her perfectly rounded figure and teasing ways she was altogether fetching, and for at least five years of his life he was fascinated by her personality, torn between love of woman and his lifework, toying with the idea of marriage but always recoiling from it.

When he thought of his first meeting with her, he smiled, and the picture in his mind's eye changed to a little canvas he had painted in the summer of 1869; he called it "High Tide," and one of the critics called it "not quite refined." The painting was a record of their meeting the year before, just after he returned to New York from the White Mountains and the Manchester coast, where he had gone when the party broke up. He had taken off by himself to explore the countryside, visit the historic city of Salem, the scene of so many witch hunts in his ancestors' time, and finally to go fishing in the Merrimack River. "Idling" over a fish pole, he meditated on the months he had spent in France, wondering if he had wasted his time; he had no desire to return, like Alfred Howland, who went over every year. Yet Winslow had enjoyed himself, and the thought of the voyage sent the excitement of the sea coursing through his blood. Some day he would paint the sea; he would get at the meaning of it with the sweep and depth of powerful brush strokes, the laying on of color that caught the lights and intimated the shadows. . . . At the moment, when he had fished his fill, he did a painting of the Manchester coast, which he exhibited in the National Academy the following spring.

It was close to the middle of August when he came into Manhattan again to complete his illustrations for *Galaxy*, report to *Harper's*, put his drawings on the block, and take care of his "engraving business" generally. But his tower studio was like a bake oven, and the city looked sullen and drab in the summer heat. Even the carriages that appeared in Madison Square Park every afternoon, when fashionable ladies took their daily airing, seemed too hot for comfort; and up in Central Park the ponds were covered by a film of dust, the young trees already brown against the hillsides.

Unable to breathe after a few days, he declared to Eugene Benson that he would have to get away again as soon as his routine was taken care of—and he had collected payments to furnish funds for his traveling expenses. Benson suggested that he come to Long Branch as soon as he could; a bunch of artists

High Tide

The Metropolitan Museum of Art, Gift of Mrs. William F. Milton, 1923

were going to camp on the Jersey shore, and he could join them. Some of the girls they knew were planning to be there at the same time.

The season was at its height when he arrived. He spent a few days at one of the hotels along the boardwalk and made a number of sketches as well as a painting of the stylishly dressed women with their pillbox hats and parasols, strolling on the bluff, high above the beach; some, lifting their ruffled skirts daintily, were about to descend the long wooden steps to the sand. He set up his easel on the boardwalk and painted the scene as he saw it, gay, carefree, with much of the same bright sunlight effect he had achieved in "The Bridle Path." He was not afraid to use thick layers of paint to gain the lightness of atmosphere he wished, and, unlike the older artists, he used no glaze at all. To him, glaze ruined a picture by making it 'artificial,' and he wanted his paintings to look natural—not ordinary, because he could see the extraordinary in commonplace sights, but there must be no pretense about his art—no fancywork or unnecessary embroidery.

The feminine bathers amused him, dressed in their watertight caps, thin, close-fitting pantaloons, and knee-length bathing skirts. One morning he saw two comely swimmers, squealing and laughing as they gingerly sampled the surf, and he promptly sketched them for a drawing which was later published with the title, "Bathing at Long Branch—Oh, Ain't It Cold?" Women were such deliciously ridiculous creatures (in spite of their particular abilities and intelligence, which he was willing to grant) that he took delight in poking fun at their foibles, their exaggerated femininity in moments like this.

Toward sunset of the same day, when the tide was beginning to rise and the beach was almost deserted, he was tramping along the sand, folded easel and paintbox under his arm, followed by a little black dog he had picked up somewhere in the course of meandering. He was looking out over the ocean at a distant liner headed for Hoboken, so he didn't notice the trio on the beach until the little dog set up a fierce barking, as if to berate them for

On the Bluff at Long Beach, at the Bathing Hour

The Whitney Museum of American Art

having been caught by the incoming sea. Two girls and a woman had evidently been relaxing on the soft sand, drying off after a dip, when a huge wave rolled toward them and broke before they could get away, drenching them all over again. The woman, her back to Winslow, was standing on the edge, wrapped in a long beach robe, watching the wave as it retreated while she waited for the girls. One of them was bending over, wringing out the skirt of her bathing suit, her long blonde hair hanging down limply, covering her face like a mane—probably the cause of the dog's insistent yapping, which seemed to be directed more toward her than the others.

Seated on the sand, tying or untying the laces of her bathing shoes, her hair completely hidden by one of the tight-fitting caps, the second girl was obviously put out. She was not beautiful, but her face was curiously alive, set off by large brown eyes and finely arched brows that not even a frown of annoyance could disfigure. Winslow, grinning broadly, reached in his knapsack and took out his drawing pad and pencil as fast as he could.

"Oh, be still!" the girl called out to the dog at that moment, looking up before Winslow had a chance to begin sketching.

"Don't move!" he shouted impulsively, which was the wrong command, because then she did move, putting the back of her hand on her hip in the gesture he came to know so well.

The frown deepened to a scowl. "And just what do you think you're doing, pray?" she asked with biting sarcasm that some-how reminded him of his pretty schoolteacher years before.

"Sketching," he said coolly, plying his pencil across the page in swift, sure strokes; if he could set a few lines down he would have something to go on. "I'm a painter," he added quickly, lest she should take him for a 'masher.'

She eyed him skeptically. "You don't look like a painter to me," she remarked.

The other girl straightened up and peered at him through two hanks of hair, "Nor to me," she joined in.

The woman had already started back along the shore toward the boardwalk and beckoned them with an arm.

Winslow patted the folded easel. "Oh, but I am," he said. "And I hope you will pose for me—perhaps tomorrow, at this same time?" Sometimes he asked people to pose, but more often he did not, preferring the spontaneity of a candid view to a studied one. Today, however, he wanted to make sure of this particular scene as it appeared when he came upon it. He could not have said why this was so, but it had something to do with the eyes of the girl seated on the beach.

His words had the opposite effect. She stood up, giving her bathing skirt an impatient flick or two. "I'm sorry, sir. Our friend is waiting. Are you ready, Millie?"

Her companion shook the matted mane up and down, and the two flounced off down the beach.

Winslow watched them go rather ruefully; if he had kept his mouth shut, as he usually did, he might have finished the whole drawing before anyone noticed what he was doing. But some indefinable quality in the girl's face compelled him to reach out toward her, to make her aware of his existence. As his eye followed the retreating figures, he sketched the perfectly proportioned, curvaceous lines of the one wearing the tight-fitting cap. He had never painted nudes or studied drawing in a life class, more because he was not interested than because it offended his New England sense of propriety, yet now he recalled William Page's "Venus" and the thought made him blush, because he was sure the flesh tints of this girl's body must be like that. The frozen nudes of Bouguereau left him cold, but he had often remembered Page's Titianesque palette since he had seen it that day at the Dusseldorf Gallery, nearly ten years before, and his own flesh tints, in the faces and arms of his figures, reflected the impression those colors had made on him. (One critic wrote a few years later: "It is impossible to understand Mr. Homer's flesh tints or much of his colouring. His faces are always like Joseph's coat, of many colours.")

However, the chances of his seeing the saucy creature in the sketch he had just made, of painting her with or without clothes, seemed extremely remote; and with a shrug he had plumped himself down on the beach and lit his pipe. The little dog came trotting up and sat down beside him.

"You were the troublemaker," Winslow scolded him, and the mongrel sighed; a cross between a schnauzer and a fox terrier from his appearance, he had a comic face that was so appealing that Winslow could not help putting his arm around the wiry back. They sat there until the light faded from the sky and the tide, hitting its high-water mark, licked the soles of his shoes.

The next day he had found his colleagues far down the shore, camping like nomads on a deserted stretch of sand. He was hailed with joy and told that he must stay until the end of the week; Saturday night they were all going to a square dance. Homer Martin, who had completed three new landscapes, wanted Winslow's opinion on a couple of questions regarding the painting of foliage. (Between these two quiet artists there was a bond of silent understanding that required few words; both were beginners in the sense that they were still experimenting, and each admired the other's work, except that in Homer Martin the feeling was stronger.) Eugene Benson, Eastman Johnson, Roswell Shurtleff, and John F. Weir—another particular friend of Winslow's —were all eager to see what he had been doing, but he laughed and said they could wait until the Academy's next exhibit. The little black dog, which seemed to have adopted Winslow, was accepted as mascot of the campers and added his share of confusion to the clambakes and fishing expeditions.

The dance Saturday night was held in a huge barn belonging to the farmer who sold them milk and fresh eggs every day or two. The group of girls from New York, who were boarding at the farmhouse, had urged them to come to the dance. Hotel guests from the resort would be there, city vacationists in search of a novelty. Winslow, who had been to many a hoe down in Cambridge and Belmont, was not especially attracted, but at the last minute he decided to accompany the others.

The sea breeze that swept through the barn swayed the lanterns hanging from the crossbeams and stirred the sweet-smelling hay in the loft; when the three fiddlers struck up "Turkey in the

Straw," Winslow suddenly felt like dancing, and at the shout of "Right and left" from the caller he joined the line. Halfway down the row he found himself face to face with the girl on the beach, just as the order came to "Swing your partner!"

"The schoolmistress!" he exclaimed involuntarily as he swung her around—she was as light on her feet as a field daisy. There was no mistaking those large brown eyes, which opened wider in surprise. "How did you know?" she gasped, slightly out of breath from the twirling.

It was his turn to be amazed. "You're not really?" he asked incredulously, and she nodded, smiling for the first time, summoning a mischievous dimple in her wide cheek. It was then he noticed the delicate rosebud mouth, set off by white, even teeth. Her eyes held a challenge.

"Do I look like one?" she demanded.

"No—well, yes. Like a pretty one I had in the first school I went to," he told her between steps. She laughed, and the sound was like a small peal of bells above the violins. There was no time for more, because at that point they had to move in opposite directions; but when they came around together again, he found out that she was a country schoolteacher, in a village along the Hudson. She wouldn't give him her name or tell him where she taught. She could not pose for him—she was leaving Long Branch the next morning, she said, with a shake of her brown curls, swept up and held by a red ribbon above her shell-like ears.

When the set was over, he was nowhere near the spot where she stood, chatting vivaciously with some gentleman. With them was the other girl (her blond hair now neatly done up in a bun at the back of her head), and before Winslow could get to them through the laughing crowd, they had slipped out of the barn door and vanished into the summer night. All he could see was the tail end of a horse and buggy clattering down the road to the resort.

He returned to the dance, but somehow the zest was gone, and after a while he went back to camp and built a small fire on the beach. He tried to draw the girl's face from memory and the sketch he had made the day before, but it was no use; he needed the model. He had a premonition that he would see her again, if he had the inclination to investigate the village schoolhouses along the Hudson for new subjects.

When "Long Branch" was exhibited, the critics could not understand how the painter of superb war pictures could waste his time on such frivolous scenes. A Brooklyn paper remarked: "The success which attended 'Prisoners From the Front' seems to have somewhat spoiled a good artist." Winslow, reading the column in Shurtleff's studio, threw the paper in the wastebasket. Why must the critics keep harping on "Prisoners From the Front"?

"I'm sick of hearing about that picture," he complained bitterly.

There were painters, he knew, who had gone on 'capitalizing' on the Civil War and probably would continue to the end of their days. But the war was over, and best forgotten, like an ugly sore; the country was in the process of Reconstruction; life was being rebuilt, a whole new era was beginning, and the young faces at Long Branch, the summer residence of President Grant, were part of its spirit. From the standpoint of art criticism Winslow was even more annoyed, because the reviewers seemed to disregard the fact that his technique was improving, raw and experimental though it still remained. His feeling for sunlight and air had certainly developed over the summer, and he resented the fact that it should be regarded so superficially.

He considered versatility a prime virtue, necessary to universality in art. Late in the fall he spent some time aboard a sailing vessel off the New England coast, but he was back in New York before the holidays, in time to go to Belmont for the festivities. Here he drew a whole sleighful of pretty girls, setting off gaily for a ride, some waving their wide silk kerchiefs, others keeping their gloved hands warm inside the fur muffs they all wore hanging around their necks on braided cord. A scholarly looking driver was trying to concentrate on his duties. The engraving, published January 2, was called "Christmas Belles" and was a triumph in lightness of mood and sense of movement. Two weeks later,

Christmas Belles

National Gallery of Art, Rosenwald Collection

on January 16, *Harper's* printed "Winter at Sea—Taking in Sail Off the Coast," a dramatic drawing he had made on his recent trip, his first attempts at recording life at sea. Seven or eight sailors were aloft, taking in sail in a snowstorm, working against the wind, while far below them two men were at the wheel, peering into the blinding blizzard; the foaming wake of the vessel, the dark sky and sea gave a feeling of peril to the picture. Here was a complete contrast, an entirely different sort of activity and motion, yet it was equally successful and served as a sounding board for the key in which eventually he was to compose.

He was busy most of the winter with illustrations for serial stories published in *Galaxy, Hearth and Home,* and other magazines, so busy that he could not do as much for *Harper's* as usual. His work was in demand; art editors sought him out; yet the jobs allowed little leeway for originality and less time for painting. At the sign of the early crocus, peeping from under the thin layer of March snow, he was ready to take to the open road. It was the middle of April, however, before he finally got away, and, as if drawn by a magnet, his footsteps led him into the farmland and the country villages along the Hudson. From hamlet to hamlet he went, without any particular course, but a single direction in his subconscious mind. Although he would not admit it to himself, he was searching for the girl he had encountered so briefly at Long Branch.

In the meantime, he was collecting "material" for new and future works as he made his way cross-country. If a village was so small it could boast no inn or a wayside tavern, he boarded at farmhouses and roamed the surrounding fields. He carried his equipment wherever he went, and when he came upon a rural scene that struck his fancy, out would come the sketchbook or canvas. Sometimes he ran into trouble. Once when he started to sketch a sunbonneted maid feeding the chickens, the flock went scurrying in all directions, scared by a strange presence. Another day he heard a farmer asking a neighbor, "What on airth is thet feller prowlin' around our property fer?" and although he explained, they seemed mistrustful. Even the cows were suspicious and moved slowly away at his approach. (He did not choose them often, as cattle held little interest for him. Weaning a calf was a different matter; of this he made a number of notes, studies in oil, a water color, and a drawing; from these a large painting was eventually evolved—or composed, for he began to select and arrange as he profited by practice.)

All unconsciously he looked into every schoolhouse he happened to pass, idly wondering if this might be the one. These one-room country schools had not changed since his boyhood, nor had the games of boys. Snap-the-whip was still the favorite, he could see: if it was near the noon recess when he came by, there was generally a line of tousled pupils, hands joined, playing with all their might. He usually timed his "investigations" to coincide with recess or dismissal, because at those hours the teacher was out of doors supervising recreation or standing in the entrance-way as her charges filed past her for home.

By May he had reached the village of Hurley at the foot of the Catskills, four miles west of Kingston. It was noon when he came to the little red schoolhouse, set against a backdrop of green hills. The air was soft with the fragrance of late apple blossoms wafted from some gnarled old trees in a nearby orchard, and dandelions dotted the stubbly field in front of the door, which was suddenly thrown wide open as a torrent of children rushed out. He waited for the teacher, but she did not appear. The lunch pails were quickly emptied, and the boys began their games while the girls played tag or picked flowers, but still no sign of a teacher. He sketched the line up for "Snap-the-Whip"—a preliminary study—and then, out of curiosity, he made his way up to the door and glanced inside.

All he could see was a small boy, his face hidden behind a book, and a portion of a young woman's figure, the back of one hand on her hip; but even before he knocked he had an idea the unbidden search had ended.

"Yes?" She turned around and he beheld the provocative face, the vexation that turned to surprise when she saw who it was. "Oh." She lifted one eyebrow. "What is it you wish, sir?"

He grinned with unaffected triumph. "Will you pose for me, since you have nothing to do but guard this unhappy culprit?" He indicated the boy, who had peeked from behind the book covers and was staring at him, openmouthed.

She looked as if she was ready to tell him to leave, but instead she smiled unexpectedly. "You're the artist who was at the beach last summer."

He nodded. "And you the schoolmistress."

He had introduced himself properly then and shown her a copy of *Harper's* containing "Bathing at Long Branch—Oh, Ain't It Cold?"

She had recognized his work, had seen his illustrations for Mrs. Edward's novel, *Susan Fielding*, but had never dreamed that the anonymous painter at the resort would be Winslow Homer. She gave her name and posed long enough for him to get an initial note for a later drawing called "The Noon Recess." Then it was time for classes to be resumed, and when the pupils trooped in, he sketched them briefly at lessons, the first of many studies he made in the next two or three years for a painting of "A Country School," which was to become one of his most famous. He could not take long for he was too much of a distraction. He went outdoors again and drew the old orchard, with the crumbling stone wall along one side of it. At the close of school he waited for the teacher and silently handed her two sprays of apple blossoms, watching while she put them in water in a glass jar on her desk; afterwards he "walked her" back to the farmhouse where she lived during the school term.

As they strolled along in the warm spring sunshine, he found himself telling her of his earliest ambitions to become an artist, of the times he had been kept in at noon for "defacing" his school-books with drawings.

She laughed. "You deserved it!" she teased. (At least he hoped she was joking; he never knew for sure whether she was or not.)

He had not meant to stay in Hurley more than a day or two, but when they reached the house, he asked the farmer's wife if she had an extra room and could take on another boarder. The woman, a stolid Knickerbocker matron, sent a measured glance from the schoolteacher to the painter, as if to gauge their intentions, and, apparently satisfied, agreed to put him up at considerably less than the local tavern, where he had left his belongings.

That was the way it had all begun—almost casually, a passing intrigue. Yet he was still in Hurley three weeks later when school closed, during which time he recorded the simple rural life as he saw it: the farmer, plowing the stony soil, patched shirt sleeves rolled up in the spring sun; the farmer's wife as she stood in the kitchen door one day, blowing the dinner horn; and their daughter, the strings of her calico sunbonnet dangling loose, going to milk the cows, a three-legged stool in one hand and the pail in the other.

He did not see as much of the schoolteacher as he wished. She preferred to walk to school alone in the morning, and although he managed to be close by when classes broke for the noon recess or were dismissed for the day, he did not often succeed in being alone with her. One or two of the older girls always wanted to walk partway home at least with their schoolmistress, leaving him small chance to become acquainted with her. (He did a portrait of "The School Girl" who was most studious, her grave young eyes regarding him seriously, a book under her arm, the tips of her blond pigtails showing from behind.) At the farmhouse there was generally a full household for meals in the roomy kitchen, and even when he was lucky enough to sit beside her, he scarcely had a word with her. She seemed to be half amused, half annoyed at his presence, his habit of appraising her from head to foot with his artist's eye, his poker-face stare. His reserve kept him from revealing that he thought she was the most attractive young woman he had met in his thirty-three years, and as he was not a talkative man, he paid her no compliments except that he kept asking her to pose for drawings and paintings. (Eventually, out of the sketches and oil studies, he developed paintings of "The Schoolmistress" and "School Time"—the latter begun one morning when she consented to his company on the way to school. She was wearing a straw bonnet, with a ribbon run through its crown and tied under her chin, and she looked as fresh as the day itself.) The fact that he found her enchanting he scarcely realized, but he knew that he intended to see her again, as often as he could.

On the Saturday before she left, he invited her to go up into the Catskills with him for a day of painting; the farmer's wife fixed a lunch basket for them, and they took the "mountain wagon" (run by the livery stable), piling in with a party of tourists to ride as far as the first hilltop. Here Winslow decided he would like to paint the view looking across the valley to the folded hills beyond. He set up his easel among the tall grasses on the cliff, fixed his palette, and began to put on the color—fresh, pure tones as he saw them in the sunlight; he had no recipe for color but his own gifts of sensual pleasure and honesty, his innate sense of harmony. The "schoolmistress" stood watching him for some time, fascinated, and he could not resist making a sketch of her—and himself from the rear, painting the scene. He called it "The Artist in the Country," and *Appleton's* published it on June 19.

She proved to be a delightful companion, as carefree as a schoolgirl herself now that the term was over. After lunch, which she spread out neatly on a white cloth under a tree, she took off her shoes and capered around in the grass; she liked to go barefoot at every opportunity, she told him. She came from Rheinbeck and, after she finished her "Normal" training, had been assigned to the Ulster County school at Hurley two years before. She was an avid reader of novels and had brought one along with her, which she read, settling down against the trunk of a tree, when he went back to his canvas.

It was near dusk by the time they descended the hill, and the lamplight was already winking at them through the kitchen window as they approached the farmhouse. Stopping to rest his gear on the ground for a moment, Winslow was overwhelmed by a sudden desire to kiss the rosebud mouth he had been admiring all day; moving on the impulse, he did so rather thoroughly, and it would have been hard to say which of them was more surprised. As he released her, they stared at each other, then laughed.

"According to the novels I should slap your face," she said softly, holding up the book.

He said nothing but took it from her and tossed it on the pile of artist's paraphernalia at their feet.

The next day she had gone away, but not before he had made arrangements to meet her at Long Branch later in the summer. He took to the road again, heading east to visit his family, sketching as he went. The sight of three farm children, two boys and a girl, standing in a field, waving shyly to a mountain wagon full of gay vacationists "On the Road to Lake George," inspired him with an idea for an appealing picture, published under that title in *Appleton's* on July 24. All along the way he made sketches of "Summer in the Country," a series which ended with "The Last Load—Laborers at the End of Haying."

He did not mention his latest "heart interest" to anyone in the family, not even Charlie and Mattie, who came there for a few days. He was not sure of his feelings yet or whether the plans for their meeting would work out. However, he left Belmont earlier than he had intended and was in Long Branch a day or two ahead of time. His friends, who were camping on the shore again, were planning a picnic excursion in the hills, and Winslow was persuaded to invite the girl to come along, if she turned up . . . She did.

They met casually again, on the boardwalk in front of her hotel, the morning after her arrival. It was hard to believe he had kissed this saucy, imperious young lady—half hoyden, half schoolmistress in manner. Yet, once the initial standoffishness had melted, she was so friendly that he had had no hesitation in asking her to go on the excursion. She proved to be most congenial with the party, which was rather large, two wagonloads of picnickers, laden with hampers and baskets. One of the men had included a few bottles of wine, which brought disapproving glances from some of the ladies as they were unloading. Winslow could not refrain from recording the scene.

The next day he made a drawing of all the girls, down on the beach, strolling in afternoon finery at promenade time, hair all flying in the sea breeze (instead of pinned-up coiffures like the ladies of fashion on the boardwalk above). His girl, as he was already beginning to consider her in spite of himself, was carrying a closed parasol, using the point of it to print her initials in the sand. He posed her for the drawing as if she had just finished tracing a large "W.H." with which he signed the picture when he finished. She seemed to enjoy his playful inventions—indeed, she fell in with them more than the professional models, who did not always understand what he was doing.

He got two of them to pose with her in bathing togs when the tide came in, as she looked when he first laid eyes on her. She was somewhat disapproving, but this only made her frown natural instead of studied; and as painting was paramount to him, he did not stop to concern himself too much with her reaction. He made several oil studies for the picture "High Tide," which, if it did not win him praise, at least created a stir for its realism. He had later put it on the wood for one of the magazines. (During all of 1870 he did no engravings for *Harper's* and sent most of his work to *Every Saturday*, a Boston weekly which took a venture into the illustrated field, hoping to reap the same sort of harvest yielded by *Appleton's*, *Harper's*, and other New York publications. For an exclusive on Winslow Homer's wood engravings they offered a higher price than *Harper's*, and he could not afford to turn it down. But like *Ballou's*, the publishers of *Every Saturday* found that staid Boston would not support a pictorial, and the venture had failed after one year.)

By the time their stay in Long Branch was over, there was an unspoken understanding between them. Though nothing was said, both knew they would meet again, and often. In the fall and winter months that followed, Winslow went to Hurley frequently; he told himself the village was "handy'" for subjects he liked to use; he made sketches of the country store at the crossroads, which also served as post office and gathering place, where the farmers exchanged crop news and the genial storekeeper, in his little round cap, took time to help the ladies weigh themselves on his grain scales (all this in the midst of widely varied stock, including soap, fresh eggs, new brooms, flour, rakes, clotheslines, tubs of lard, and a "notion" counter). He drew the harvest scene, showing whole families in the fields at sundown; "the pumpkin patch," a study for a painting; and after the snow fell, country winter scenes filled his artist's notebook. He knew in his heart, however, that he would not have returned to this particular hamlet so many times if it had not been for the presence of the schoolmistress.

She still fascinated him—her warmth stirred him; her willful, capricious ways baffled him. She laughed easily and as quickly became impatient or exasperated; then the back of one hand would fly to her hip in a flamboyant show of anger and she would be utterly irresistible. When the apple blossoms perfumed the air again, he made further sketches of the schoolroom. This year there were more children, some of a very tender age (brought along by older brothers and sisters for the schoolmistress to "mind"). The pupils seemed to like their teacher in spite of her sharpness; a little group was always running to meet her when she arrived, even some boy who might have been kept in the day before. (Winslow had no difficulty in finding subjects for "The Noon Recess"; in the final version, which was not published until 1873 as an illustration for an inferior rhyme, he printed the first eight letters of the alphabet on the blackboard, stopping with *H*. Below them to the left he put both of his initials, adding a few numbers at random, so that at first glance the impression was one of blackboard work.) She was quick, bright, and intelligent, and if she was not profound, she had undeniable charm, and Winslow found himself falling under her spell the more he saw her.

In a vague sort of way, because he didn't even realize what was happening, he was disturbed about being in love this time. The transient affairs of the past were fleeting emotions; he sensed that this one would not be. On the first warm Sunday in spring he returned from an early-morning walk along the country lanes and found her alone, lolling dreamily in the hammock, which had just been put up the day before. The farmer's family was attending church, and all was quiet, even in the barnyard. He had held her; later they had talked softly about the future, and almost unconsciously he started sketching her in this unusual mood, which somehow changed her face. Suddenly the stillness was broken by the lilting chirrup of a robin on a branch of the maple tree beside the porch, and as she turned in its direction, Winslow caught her wistful expression, tinged very slightly with discontent. He called the drawing (which was not published until late August) "The Robin's Note," and to him it sounded a warning. He was getting more deeply involved than he had expected.

After school closed, they went on several excursions with friends, and he started a painting, "Under the Falls, Catskill Mountains"—a large canvas of the tourists making their way around the rocky ledges which afforded a full view of the cascades. In the foreground, the back of one hand on her hip as usual, obviously impatient at her companion's extended rapture over the magnificent sight, stood the schoolmistress with one of the models; half amused, half annoyed, she had never looked saucier or more alluring, dressed in summer white that showed off her figure to the full. Like most of the sightseers, both young ladies carried alpenstocks, but she sported hers like a walking stick.

Among his circle of artists and models she was accepted as 'Winslow's friend'; nobody asked any questions, no one voiced

The Noon Recess

The Cooper Union Museum

any conclusions; but he was vaguely troubled by that very acceptance. When they were by themselves, she seemed to take it for granted that they would some day be together permanently. Before they parted in June to visit their respective families, they spent "a quiet day in the woods," she reading a novel while he sketched or browsed through the newspapers. When she finished the story, she threw the book on the ground and leaned back against the trunk of the tree, daydreaming. After a time she had begun to speak of the future again and, as if musing aloud, said she hoped they would not have to wait too long. And he, disturbed, repeated his deep desire to become a painter in the fullest sense; he hoped he would soon be financially independent and could give up illustrating. . . .

Russell Shurtleff came from Keene Valley, in the heart of the Adirondacks, and when Winslow went into New York briefly to put his drawings on the block, his friendly neighbor suggested that he try the mountain lakes and streams for fishing that summer; the rocky retreat would be cooler than the seashore, and he might find some new subjects, as well as speckled trout. Winslow welcomed the idea and wrote to Charlie at once, and it was then that they had made the first of many camping trips to the North Woods for fishing, hunting, and mountain climbing. The region near Russell's home, an untouched wilderness of green-covered ridges, provided the pristine atmosphere Winslow had been unconsciously searching for, the elements which were to give a larger perspective to his life and his work.

With Shurtleff's help they secured a couple of guides—a young giant who always wore a red shirt, and 'Old Mountain Philips,' as everyone in Keene Valley called him, a bearded trapper, hunter, and angler who had been around so long he had become part of the scenery, a local celebrity. Without these two stalwarts to guide them, Winslow and Charlie could never have pushed their way through the thick underbrush and up the steep paths to campsites near the clear mountain streams that rushed out of the rocks. Here, in the stillness of virgin forests, as he went upstream by himself to cast or waited long stretches to play a wily fish, Winslow had time to contemplate the events of the past months, and he saw his love in a different light. Sex to him was not the all-consuming hunger it apparently was for most men; to him it would always be subordinate to the excitement of reproducing the grandeurs of nature, of discovering the secrets of color and brush stroke, the best means of capturing this pure, almost holy, all-pervading light of the mountaintop. Marriage, no matter how desirable the girl was, could wait; painting could not. During the next few weeks he did two 'Adirondack' oils, but they were only a beginning; he was far from satisfied with them.

He had to admit that it was not simply a question of finances that held him back from the responsibility of marriage: he wanted to be master of his art first. (Meanwhile, he made a number of drawings, at this time and in December, when he and Russell went trapping and deerstalking in the Adirondacks, illustrations for *Every Saturday*.) He said little of this to Charlie, but one night, as they were sitting by the campfire when the guides had fallen asleep and only the tall trees stood sentinel, he told him enough to reveal his conflict. His brother, with his customary concern, wanted to offer financial assistance but was wise enough to refrain from giving even advice; with typical Homer practicality, he agreed that the problem was a knotty one and mentioned that some of his business associates might be interested in buying Winslow's paintings—an indirect assistance he knew would be acceptable. He added casually that he and Mattie would like to meet 'Win's girl,' as she was later referred to by the family.

Winslow could see that he was in the same vicious circle that surrounded him before his trip to France, only this time the destiny of another was also at stake, and so the decision was more difficult to make. He had rebuilt his earnings, but he still had not nearly enough time to paint; if he could improve his art, he was convinced he could receive higher prices for his work, but he could not risk losing the income from the time-consuming illustrations, especially if he expected to marry. He told himself that it would perhaps be best to end the relationship before it became any closer. Yet August found him in Long Branch again, and after school opened, he resumed his frequent trips to Hurley; he could not stay away. He made studies of the "Dutch door" at the farmhouse, looking across the top half through an entryway and outer door to the sunlit field beyond; he did not develop the painting for some years, but he was constantly experimenting with the reproduction of light. In January a big storm kept him snowbound in Hurley, and when the farm boys began "shoveling out" through the white drifts, he recalled the pure joy he and his brothers had felt on winter mornings like this. In a reminiscent mood he drew the scene, which became one of his most famous engravings.

That winter the Metropolitan Museum had opened in New York, and Winslow had gone up to Central Park with the other artists to see the odd assortment of objects John Taylor Johnston had borrowed, or loaned from his own collection, for the opening. Some of his friends were eager to exhibit in the new museum, but Winslow thought the galleries were no improvement over those in the "new" Academy Building on Twenty-third Street, and *they* were none too good, with the exception of the large South Gallery. Until he could find a private dealer to handle his work, he preferred to show in the Academy.

For the spring exhibit his principal offering was the painting of the schoolroom, which brought him the attention of the critics, if not their acclaim, because of its unvarnished realism. He had shown the children in groups of two or three, reading, whispering, oblivious of the hard wooden benches, cracked and splintered, on which they sat. Some of the boys were barefoot, others wore their heavy bluchers; on a back bench three little girls were giggling, their heads in a huddle. His pretty schoolteacher stood at her desk in the center, reading aloud; a frilly white apron covered the front of her dress and extended over her bosom in the shape of a heart; her hair was held back by a ribbon, from which a few curls escaped onto her neck. The straw bonnet he liked so well was hung on a peg above the blackboard. A brass bell stood on the desk, along with two sprays of apple blossoms in a glass jar (in case this should be too broad a hint of romance, other sprays were thrown carelessly on the back table by the girls, and a small sprig lay on the wooden floor in the foreground, as if some child had dropped it).

He called the picture simply "A Country School," to represent those one-room rural institutions all over America; although it reflected his early days in Cambridge (and he had made recent sketches in Belmont), he did not want to designate any single place. Everybody who saw the painting recognized and recalled his own classroom hours, and it was this note of universality that gave the work its tremendous appeal. Even critics who were offended by Homer's realism and found pictures like this (or "Snap-the-Whip" in the following exhibit, and others, of run-down farms, peeling barns and rail fences, of awkward milkmaids and farm hands in cowhide boots) "damnably ugly," as Henry James expressed it, had to admit that the "truth and honesty" in them made Winslow Homer's canvases undeniably attractive. In the final version of "Snap-the-Whip" the general color effect of ruddiness expressed the character of these sturdy farm boys; when he showed them just as they had raced across the meadow and, with a hard yank from those on one end, sent the two at the other end tumbling, Winslow remembered how it was when he and Charlie and the Benson boys played the game with their school-mates, but this did not make the picture sentimental or nostalgic; it merely gave authenticity to the vigor and energetic play of schoolboys. (He was a familiar figure to the children, who felt at ease with him, and if he frequently asked them to pose for him, he was also ready to go fishing for suckers or show some small angler how to make a cork bobber, or give a sunbonneted little girl, sitting on the board of a rope swing, a push or two to send her up, 'up in the air and down.') There were no immediate purchasers for these pictures, but they increased his stature as a painter, his reputation as a realist.

Early in 1872 he had moved from the University Building into the famous Tenth Street Studios, constructed exclusively for artists by James Boorman Johnston, patron of the arts whose son was president of the new Metropolitan Museum. John LaFarge, whom Winslow knew only slightly, had been the first tenant, moving in before the plaster was quite dry, in 1858. Homer Martin had convinced Winslow to put his name on the waiting list, and both had been notified at the same time that there were vacancies. It was considered an honor to get into the Studios, designed for the working convenience of artists by Richard Morris Hunt, the first American architect to be graduated from the Beaux-Arts in Paris. Winslow, walking downtown from Mrs. Cushman's to his Nassau Street loft during his early days in New York, used to pass the Tenth Street Studios occasionally and wonder what it would be like, as he gazed at the word chiseled in stone on the front of the building, to work in a real "studio," with a skylight and long windows that probably gave more light in a day than the place on Nassau Street did in a week.

Now, thirteen years later, he was moving in, a full-fledged Academician, an expert and famous illustrator; yet, outside of his artist's paraphernalia, he had only a small wagonload of worldly goods to cart across the square to Tenth Street, and his room, on one of the lower floors, was scarcely more comfortable than the old one in the tower. He did buy a carpet and a brass alcohol urn for the brewing of coffee or tea on open-house nights when the artists exhibited their work. Among the advantages of living here was that the showroom was handy. The building was constructed in the French style of a hollow square, allowing all the studios to look out on the center dome or huge skylight over an enormous central studio fitted up as a gallery. The rooms were laid out in railroad fashion, with the door of one leading into the next, providing additional space for display.

Twice a year the artists joined in a co-operative exhibit. Most of the works were hung in the "dome gallery," but the whole interior was on display during open house, when the connecting rooms were thrown open to allow guests to inspect individual exhibits as well. A prospective buyer could wander from studio to studio, looking at the pictures, seeing how the various artists lived and worked, perhaps becoming acquainted with the painter whose picture he had just bought or was about to purchase. The consecutive order of the rooms on each floor made it possible to make the rounds easily in a short time, so that within a few hours a great many people could view the projects completed in the six-months period—oils, water colors, sculpture, stained glass —anything the artist wished to offer to a select group of friends and patrons. Cards or invitations were sent out for these "at home" occasions, which made them more acceptable to Winslow than they would otherwise have been. He avoided meeting the general public during Academy shows, but he realized that the artist's receptions provided a reliable market for his work and he overcame his reticence to be as genial a host as any of his colleagues. (Many of them were of the Hudson River school— Albert Bierstadt, Frederick Church, J. G. Brown, famous for his "bootblack boys"; Emanuel Leutze, who painted "Washington Crossing the Delaware," and others who were anything but bohemian and stuck stoutly by their conventional, dark-brown painting. On the other hand, there were a number of experimental spirits, like Homer Martin and himself, among the tenants —John LaFarge and J. Alden Weir, who became his close friends; Eastman Johnson was here also, and in a few years the dashing figure of William M. Chase arrived to change the atmosphere entirely when he took over the main gallery as his studio and made it the scene of many a revelry as well as "new thought" in art.)

In Winslow's mind the picture of preview nights on Tenth Street stood out clearly, especially in the first two or three years after he moved in. The whole block between Fifth and Sixth avenues would be crowded with glistening carriages, drawn by spanking teams, coachmen and footmen on the box, from which gentlemen in silk toppers and ladies with plumed hats, brilliant jewels, and furs passed through the portal of big barnlike doors lighted by the flares of a huge gas lamp on either side. Previews were high lights of the social season to which invitations were highly prized. Winslow's parents came from Belmont that first year; Charlie and Mattie drove from West Townsend; and "the schoolmistress" came from Hurley for the event.

Winslow's studio, like all the others, was brilliantly lighted with candles in addition to the gaslight; he had borrowed two candelabras and filled them with tall white tapers placed at either end of the room. The tubes of paint and the brushes on his worktable had been sorted out and lined up to clear a space for a bowl of bright flowers, which he arranged to bring out their form and gaiety—a talent he had gained from watching his mother, who noticed the bouquet as soon as she came in. (He wore a white carnation in the lapel of his cutaway, and he had placed two shell-pink camellias in the soft brown hair of his girl, who was turned out in a mauve-colored dress with a black-and-white-striped petticoat, a striking costume she had ordered for the occasion.)

On one of two small tables he had also borrowed the urn stood ready, the small flame underneath keeping the water hot; on the other a punch bowl held a more spicy liquid, which his father eyed suspiciously when Winslow asked him what he wanted to drink.

"Is there any alcoholic liquid in that, Winslow?" he demanded.

"Yes, Father."

"Then I won't touch it. I don't see how you can ruin the tissues of your stomach with such poison," his father growled, adding, "I'll take a cup of tea if you have it." He was a total abstainer, proud of it.

"Certainly, Father." With an exchange of the merest glances

between Charlie and Mattie and himself, Winslow fixed the cup of tea he had expected his father to take in the first place.

The reception had lasted for hours, until late at night. Distinguished guests came and left—art critics from leading papers and periodicals; curators from out-of-town museums; and internationally known collectors, as well as the socially prominent, who had the money to buy pictures. Long before the last guests had departed, the Homers were ready to go back to their hotel, having filed through the main gallery and most of the studios with the first line of visitors, and decided, as Charlie put it, that the other exhibits 'couldn't hold a candle to Win's.' Mr. Homer, however, wanted to know why his son didn't paint some "big" pictures, like Bierstadt's or Church's, or William Bradford's enormous icebergs, painted in the Arctic; then he could ask decent prices. (At an art auction held in 1871, only the year before, one of the "Croquet" scenes had gone for the ridiculously low price of $36, and the thought of it still rankled.)

Size was not so important; it was theme that counted, and technique, and spirit, Winslow thought, but all he said was, "Give me time," with a slow smile toward his girl, who was standing nearby.

She blushed furiously, knowing full well what he meant; yet she was not willing to grant him indefinite time, and it was after this evening that they became engaged—not formally, nor with a definite wedding date in mind, but merely with the understanding that they would marry as soon as Winslow was able to provide for a family.

For him even this was a reckless agreement, and he thought about it a great deal when he went to Belmont later on. He said nothing of it to his parents, although they voiced approval of the girl, and his father was of the opinion that marriage might improve Win's habits. He was especially emphatic on this score one Sunday morning when he asked if Winslow was going to church and received a simple but positive "No, Father" in answer. For the moment he merely shook his head disapprovingly as he took

Mrs. Homer's arm, and the two, regular churchgoers as long as Winslow could remember, went off down the road together. For some reason Mr. Homer had returned earlier than usual by himself and, as luck would have it, found Winslow in the fields behind the barn, busily sketching. He was trying to complete a haymaking scene he had started in Hurley and had persuaded the hired man to act as his model, posing with a scythe, as if he had just cut a swath through the alfalfa.

Mr. Homer, in high dudgeon, sounded off against such "Sabbath-breaking procedure" and berated his son for the bad habits he had picked up since he left home. (Here Winslow smiled, remembering some of those Sunday mornings in Paris—if his father had seen him *then*!)

"Will you tell me why you insist on working today?" The old man ended his sermon with an acid question.

"Tom won't have time to pose tomorrow," Winslow said calmly, continuing his pencil strokes, while the hired man, embarrassed, awkwardly shifted his stance. "This drawing must be ready for *Harper's* by Wednesday, and besides, it may rain." He looked up at his father for the first time. "I have to make hay while the sun shines," he said with a perfectly straight face.

Mr. Homer was hardly in the mood for humor, although he appreciated his son's quip. "So I see," he said dryly. But as he walked off, he delivered a parting shot. "It's high time you were married and settled down."

Winslow scarcely heard him—he was already engrossed in his work again, getting the effect of warm, sunlit fields on a calm summer day. In his initial drawing he had included a small boy and girl, sitting in the long grasses beside a pail of water they had brought the mower, and the delicacy of green spears surrounding the two little figures added to the lyric quality he was able to give a homely scene. When the full-page engraving, "Making Hay," appeared on July 6, *Harper's* editor wrote: "Mr. Winslow Homer's beautiful picture is a poem in itself, a summer idyll, suggestive of all that is most pleasant and attractive in rural life."

During the summer he completed the painting of the Catskill Falls and put it on the block as an engraving in September. He tried to save money and lived simply enough (the rent at the Tenth Street Studios was about $200 a year), outside his traveling expenses or an occasional extravagance. (With his penchant for trim-looking clothes, he sometimes bought an entire stock of an item he liked—underwear, or socks.) But as soon as he got ahead a little, he would have two or three paintings to be framed, and his small reserve of cash would be gone again. And always, always there were art supplies to be bought, new pigments he wanted to try, a roll of canvas one day, drawing paper or a sketch pad, charcoal or pencils the next. . . .

The following winter saw the "panic" of 1873 and the long five-year depression that set in a few months later. Winslow's father suffered severe "business reverses"; the farm in Belmont had to be sold, and both his parents went to live with relatives in Brooklyn. Luckily Charlie had just accepted a new position as chief chemist of the Valentine Paint and Varnish Company, a pioneer concern in a budding industry that bid fair to outstrip the textile mills in time. Always a mainstay in the family, Charles helped their parents move and saw to it that they were able to contribute their share of expenses to the Brooklyn household. Now, once again, Winslow saw his mother make the adjustment to hard times. As before, she managed to continue her water colors, standing before her easel several hours a day, in spite of the cramped quarters and the difficulties of living with in-laws.

That year both mother and son had exhibited work in the Brooklyn Art Association show, and both were proud of the fact, though they made little of it and each was pleased in a different way. There had never been a sense of competition between them, but rather a mutual, unspoken admiration. Mrs. Homer had long ago acknowledged her famous son's superior ability, yet she took her own painting seriously enough to keep at it and to exhibit professionally once in a while—if Winslow happened to be represented in the same exhibit, as in this one, so much the better. For his part, Winslow encouraged his mother to offer her water colors as fine examples of floral design. When either of them mentioned the pictures they had in the Brooklyn exhibit, it was to discuss technical points of hanging, placement, in terms of the best light, or prominence of position. (Winslow fared better here than he did in the Academy, where he was usually hung in the long corridor or up over a doorway, even now.)

It was due in part to his mother's work in water color that Winslow decided to take up the medium in earnest; he had painted in it occasionally or added touches of color to a drawing (one study of "The Schoolmistress" had been done with water color), but he had not thought of practicing the art with any degree of concentration before. In the spring the Academy held a showing of British water colors which added a further incentive since they proved to be very popular with the American picture-buying public. Here was a chance to increase his income enough to marry; and in time, if he was successful, he might be able to give up illustrating, which could not satisfy his soul, no matter how skillful he was.

In June and part of July, Charlie and Mattie rented a house near the ocean in Gloucester; the place was big enough to accommodate the family and a guest, Mattie wrote, if Win would like to invite his girl. He arranged for her to join him there in July after she had visited her parents, while he went on ahead as soon as school closed. From the day of his arrival at the fishing port he began to work in the medium which he had later mastered in full measure; he made sketches first and used quite a bit of gouache, so that his initial attempts resembled colored drawings. But he was delighted to find that he could paint swiftly and accurately, entirely in the open, recording his impressions spontaneously, and there was much to inspire him: the children playing in the harbor—boys busily preparing a clambake, fishing, wading, or bathing; building model sailboats from scraps picked up in the shipbuilders' yard; girls gathering berries in seaside meadows or

The Berry Pickers

Harold T. Pulsifer Collection, Colby College

playing "cats cradle" while a bunch of boys bounced precariously up and down on a homemade seesaw nearby. Before the month was out, he had produced a whole group of water colors, and while they were small, and somewhat tight in handling, there was a remarkable quality of freshness in them, of childhood joy perceived with a mature eye and recorded with the sure strokes of an expert draftsman and instinctive colorist. These were the brightest colors he had achieved so far, and he reveled in them.

When his girl arrived with an armload of books for summer reading, he did a number of water colors of her at her favorite pastime. In one she was sitting on the porch stoop, "Reading in the Sun," holding an open parasol over the pages to shut out the glare; another showed her stretched out full length on the grass, her jacket rolled up and tucked under her head as a pillow, devouring "The New Novel"; in a third she was lounging in the hammock, one hand behind her head, the other propping up the book, which half covered her face. (He also made an oil study of her as she sat in a straight chair on the porch, lost in some romantic tale—a picture that came close to portraiture.) In all of these there was an amused tenderness implied rather than stated, born of the tolerance between lovers. Winslow might tease her about always having her nose stuck in a book or talking her head off about the latest novel, but he thought she was charming whatever she did, and he admired her ability to spend so many hours reading. He himself was never a reader; he was a thinker—and a creator. For her part, the girl paid no attention to his gentle jibes and did as she pleased, confident of his love. She was impatient, however, about putting off the date of their marriage much longer, and he could hardly blame her.

In this mood he pushed himself into turning out almost as many drawings for wood engravings as water colors, among them the finest of his line compositions. He used much the same subjects—the children in the harbor; the small anglers, "waiting for a bite"; the berry pickers; the model-ship builders (in which he combined two oils and a water color to produce a work more

The New Novel

Museum of Fine Arts, Springfield, The Horace P. Wright Collection

complete and original than any of the three). Perhaps the most inspired of all, "Raid on a Sand-Swallow Colony—'How Many Eggs?'" was done only as an engraving. The picture showed four boys he had seen trying to keep from slipping down a steep sandbank near the ocean while they dug their hands into the holes for swallows' eggs and the birds fluttered excitedly overhead. Here was action, suspense, boyhood's intensity of purpose combined with the beauty of selective design that made these wood engravings of Gloucester his crowning achievements in the medium.

He went into New York to put his drawings on the block and took on some extra illustrating on the side to build up his savings. He worked like a beaver to get enough done for several weeks ahead (he had Gloucester material to furnish engravings for two summers). He was eager, too, now that he had begun to paint in water color, to try a few in a different region, perhaps the Adirondacks, where he and Charlie planned to go fishing again. Combined with his artistic goals, the sweet, if disturbing, thought of marriage goaded him on; he hardly let anyone into the studio.

One afternoon a knock came just as he had posed a professional model on a low board seat, as if she were in a rowboat, listening to a young man make love to her. Annoyed, he went to the door and opened it no more than a crack, blocking the entrance. It was boyish James Kelly of *Harper's,* who had come to deliver a block. Winslow noticed a card sticking out of the package as he accepted it and, as long as he was interrupted anyway, stopped to read the message. Charles Parsons had scribbled a few words of introduction on his card for Kelly, who had been wanting to meet Mr. Homer personally.

Winslow opened the door a crack wider, took one look at the personable Kelly, and asked him in—the boy was just the type he needed.

After a few friendly exchanges about the office, during which time Kelly looked wonderingly around the sparsely furnished, "spic-and-span" studio, in his eyes a palace of art, Winslow de-

Ship-Building, Gloucester Harbor

The Whitney Museum of American Art

manded abruptly, "Will you pose, making love to this young lady?"

The editor's assistant jumped at the chance, and when the sitting was over, Winslow, appreciative of the boy's co-operation and eagerness to learn, took the time to show him a few of the things he had done at Gloucester. He could see the same light of dedication in Kelly's eyes that was ever burning within himself, and from then on the youthful artist was one of the few "exceptions" who could come and go at the Tenth Street studio. His pleasant, lively face appeared in more than one love-story drawing as Winslow completed the magazine commitments he had piled up. He was able to promise that, if the work kept up at this rate, the wedding date could be fixed.

Yet the months passed, and for one reason or another he had to keep putting it off. The depression deepened; money was tighter. The water colors proved to be popular, but he had to price them as low as fifty dollars, or no higher than seventy-five apiece. All along he correlated the work in water color with oil paintings, which were expensive to frame. By the beginning of 1874, long lines of unemployed queued up in New York soup kitchens for a handout, and at night police stations were crowded with jobless men who could find no place to sleep. (Winslow received one of his now infrequent assignments from *Harper's*, to draw the "Station-House Lodgers," published in February 1874.) Many schools closed for lack of funds, and among them was the one in Ulster County. Its schoolmistress was left without a job, and few teaching posts were available. Rather than go to live with her family, she wanted to be married right away and start raising her own family, depression or no. Winslow, who had saved up a fair sum, said perhaps they might have the wedding in June.

He decided to show "School Time," along with several other paintings, in the Academy exhibit that spring; he would price it at $200. Framing for three pictures ate up most of his savings, but if he could sell one canvas, he would get it all back and make a profit besides. He hardly considered the risk; it would have been unthinkable to him to skip an Academy show. One prospective buyer was interested in "School Time" but said he could not purchase till later. The other pictures received not even a nibble. At the Water Color Society exhibit, running at the same time, his first professional display in the medium brought praise from the critics but no buyers. It was discouraging, but he had no thought of abandoning his art.

As June approached that year, his girl had tried to pin him down to a definite date, and he had to confess that his savings had gone for picture frames.

"How much did they cost?" she wanted to know.

"A hundred and fifty dollars," he said, not realizing the effect it would have on her.

"For *three pictures?*" She was aghast. It was then that she had launched into the tirade that had so startled and shocked him, a burning harangue that twisted her mouth into a mocking leer, provoking a violent quarrel between them, which ended in a flow of bitter tears on her part, and on his, feelings of pain and guilt.

"If you think so much of it, you can be wedded to your art, for all I care," she had flung at him hotly.

"Perhaps," he said slowly, seeing her with disillusioned eyes; yet he protested that his every effort had been aimed toward earning enough to marry; he tried to make her understand what it meant to be an artist in the full sense.

She hardly listened and, before he had quite finished, gave him the ultimatum of making up his mind by June; she was not going to wait any longer. They were in his studio, and he had taken her in his arms when she started to cry, holding her close, stroking her hair as he attempted to explain what it was like to be driven by a force so powerful that even love must wait on its demands. She broke away from him impatiently, and, grabbing up her jacket along with her straw bonnet, she rushed from the studio and went running down the stairs. Going to the long windows, he watched her hail a rickety old hack and climb aboard and, his heart heavy, saw it go clattering over the cobblestones at the flick of the driver's whip on the back of a hungry-looking nag.

He sighed, wondering what he should do.

He thought of going to Charlie for advice, but he knew that the decision must be his and his alone. Meanwhile, there was work to be done; he picked up a block and began transferring a drawing he had entitled "Two Hands in Prayer," depicting the work of New York charities, St. Barnabas House on Mulberry Street, which had to be ready for the issue of April 18. Without clasping them, he felt as if he were lifting his own hands in supplication.

He still had not made up his mind a month or so later, when one of his fellow artists, John F. Weir, whom he sometimes visited in West Point, invited him to come up for the weekend. The garden was in full bloom, the weather very warm for May, and Winslow, turning over the situation in his mind, could not sleep. The fragrance of the lilacs drifting in reminded him of the soft sweetness of his girl's hair, her skin, when he touched her cheek or kissed the palms of her hands. He loved her as he loved no other woman, and when the wave of passion washed over him, it swept before it all his objections to marriage. But when he thought of the years of struggle still ahead, and remembered the endless months of pinched living, if not actual poverty, he and his family endured, and when he saw the worried look come back to his mother's face recently, since the Homers had moved in with relatives, he could not bring himself to take on the obligations of marriage and fatherhood until he was in a position to do so—as well off as Charlie. To arrive at such a point might take years, and he was going on thirty-eight; he could scarcely expect a girl to wait. . . .

At three o'clock he got out of bed and quietly put on his clothes. He sat down on the wide sill of the open bay window just as the morning stars shone in the pale aura of predawn; before long the first roseate glow appeared, and soon the spectrum in the sky was reflected in the garden below as the golden bands broadened. Winslow, fascinated, marked the effect of the early light on the varied hues in the hyacinth bed, the rich blossoms of the lilac bush, and the trim tulip cups; his keen eye traced the patterns of shade on the garden walk. And unconsciously, as he continued his close observation, he came at last to his decision; his art meant more to him than anything else in life. He could not marry now, nor would he ever, if his girl would not wait.

His friend, coming in a little later, was surprised to find him up and dressed at such an early hour, sitting on the sill. Winslow said only, "I wanted to see the sunrise over the garden."

Once he had made up his mind, it was not so difficult to tell his girl. She seemed to sense what he was going to say and, on her side, was equally firm. Both were calm and controlled; it was as if the fever pitch of their love had been broken by the crisis, but now that it was past, not enough warmth remained to allow them to compromise. Since neither would give way, there was nothing to do but part. Before they went their ways, however, he wanted to paint her picture in the mauve dress with the black-and-white-striped petticoat.

"That old thing?" she protested. "It's nearly in rags!"

But in the end she wore the one he wanted. They had gone into the country, and she had brought along, besides a novel, a pack of cards. Sometimes at parties she told fortunes, out of mischief and a sense of fun, and in a whimsical moment had brought the cards with her that day. As soon as they found a "spot," she had stepped behind some bushes and taken off her shoes and stockings, as of old. She was hoydenish, gay, and defiant, determined not to show any regrets.

He posed her seated on a slow rise of ground, before the green curtain of shrubbery, her bare feet stretched out, peeping from the striped petticoat that showed in a ruffle all around beneath the mauve dress. She was wearing a jet necklace of unusual design, ending in a bar across her breast. She was idly shuffling the pack of cards while he set his palette, and on an impulse she selected a certain number from each suit, which she spread fanwise and held up. "Shall I tell your fortune?" she asked challengingly.

He did not answer, busy with paints.

The little frown came on her forehead, the piquant, teasing expression flashed in her eyes, and her free hand flew to her hip in the familiar gesture, the back of it pressed hard against her side, the palm wide open. "You will live to be an old man," she began, "a famous, lonely, crusty old man. You will have houses galore and no children to live in them. Your only companions will be your paintbrush and pipe."

He smiled. "Hold the cards a little higher," he said.

He did not complete the picture for some time; more than once he put it aside for several months and more than once thought of painting over the canvas, but he did not. In the spring show of 1876 at the Academy two paintings by Winslow Homer brought marked attention and acclaim from the critics and colleagues alike. One of them, begun in Gloucester, he had been working on for three years; called "A Fair Wind, or Breezing Up," it was a picture of three boys and an old fisherman returning with a day's catch, scudding before the wind in a sailing dory. The easy balance of the young crew, tired and dreamy-eyed, the slack rope in the old man's hands, the running sea were depicted with a vitality and feeling that had widespread appeal; an enthusiastic critic said "A Fair Wind" was "settled upon by the artists as the author's greatest hit since 'Confederate Prisoners.'" The other notable offering was also the result of several years' work and a number of studies he had made of the two guides who had been leading him and Charlie on their Adirondack trips. One of his largest canvases, "The Two Guides," showing old Mountain Phillips and his young partner standing on the mountaintop at daybreak, was a triumph in its conception of great height and vastness of space, of the sheer transparency of light in the mountains, and the primitive beauty of the forest.

People who came to the exhibit scarcely noticed the portrait of the barefoot girl in the mauve dress, except to remark that the title was rather odd—provocative. It read, "Shall I Tell Your Fortune?"

Shall I Tell Your Fortune?

Collection of Mr. and Mrs. R. L. Ritter

CHAPTER VII

Exhibitor Extraordinary

1875-1878

HE HAD TO GET AWAY, NOW THAT THE LOVE AFFAIR WAS OVER. IF
he had had the money for a trip abroad, he would have sailed on
the first ship, but since he could not, he wanted to paint entirely
different subjects, to lose himself in work that would be a complete change. Going through some Civil War sketches which had
not sold, he remembered the scenes near Petersburg that he
could only glimpse during the siege—negroes, picking cotton in
a field which had not been burned, or working their own patches
of ground before a tumble-down shack. He recalled the interesting structure of their faces, the combination of innocent
childish joy and primitive poetry in their expressions.

Early in 1875 he packed a grip and his artist's paraphernalia
and boarded the train for an indefinite stay in Virginia. He took
a room in the little hotel on the main street of Petersburg, where
the news soon spread that there was a painter in town. The name
of Winslow Homer did not mean as much as it did in the North,
but the mere fact of a painter's presence sent a flutter of excitement through the community; and the ladies of First Families,
clinging to the shreds of colonial aristocracy, were quick to offer
their southern hospitality to him, no matter if he *was* a Yankee.

During the first week or so a number of invitations were delivered to him at the hotel.

Winslow, however, was seldom on hand to receive them. He had looked up the colored section on his arrival, and he usually spent a good part of the day there, making friends with these people over whom the war had been fought. He saw that, although the Fourteenth Amendment had liberated them, it had brought to a great many among them more hardship than they had known before. Economically, freedom meant only that they had to shift for themselves; the paternalism of the slaveowner, doubtful as it was in most cases, was gone, and in its place was the necessity of earning enough every day for mere existence. Work was scarce, and wages were pathetically low, as low as southern employers could set them and stay within the law. Yet theoretically, legally, the Negroes were free; and psychologically, philosophically they experienced, Winslow observed, the same elation, the same high hope that he had known when he left Bufford's. Talking to aged and wizened "Uncle Ned," who worked his small square of soil with pride, Winslow read in his face the patience that would outlast prejudice and make each small gain a milestone toward equality.

Every day after his breakfast in the hotel he took his paintbox, drawing pad, easel, and campstool and went to paint among the cabins. He found, as he had during the war, that the Negroes were a simple, friendly people who, as soon as they got acquainted, were happy to pose for him. He made studies of them at home, working in the fields, in a festive mood at carnival time, and in a deeply religious one on Sunday morning, when they were able now to read the Bible themselves and there was no one who could tell them they dare not. They soon came to expect him at a certain hour and welcomed him with good-natured friendliness and ease.

He had left Uncle Ned's one afternoon and gone toward a cabin farther down the line, where he had begun a study of the mother and two daughters who lived there. As he approached, he saw that an elderly white woman was standing in front of the three, who were resting on the bench by the door. The visitor was obviously their old mistress, and he recognized her as one of the social leaders who had proffered him hospitality. Undaunted, he asked her to pose with her ex-slaves, just as she had been standing there, conversing with them in prim, threadbare elegance. She looked surprised to see him and uncomfortable at his request, yet she could hardly refuse, and he was able to get enough of an impression in that moment to create one of his most successful pictures.

Before long, news of the Yankee painter's activity was all over town and was bitterly resented by the majority of whites, still smarting from the defeat at Appomattox. He was labeled a "damned nigger-painter" by a group of firebrands, who threatened to run him out of town. When Winslow heard of it from the Texan who usually sat next to him on the hotel porch every evening, he shrugged his shoulders. He was preoccupied with an idea he had just conceived for a painting of two young Negro girls in the cotton fields, sunbonneted like his northern farm girls, but working with a grace and poise, and possessed of a certain stately beauty completely foreign to the white counterparts he had painted up North. He had no time to worry about crackpot warnings. He kept right on going to the colored section, selected the two subjects he needed, and began the painting of "The Cotton Pickers."

The work progressed swiftly, smoothly, and he was pleased, well satisfied with the strides he had made already since he was no longer burdened with deadlines for engravings. He had met the last one for *Harper's* just before he left for Virginia; the drawings he did now were simply work sketches, principally for his own use. With his decision not to marry, he had resolved to stop turning out illustrations week after week, so long as he was not in dire need. His water colors would bring in enough for a single man, and soon he could ask more for them; he was perfecting his technique all the time. He had not indulged in regret

A Sunday Morning in Virginia

Cincinnati Art Museum

or self-pity, and if he felt pain when he thought of his girl, he did not dwell on it; he had trained himself to concentrate so thoroughly on his art that it was not difficult to sublimate the memory of his love.

It was while he was in the midst of studies for "The Cotton Pickers" that a group of club ladies asked to see his work. Ordinarily he would have refused, but the streak of contrariness in his nature could not resist showing the busybodies exactly what he was doing, and a small exhibit was arranged in the lobby of the hotel.

It was received with cold stares and none too polite silence from the women, until a "First-Family" belle finally asked in a broad southern drawl, pointing to the picture of the two young cotton pickers, "Mr. Homer, why don't you paint our lovely girls instead of those dreadful creatures?"

"Because these are the purtiest," he said gruffly, exaggerating his own Yankee inflection. His tone was final.

The woman blushed with anger and turned away. His remark spread like wildfire through the town, receiving various interpretations along the way. A few days later Winslow and the Texas drummer were sitting on the hotel porch, when they saw a roughneck riding up to the hitching post. Clearly a fanatic, he jumped off his horse and, without tying it up, started menacingly up the steps toward the "damn nigger-painter." He muttered the phrase like a curse.

Winslow sat perfectly still, his hands in his pockets, and watched the man slowly mounting the steps. He told Charlie afterwards, "I looked him in the eyes, as Mother used to tell us to look at a wild cow," but at the moment he hardly realized that he was more than returning the grim stare coming closer with each step. Halfway to the top, his assailant suddenly stopped, seemed to change his mind, and with a quick turn ran back down, sprang on his horse, and rode off. When he was well out of sight, the Texan, who had vanished, wriggled out from under a bench near their wicker chairs.

The Cotton Pickers

Collection Mr. James Cox Brady

"What did you get down there for?" Winslow asked him, amused at the drummer's bulky figure emerging from the tight space.

"Well, it wasn't my fight," the Texan said, "and I thought there was going to be some shootin'."

Winslow was puzzled. "Why did he go away?"

"Well, I'll tell you. He thought you had a derringer in each hand and were going to get the drop on him."

It was too good a story to keep, and that night Winslow sent an account of the incident to Charlie and Mattie. He continued to paint in Petersburg for several weeks and needless to say, was not attacked again.

He had returned to the little town a number of times in the next year or so but on this visit started the series of water colors and oils that placed him among the most individualistic of painters. No one before him had painted the American Negro with such sympathy and understanding. He could picture the humor in their actions without making fun of them, point out the miserable way they lived without overpitying them, and reveal the religious, poetic side of their nature without glorifying them. His objective eye saw much artistic value in a race that had heretofore been represented principally in caricature, and he set about changing the concept.

His love of color had full play in the garish reds, yellows, and purples they wore, which harmonized perfectly with the dark flesh tints. In the softer blues, greens, and mauves, their choices matched his own intuitive sense of harmonic synthesis. His largest canvas, "Upland Cotton," which was not exhibited until 1879, was analyzed by one critic as "a remarkable penetration of Japanese thought into American expression. . . . The picture is a superb piece of decoration, with its deep, queer colors like the Japanese, dull greens, dim reds, and strange, neutral blues and pinks. Japanese Art is not gorgeous . . . but its peculiar and artistic subtlety has been assimilated precisely by Mr. Homer. This picture seems to us original and important as an example of new thought."

He stayed in Virginia until the weather became too warm for comfort; when the sun grew strong enough to ripen the watermelons he was ready to leave, but he delayed his departure to complete some water colors and drawings he had made of a few children he had stumbled on near the melon patch. Four of them were diving into a huge quarter of the red fruit; it was a delicious scene, one he had to get on record, and his subjects were more than willing to co-operate—he thought the watermelon would come out of their ears! And the pictures gave that impression. "The Watermelon Boys" contained broader humor than any of the other works he did in Petersburg, and it proved to be almost embarrassingly popular. In "The Unruly Calf," showing a small black boy trying to control a stubborn calf, or "Weaning the Calf," or "The Carnival," the humor was much more subtle; compared to these, "Watermelon Boys" was superficial, and he was annoyed by the success of such subject matter.

He had completed most of the oil paintings in his studio when he returned to New York. His colleagues on Tenth Street, particularly John LaFarge and Alden Weir, took great interest in his latest work and encouraged him to persist in choosing original subjects no matter how much the Hudson River school artists might frown upon them. In the nightly discussions that often went on till all hours in one studio or another, these conventional souls tried to convince the nonconformists to "mend their ways," but both LaFarge and Weir recognized in Winslow Homer a distinctive genius which, though still in the budding stage, gave promise of great flowering. They sided with him and Homer Martin against the others, and he appreciated their support. Not that he needed encouragement from outside; he would have gone his own way if no one had agreed with him, but it was heartening to know that there were others besides himself ready to beat new paths in American art.

It was not easy to find models for some of the paintings, so when he saw a type he required, he wasted no time. He was

walking along West Street shortly after his return, when he saw
a large colored woman lumbering toward him, her bulk about the
same as that of the southern "mammy" he was depicting. He
stopped her, explained that he wanted her to pose for him the
next day, and scribbled "51 West Tenth Street" on a card for
her. She looked rather doubtful, but promised to come, and
showed up at the time she was expected.

He grinned as he remembered her expression when she looked
around the studio, awed by the half-finished paintings, the easel,
the model stand, and struck with horror at the sight of the lay
figure, hung limply over a chair.

"What's that?" She pointed to it fearfully.

"Just a dummy I use for a model—dress it up in different suits,"
he explained briefly, busy with paints.

"Looks like a corpse to me."

He tried again to tell her what it was and got her to pose, but
she still cast nervous glances in its direction, her eyes rolling in
terror. He had made a good start when he discovered a small
footstool was missing and went behind the screen, where he kept
his props, to fetch it.

He had no sooner turned his back than the "model" jumped off
the stand, dashed out of the studio, and fled down the four
flights of steps in spite of her enormous size. He reached the
window in time to see her running down Tenth Street, and, as he
told it later, "she was only hitting the high places."

In July that year—1875—his brother Arthur was married to
Alice Lowell, and Winslow joined the rest of the family for the
wedding. Arthur, who had been coming from Galveston every
summer for his vacation, had discovered an ideal spot at Kettle
Cove on Prout's Neck, a peninsula running out about ten miles
from Portland, Maine. The only hotel in the craggy strip of land
was the Checkley House, a frail shingle building perched precariously on the cliffs out over the coast line, and here it was that
the couple came for their wedding trip. Winslow found Alice an

agreeable person (if not as outstanding as Mattie) and spent a good deal of time getting acquainted with his new sister-in-law. He made a drawing of her, sitting on a hillside with her back against a tree trunk (as his girl used to do so often), Arthur lounging at her feet, gazing up at her in lazy adoration.

Winslow called the drawing "The Honeymoon," and while he was sketching, he could not help wondering whether he had been too unbending in his attitude toward marriage. But when he thought of the progress he had made during the past year, of the freedom from the printer's deadline, of the pleasure he took in drawing only when he chose, for entertainment like this or taking notes for water colors and paintings, he could not regret his decision. There were moments, it was true, when the vivacious, piquant face of his erstwhile "betrothed" came before him unbidden, but he would push the image to the back of his mind and busy himself with his work. And he was happiest when he was hard at it. Finishing the sketch of the newlyweds, he signed it with a flourish—"Kettle Cove, Prout's Neck, 1875"—and gave it to Alice and Arthur for a wedding present, one they had always treasured. Family ties were strong in the Homer clan, however undemonstrative its members might be or how often their affection took the form of a practical joke. They were closely knit in all they did, and Winslow found a certain contentment in the fact that both of his brothers were happily married.

He was too objective to indulge in much self-pity or recrimination over the lone life he had chosen to lead. Besides his art, he had the company of his colleagues in the Studios, several of whom were already his fast friends. For a number of years these friendships had replaced love in his life. When the portrait, "Shall I Tell Your Fortune?" had not sold at the close of the Academy show in 1876, he had put it away with a pile of unpurchased paintings, where it had remained for a quarter of a century. He did not want a constant reminder of the fact that his lack of financial success had forced him to give up all ideas of marriage.

During the winter months he spent the long evenings with the groups that gathered in someone's studio—very often it was Eastman Chase's—and listened to the heated arguments with noncommittal silence. Once in a while he would offer a dry comment or a suggestion for some side line in which they could all take part. The Centennial Exposition of 1876 featured a display of decorative arts that captured the country and sent young ladies, if not whole households, into a fever of china painting, "pyrography," and tile design. Winslow, like the other artists, had small regard for the burnt wood and leather pieces, or the hand-painted dinner plates, but the Spanish tiles, on which colors could be fired to a dazzling brilliance, caught his fancy as much as theirs. In the fall of 1877 he was one of the founders of the Tile Club, along with Alden Weir, Abbey and Reinhart (his friends from *Harper's*, who had taken over much of the illustrating), Chase, William R. O'Donovan, and several others. It was his idea to have no rules but one—that the membership be kept small, not more than twelve at the most, so that the club would not become an "organization," with tiresome details like officers, a constitution, or the deadly dues.

The keynote was informality: every Wednesday night a dozen or fewer would meet in some member's studio, where the host was ready with a stack of blank tiles, a keg of beer, and a large board of cheese and crackers. In return for these essential supplies he was presented with all the tiles produced during the evening, often a rather dubious remuneration, especially in the beginning, when the efforts of the majority at a purely decorative art proved feeble, to say the least. Before the meeting was over, one or two would stray from the business at hand and start plinking a mandolin or strumming a guitar as accompaniment to the latest ballad. Soon others would join in, and almost invariably paints and brushes were put aside for entertainment or one of their heated discussions.

Winslow was one of the few who stuck to the project until he had mastered the art. He was fascinated by the gleaming color of the tiles when they came out of the kiln, and he used a full scale instead of monochrome as the others did. He had no objection to the impromptu choruses, or the hot arguments, but he was too busy 'playing' with the art of tile design, employing his fine draftsmanship on the eight-inch, white clay squares as he had on the wood blocks; when somebody ribbed him about his persistency, he smiled and puffed on his pipe. His noncommittal silence won him the pseudonym of "the 'Obtuse Bard' (whose birthplace was rendered obscure by a bad habit he had of promiscuously begging his bread, for purposes of erasure)." All their names were disguised by something equally farfetched, in keeping with the spirit of the club.

Whether he took part in the clowning or not, he enjoyed it, so much so that he elected to hold the club's first annual dinner in his quarters; he planned the menu carefully and shopped with New England thriftiness, remembering, too, the delicious madcap meals the artists in Paris had bought for a few francs. The event had been a great success, recorded by the club's historian as "one of the most crisp and toasty affairs that ever took place since the time of Lucullus, involving, as it did, too, a singularly small consideration in cash *per capita*."

During that first year he had made a full set of tiles for the fireplace in Charlie's new home—an outright piece of pure decoration—eighteenth-century shepherds and shepherdesses that, with their ruffles and ribbons, bodices and knee breeches, shepherd's crooks and crocks, were more like Boucher's French rustics than Winslow Homer's Yankee milkmaids, farm hands, or rugged woodsmen. He chose the theme deliberately, as an artistic and family jest, knowing Charlie and Mattie would enjoy such an outlandish contrast to his usual subjects. However, with his customary thoroughness, he carried out the project with wholehearted energy. He went to the costumer's for authentic "props." He did most of these tiles in his studio, on offhours during the day, in order to get the best light so he could experiment with two or three colors, instead of sticking to monochrome, the way most of the members did at meetings because of the artificial glare of the gas jets.

The outcome was a fireplace of such delightful ingenuity and skillful delineation that it was one of the distinctive features in Charlie's house (and was so admired by his mother that he did a second set for his parents, though they were still with the Brooklyn relatives and had no home in which to put it). He was pleased by the success of his efforts, because it was a small measure of his appreciation for his brother's kindness and understanding in giving him indirect assistance. Charlie was now an executive in the Valentine Company, and the two brothers who were the owners—Henry and Lawson—were almost as interested in Winslow's career as he. From the first Lawson had been impressed with Winslow's honesty, his rough yet highly poetic picturization of contemporary American life. Between them there was an easy camaraderie that few people beside Charlie enjoyed.

When "A Fair Wind" was exhibited at the Academy, Lawson had been so taken with the painting that he had made an immediate offer for it without naming any price. Winslow wrote him a characteristic answer:

"I am very much obliged to you for noticing my picture at the Academy & expressing a wish to buy it. Take my advice and don't do it. I am about to paint much better pictures & will give you a chance at them. If the 'Fair Wind' comes home to me from the Academy I shall be glad to sell it to you at a reduced price, but as it stands now it must bring me the price in the catalogue to have it pay me for three years' work. The price $850 would be reduced by commission and frame—

$85
55
$140 $850
140
Little enough $790

"P.S. I shall come down for beans on Wednesday."

A Fair Wind, or Breezing Up

National Gallery of Art, Gift of the W. L. and May T. Mellon Foundation, 1943

It was this drollery, along with his ability to concern himself with things of the moment, that kept Winslow Homer from brooding on his decision to lead a lone life and becoming an embittered man because of it.

CHAPTER VIII

Sunlight and Spirit

1878-1880

LAWSON VALENTINE'S INTEREST IN THE WORK OF HIS PARTNER'S gifted brother led him to offer Winslow a summer sojourn at Houghton Farm, his country place near Cornwall, in Mountainville, New York. The Valentines were going to be away, so the artist would be free to paint as much as he liked without fear of being interrupted or observed. Both Lawson and Henry knew his aversion to publicity and prying eyes. Like Charles, they understood the artist's need for privacy and respected it. At Houghton Farm he would have the opportunity to work exactly as he wished, as much or as little as he liked.

Winslow jumped at the chance. He preferred going away by himself in the summer (save for the fishing trips with Charlie) to taking weekend jaunts with his colleagues as he had sometimes done in the past. At the annual dinner of the Tile Club the members had planned an excursion of several days aboard a canalboat and another in the mountains during the month of July, but Winslow had only half consented to join them at the time, and now he was glad of an excuse not to do so. He was still sociable during the evenings of the winter months, when painting was impossible anyhow, and he enjoyed the company of John La-

169

Farge, Alden Weir, Eastman Chase, and Homer Martin outside
the Tile Club meetings; but more and more he was discovering
that he had to be by himself in order to create the art form which
most forcefully expressed his profound feeling for nature and
life at its core. Water colors at this point in his career were
rapidly taking the place of the wood engravings as a means of
income and a record of firsthand impressions, later to be used
as a basis for paintings. Drawings, if he made any, were the
merest sketches, preliminaries to water colors, and they in turn
were preliminaries to paintings. However, his drives for perfec-
tion were so strong that, just as his wood engravings had become
a true art form in themselves, so his water colors, because of his
experimental technique, already represented a much higher, more
spontaneous art form than the one taught in ladies' finishing
schools or practiced heretofore by wishy-washy painters with
a predilection for prettiness.

Houghton Farm proved to be an ideal spot for his scheme of
painting directly from nature, his experiments with light and
color. Surrounded by the pastoral scenes of rounded hills, slim
valleys, and sloping pastures where small flocks of sheep gam-
boled and grazed, tended by a slip of a shepherdess in her early
teens, Winslow had given his fancy free rein; he had embarked
on a kind of water-color spree and had produced dozens of pictures in the medium during a single summer.

He soon discovered that the half-grown girl who watched over
the sheep with a lackadaisical air was the daughter of a poor
mountaineer in the neighborhood. He arranged with her father
to have her pose for him as she looked after the flocks. He
remembered how tickled the girl was and how she had shown
up the first time dressed in her Sunday-meeting clothes, starched
and beruffled, in place of the smock and sunbonnet she wore
every day.

"This won't do," he had said, and had sent her home to
change. She went meekly enough but was so bewildered and
crestfallen at not being painted in her Sunday best that he felt

Shepherdess Tending Sheep

In the Brooklyn Museum Collection

sorry he had been so brusque. He promised that if she would pose a number of times in her loose-fitting calico and limp sunbonnet, he would paint her later on in a real 'costume.' And even as he spoke, an imp of an idea came to him: he would send for the laced bodices, straw hat with blue ribbon streamers, the buckled shoes, and shepherd's crooks he had used in the tiles, and he would paint this gawky, "flat-breasted, pie-nurtured" Yankee girl in an eighteenth-century shepherdess outfit!

The result was a delightful combination of the classical with the modern, of the fanciful with the realistic. No amount of ribbons or laced bodices could disguise the awkward adolescent from upstate New York, who stood on the hillside one spring morning, pleased and serious at having her picture painted, while the breeze ruffled her "costume" and bent back the brim of the wide straw hat with its blue streamers. He did many studies in water color and several in charcoal of shepherdesses that season; sometimes they were crossing a meadow, arms entwined, exchanging country gossip; sometimes they flirted with a farm boy on a fence stile or rested in the shade of an apple tree, stretched out on the grass. But the most successful of all was the girl in the eighteenth-century costume. To his surprise, critics and public alike were captivated by the playful innocence of the portrait, the freshness of the atmosphere, the freedom of handling in color and wash. He had not expected such pronounced acclaim, nor, in his eyes, did he deserve it for these pictures. He was pleased, but principally because he felt that his command of the medium was growing and because this would lead to greater achievements in painting. (Oddly enough, however, the oils he did from the Houghton Farm water colors were not as successful; done later in the studio, they were too stilted and lacked the lightness and spontaneity of these on-the-spot water colors.)

Lawson Valentine and his brother Henry promptly purchased many of the Houghton Farm pictures, helping him over the financial hurdle he had been up against since he had stopped

Fresh Air

In the Brooklyn Museum Collection

illustrating.

His reputation abroad was slowly growing; in Europe as well as America he was gaining recognition for the naturalistic quality of his work. Before leaving for Houghton Farm in the spring, he had sent a number of his most successful paintings to the Universal Exposition of 1878 in Paris. As he had done eleven years before, he chose canvases which would represent two types of subjects—"Snap-the-Whip" and "A Country School" were contrasted by "A Visit From the Old Mistress" and "Sunday Morning in Virginia." All four were praised by the critics, and one publication reported that "Mr. Homer would have received a gold medal had he sent more carefully finished examples of his very real and decided talent." That the critics were still crying for greater "finish" irked him no end, but if his paintings, for all their roughness, came close to winning him a gold medal, he was satisfied that his work was progressing. He did not set much store by such awards, but they served as a yardstick of success in the eyes of the profession; and, indifferent as he might appear to be on the surface, he was deeply concerned over the lack of understanding and real recognition he had been shown so far. He would continue to go his own way whether the word of the critics was in his favor or not, but he hoped the time was not far off when his art would find full appreciation in their columns, and he was practical enough to realize that artistic success was often followed by financial security.

The months at the farm had been pleasantly busy, idyllic if not downright bucolic in flavor, and although he had enjoyed this interlude, Winslow did not care to risk getting a name as the painter of "the American shepherdess"; moreover, he was growing restless, feeling the urge to explore rugged country that offered strong masculine subjects. Late in the season he and Charlie went to Keene Valley on a camping trip; fishing tackle and hunting knives formed part of their gear, along with "Win's" tin box of paints, his brushes, and palette. The first night, as they camped beside the inscrutable dark forest they would pene-

trate in the morning, Winslow was struck by the contrast between
the pastoral setting he had just left and the mysterious power of
the scene before him. Charlie had already climbed into his
sleeping bag, but the guides sat silently before the fire, watching
the tongues of flame that leaped toward the sky and lit up the
towering background of trees. No sign of a house, no cultivation
within miles; from the depths of the forest came the howl of a
wolf, then all was silent again save for the crackling of the logs.
. . . Before he knew it, Winslow had taken out his paints and
started an oil study—red, black, deep blue; he worked fast, recording an impression: the fire in the foreground, the two figures,
the forest, the night sky. . . .

   The painting, "Camp Fire," turned out to be his most important
oil that year. He had hardly worked on it afterward; only a tall
tree was painted on later, and then he built a fire in front of it,
studied the light effect, and put it on the canvas. Russell Shurtleff, whom they saw before leaving the Adirondacks, said the
picture was "so real a woodsman could tell what kind of logs
were burning by the sparks that rose in long, curved lines," a
tribute Winslow appreciated more than the estimate of the critics,
who again spoke of the "promise" indicated by the latest product
of the artist. Only one of them, George W. Sheldon, took the
trouble to ask for information about his method of painting, in
the first interview of his career, published in the *Art Journal* that
year. Sheldon had admired Winslow Homer's individualism, his
staunch convictions on art, but it was only after the showing of
"Camp Fire" that he asked if he could interview Mr. Homer in
connection with a proposed article; he had heard of the painter's
extreme reserve (which some labeled "surliness") and hesitated
to invade it. For his part, Winslow's reticence was due not so
much to shyness as to his knowledge of the press, acquired during
his years as an artist-reporter; he knew the tricks of the trade, the
exaggerations, the gross inaccuracies in quoting the unsuspecting
subject of a piece. However, he did have respect for Sheldon's
honest, accurate reporting, his impartial critique; this might be a

real opportunity to put across a few ideas on outdoor work, the
constant, fascinating puzzle posed by light. Winslow thought of
these things at night occasionally when he could not sleep and
deliberately turned away his mind from memories of his girl.
At such times he found himself highly articulate, but whether he
would be able to formulate his theories in the presence of a
writer he was not so sure.

It was a pleasant surprise to both men, therefore, when they
met in the spotless Tenth Street studio and found that they could
engage in an easy exchange of light conversation, which led up
gracefully to Homer's ideas concerning his profession. Winslow
felt as if he had known George Sheldon a long time. He showed
him some of the Houghton Farm water colors and several oils,
including "Camp Fire," telling the way he had painted in only the
tall tree at a later date. He related anecdotes about the little
shepherdess who had been his favorite model at Cornwall.
Sheldon showed great interest in the sketches as well as the
pictures themselves. In the article he wrote that these works
were "Drawn directly from nature or *from impressions* of it upon
his mind when he committed it to paper or canvas." He went on
to comment, "No painter in this country has a greater respect for
such outdoor work, a more lively appreciation of its value, or a
sincerer and more serious aversion to manufactured and studio
pictures." He had included Winslow's contemptuous remarks
concerning the popular school of French Salon artists, one in
particular whose paintings bored him no end.

"I wouldn't go across the street to see a Bouguereau," Winslow
had said flatly, making it sound like "Boo-gro." "His pictures look
false; he does not get the truth of . . . " He hesitated, searching
for a term to describe the chilly nudes reclining in leafy bowers;
looking pale and lifeless; but finding none, he continued, ". . .
of that which he wishes to represent; his light is not outdoor light;
his works are waxy and artificial. They are extremely near being
frauds." He concluded with an air of finality, his sharp eyes
flashing at Sheldon. He was beginning to lose his hair, and the

Camp Fire

The Metropolitan Museum of Art, Gift of Henry Keney Pomeroy, 1927

early baldness made his eyes more piercing.

He was not sorry the magazine had printed the statement, yet he moderated his views on remembering some of his experiences in high winds or rain or even the murky light of morning mist; he was willing to agree that "the great compositions of old masters were almost all interiors. You can't control the thing out of doors," he granted. He pointed out, however, the necessity of painting in outdoor light whenever possible, and once in a while the artist might find a happy combination of facts—like the night he had painted "Camp Fire"—so that a sketch (or what began as a study) could be practically a completed picture. This was more often true of water colors, he added, citing the Houghton Farm pictures.

He had intended to perfect his water color technique the following summer, when he had an unforeseen setback. He had submitted no less than twenty-nine entries in the spring show of the Water Color Society, most of them Houghton Farm subjects, and had sold a good many; with the returns he had planned to go away somewhere, perhaps near the sea, if not on it, and devote another summer entirely to water colors. He had both critical and modest financial success and could have gone on painting in the pastoral mode indefinitely, as long as the market held out; but just as he had not wanted to continue the Civil War heroes, or the watermelon boys, so he had no desire to exploit the American shepherdess he had created. Once he had designed a pattern from which he could draw infinite variations, he was ready to throw it away for something new and challenging.

Before he had quite decided where he should go, he visited Mattie and Charlie in the West Townsend home where they spent spring and fall every year. They were all three ready to leave in June, when he had broken his arm. He had quite forgotten how it happened, but he remembered that the family physician in Townsend, Dr. Boynton, who came at once to set the bone, said it would take at least six weeks to heal and had offered Winslow a place in the Boyntons' home while he was recovering.

He had accepted gratefully since Mattie and Charlie had made vacation plans which could not be changed without a good deal of inconvenience; they had offered to wait, but he wouldn't hear of it.

He was disappointed at having to give up his own project; it was a nuisance to have his arm in a sling, to be forced to sit around while the bone slowly mended. Yet he was too much of a philosopher to fret with impatience, and once he had decided to stay with the Boyntons, he settled down to enjoy himself. The doctor's house was near the river, happily enough, and his small son was as much of a fishing enthusiast as "Mr. Homer." He had a thousand questions to ask, and Winslow, who was very particular about his tackle, simple as it was, taught the boy how to make his own gut leaders, when to change reels, and other pointers close to the heart of an angler, young or old. Every day the two "used to repair to the backwaters of the river at 11 A.M. and 3 P.M., fishing for pickerel for about an hour." In spite of his broken arm, Winslow was able to bring in his catch every time, while his young partner looked on with lingering admiration—the boy always remembered very vividly the artist's "skill in casting among the lily pads, and his adroitness in playing the fish, which he never failed to land." Winslow made friends easily with children because he treated them as human beings, neither older nor younger than they were; he abhorred people who talked down to children and also those who spoke beyond a child's power to comprehend.

As soon as the bone began to knit, he started sketching, then painting again. A group of boys bathing; a little girl, sitting on a rope swing; an old woman driving a flock of geese down a country road. The last was a painting, which he later inscribed and presented to Dr. Boynton as a token of his gratitude for the care and kindness he had received in the physician's home. By the time he was able to leave, he was experimenting with water color again, but it was too late in the season to make any extensive plans.

Back in the Tenth Street studio, he completed a water color

he had begun early in June. He had been helping Mattie with the gardening when she had pricked her finger on a sharp thorn of an enormous rosebush in full bloom. She had cried out in pain, dropped her shears, and held her wounded finger up with the other hand, gazing at it sorrowfully. Winslow had gone to fetch some ointment, but when he came back he was carrying his water color equipment as well. "Don't move, if you can stand the pain a few minutes longer," he said. Mattie obliged—if she found her brother-in-law slightly eccentric she gave no sign of it—and he made a quick sketch, catching the color of the rose in the sunlight, the soft June sky, Mattie's skin, the glints of light in her hair. . . . Now he completed the picture and was pleased to find that he had also captured her subtle expression, a mixture of pain, sadness, and concern. Only a few days before, John LaFarge had commented on Winslow's growing preference for masculine subjects, his Adirondack hunters and old fishermen. He wanted his colleague to see that he could still paint softer figures.

He started downstairs but halfway there met LaFarge, who was coming up. With a single gesture Winslow let him know he had been coming for him, and the two went back up to his studio without a word. Winslow pointed to the picture, and his friend studied it, squinting slightly through his glasses. Here was a girl 'pitying herself,' "as delicate an expression as it is possible to conceive," he thought, and perhaps "one of the most impossible things to render." Spoken praise was not necessary; LaFarge nodded silently, understanding that Winslow Homer wanted to show him that 'he, too, could paint otherwise,' and they went downstairs, still without a word. It was this kind of rapport, which he enjoyed with several of the painters, that had kept Winslow at the Studios for as long as eight years. At times there seemed to be a wireless communication through the entire building, so that if anything of interest was happening in any of the rooms, the whole community knew it, and at such moments he wished for a little less congeniality.

Privacy was more to his liking, and he invented little devices to insure it. That was the fall William M. Chase had come back from Europe, and after he had taken over the Dome Studio, furnishing it with a flair for the florid and bizarre (even to an aeolian harp, hung inside the entrance, which "tinkled an indefinite arpeggio" as the door was opened), the whole place took on an air of positive conviviality. The "open house" held by Chase every Saturday night was more like a revelry than the old discussions that came up spontaneously in anybody's room, and Winslow was growing away from nightly conclaves anyhow. Few people were able to get inside his room, even if he had invited them, if he was concentrating on an idea. When his father announced he was coming in town and would stop in to see him, Winslow painted a sign, "Coal Bin," and hung it on the door so old Mr. Homer couldn't find him. It worked so well he left the sign on the knob for several days, keeping all outside callers away. His habit of opening the door only a crack, till he saw who was knocking, became more extreme, and sometimes he didn't bother to do that much or call out in answer to a friendly rap.

Young James Kelly was a rare exception, whom Winslow still welcomed to his spare, spotless studio. Perhaps it was because the boy was always an appreciative audience, lapping up bits of advice as if they were choice morsels. Winslow took the time to give him pointers on drawing, advised him to practice on top hats and old shoes, and told him if he ever wanted to learn how to paint to come to him—a rash offer, since he himself still had a lot to learn; but the little he did know he was willing to pass on to someone so eager for knowledge. One day Kelly appeared at the door with a box of oils that Abbey had given him and reminded "Mr. Homer" of his promise.

Winslow had just sent "Woman Driving Geese" off to Dr. Boynton and had nothing to do at the moment.

"Come in," he said. As usual, he was wearing his dark, correct cutaway and striped trousers; his mustache was as trim as a cavalry officer's. He bent down to pick up a thread of lint from the carpet as the young man stepped inside. If he was getting fussy in his habits, he made no bones about it. Without wasting time or words, he showed his aspiring pupil how to set his palette, using, as Rondel had done years before, white, yellow ochre, red ochre, permanent blue, and raw sienna. "Will you remember that?" he asked sharply, whirling around to level his eyes on James.

"Yes."

Winslow proceeded to sketch a painting of a girl then, mixing the colors without 'puddling,' which did not crush the minute granules of the paint, he explained. Applying a light, deft, crisp touch to the canvas, so the colors lost none of their original sparkle, he began, quite unconsciously, to outline the figure of a young woman in a mauve dress, with a black-and-white-striped petticoat. The piquant face, the cheeks too full for beauty, the teasing eyes all came rushing back to him, brought into being again on the canvas. By the time he realized what he was doing, he could not stop. He was embarrassed, angry with himself, but he had to keep on—he didn't care to let young Kelly see his personal interest in the subject.

To cover up his emotions, he demanded fiercely, fastening his eyes on the boy, as if to drive home every point he made, "Do you understand that?"

"Yes."

The answer was always immediate, but he pursued, feeling plagued by the face coming to life before them, "Will you ever forget it?"

"No."

"Well, then." He continued painting, explaining. Once he added, "If you make a mistake in laying on your color, don't try to correct it, but take it off with a palette knife and paint it in fresh."

He finally finished the little figure, 'a brilliant one in effect,' his pupil thought. Winslow was satisfied that he had completed it without revealing his churning sensations. Sitting back with something like relief, he said again, phrasing the question so there would be no mistake, "Will you ever forget what I have told you?"

"No," Kelly promised solemnly, sure that he never would.

After his visitor had left, Winslow had remained staring at the picture, at first critically, then quizzically, with some exasperation. He had met other women since their separation—friends of Mattie's, girls at studio parties, models—but he was not interested in any of them. He knew now that no other woman would ever take the place of this one, just why, he could not say. Surely there were others more beautiful or brilliant, or more capable of tenderness and understanding than she had been. Trying to figure it out annoyed him, and he ended by painting over the picture. (He had also painted over the figures in "Upland Cotton" some time later because the defiant expression on the face of one of the girls reminded him in some remote manner of his girl in her mood of angry defiance. Although this painting had been highly successful, he turned it into a straight landscape of a Virginia cotton field, empty of figures, because he wanted no reminders around. If the "Fortune" had not been securely stored away, he might have painted over that one too.)

The little work for Kelly's benefit was only a demonstration piece, and he could use the canvas for something else. No matter how intense his feelings were, he never wasted materials. He took the canvas with him when he went up to West Townsend for a few days in the late fall, and over the painted-out figure he started a study for a portrait of Mattie—a striking picture of a handsome, highly intelligent woman—a character study that could have placed him as a rival of William Chase or John Singer Sargent, who was beginning to make a name for himself. But Winslow Homer was willing to leave the realm of portraiture to his colleagues. Other spheres attracted him to a far greater degree.

The world of water color continued to lure him. He saved a little money from the sale of three paintings late in 1879; "Snap-the-Whip" was finally sold for $560; he had done two versions of the picture, one with a farm background of Hurley, the other against a setting of rugged New England hills, which proved much more successful. It was this version he had sent to the Paris Exposition, and it now found a purchaser, along with "A Country School," which went for $420 at the same sale. He was glad they were not coming back to the studio again; it would have been too painful. The poignant memories of those first weeks in Hurley, especially vivid in the schoolroom scene, were best forgotten; nothing must interfere with his growing mastery over his chosen profession. The third sale was that of "Weaning the Calf," for $290, and with the amount he had salted away from the total, he was determined to go through with the plan he had been prevented from carrying out the summer before.

On tiny Ten Pound Island, in the middle of Gloucester Harbor, the lighthouse keeper's wife, Mrs. Merrill, who was related to Winslow's friend, Samuel Preston, had a house in which she sometimes took boarders; and it was here that the painter spent the months between May and September, living practically alone, concentrating on his experiments with water color. He saw nobody except the lighthouse keeper's family and a couple of fishermen who dropped their nets off the island waters. For weeks on end he stayed on the spot, rowing across to Gloucester only when he needed materials or, once or twice, was in search of fresh subjects.

From early morning until sundown, under clear skies or clouds, he was out of doors, painting the light, or the effect of light, in water color. He stood on the shore, studying cloud shadows, the calm waters of the harbor, silver gray or shimmering in sunlight. When he started to put the scene on paper, he worked swiftly, hardly bothering to compose, using only a few scratches of a drawing and then the water color, freely applied, the white of the paper giving a transparency he had not allowed it before. His tones were more subtle—grays, blue-grays, pale greens, and soft yellows. The life of the harbor furnished subjects in plenty—fishing schooners plying in and out, water-front activity, and,

Sailboat

The Cooper Union Museum

above all, the busy pleasures of boys during summer vacation. He showed them "Boys Beaching a Boat," "Bathing," idling at the dock in "The Green Dory"; in dozens of pictures he displayed the feeling for boyhood that had marked his first Gloucester water colors six years before.

In these works, however, he was in far greater command of the medium, the instantaneous, impressionistic quality of water color. They were luminous as pearls, subtly shaded, and freer than any so far. He found that he could work better alone for long stretches, with only a handful of people in sight, surrounded by the view of sky and water, which he constantly studied. When he wanted company, he preferred the water-front talk of the fishermen to the art discussions of fellow painters. On one of his trips to Gloucester he had run into Joseph Baker, who wanted him to join some other old friends from Cambridge and Belmont who were vacationing at the shore. Winslow declined politely but firmly. Joe could not understand why he preferred to stick himself away on the island, apart from all his friends.

"They're all nice people," he said.

"So are the Ten Pound fishermen," Winslow told him, climbing into the green dory to row back.

At the end of the summer he returned with more than one hundred water colors and drawings, which he scarcely touched before placing them on exhibit. For the first time he arranged a show in Boston during December, at the galleries of Doll & Richards, who had remained his exhibitors in his native city from then on. Bostonians, with their pride in local setting, took to his latest work warmly; at least a third of the water colors were sold —at moderate prices, starting at $50—for a return of $1400 after commissions. If this was any indication, his labors of the summer would be of practical as well as artistic value.

New Yorkers, however, who had hailed the Houghton Farm pictures, were decidedly cool toward these. He sent twenty or more to the Water Color Society exhibit in the spring, only to

Boys Beaching a Boat

The Toledo Museum of Art, Gift of Florence Scott Libbey, 1950

have them slighted if not ignored. For one thing, they were so poorly hung—"on the sky line, over doors, and in corners"—that visitors could hardly see them, let alone make a purchase. And the critics for the most part were lukewarm, using terms like "impressionism" in an uncomplimentary manner, or lumping them as being "in the nature of guesses" at water-color technique. Only the *Nation* again praised his efforts and blamed the Academy hanging committee for hiding the pictures in obscure corners. But even that reviewer ended his article by saying, "It is what he will do hereafter, rather than what he has hitherto done, that one thinks of in connection with Mr. Homer's work." Another spoke of the "promise" of the new technique.

When Winslow read their remarks, he thought ironically that he had received much the same sort of comment when his first drawing was published in *Ballou's*. Ten years later the phrase was still encouraging in the first review of his work, but now it was annoying. "For fifteen years the press has called me 'a promising young artist,' and I'm tired of it," he said to his writer friend, Augustus Stonehouse, who had come to interview him for a feature article during the exhibit.

In spite of the doubtful attitude of the critics toward his "outdoor" painting, Winslow stuck by his convictions with a fierce tenacity, and in a second interview with George Sheldon voiced his views in no uncertain terms. "I prefer every time a picture composed and painted outdoors. The thing is done without your knowing it. Very much of the work now done in studios should be done in the open air. This making studies and then taking them home to use them is only half right. You get composition, but you lose freshness; you miss the subtle and, to the artist, the finer characteristics of the scene itself." He tugged at his mustache savagely. "I tell you it is impossible to paint an outdoor figure in studio light with any degree of certainty. Outdoors you have the sky overhead giving one light, then the reflected light from whatever reflects, then the direct light of the sun, so that, in the blending and suffusing of these several luminations, there is no such thing as a line to be seen anywhere. I can tell in a second if an outdoor picture with figures has been painted in a studio. When there is any sunlight in it, the shadows are not sharp enough; and, when it is an overcast day, the shadows are too positive. Yet you see these faults constantly in pictures in the exhibitions, and you know that they are bad. Nor can they be avoided when such work is done indoors. By the nature of the case the light in the studio must be emphasized at some point or part of the figure; the very fact that there are walls around the painter which shut out the sky shows this. I couldn't even copy in a studio a picture made outdoors; I shouldn't know where the colors came from, nor how to reproduce them. I couldn't possibly do it. Yet an attempted copy might be more satisfactory to the public, because more like a made picture." He stopped there, slightly out of breath. It was the longest, most detailed statement he ever made in regard to his intense feeling for nature, his unceasing quest for truth in reproducing the magic and wonder of outdoor light in art.

He felt as if he had laid bare his soul.

CHAPTER IX

Tynemouth:
The Turning Point

1881-1883

THE UNCERTAINTY TOWARD HIS LATEST WORK, DISPIRITING AS IT MAY have been for a moment, served as a goad, if anything. It was true that he paid far less heed to critical estimates than most artists, but his stubborn individuality spurred him to prove his point; if nothing else, the critics would all agree that Winslow Homer's art was his own, and so it must remain.

As soon as the water-color exhibit closed that spring, he had taken his savings from the Doll & Richards sale, picked up his artist's paraphernalia, and boarded an "old tub" bound for England. Through his salty friends on Ten Pound Island he had learned of a fishing village called Cullercoats, near Tynemouth in the rugged coastal strip of Northumberland. Located on the treacherous North Sea, not far from Newcastle, where "the coaly Tyne" emptied its dark waters into the ocean, the remote village provided the setting and the privacy he needed to carry his work at Gloucester one step farther, using the delicate medium of water color to portray scenes of strong drama, the strange beauty of the perilous sea, and the dangerous lives led by those who "go down to the sea in ships."

Choosing to live close to his subject, rather than stay at Tynemouth, the fishing port and watering place known for its fine beach, Winslow had gone straight to Cullercoats, where he rented a small cottage. With its garden, enclosed by a high wall and a gate he could lock, the place provided the seclusion he was looking for; he decided to live by himself, keep house and cook his own meals, so he could come and go—and paint—as he pleased. At the outset he wanted to know the fisherfolk, observing, if not sharing with them, the rugged life of commercial fishermen and their families. He wanted to study the contour of the coast line, the turbulent waters of the North Sea, and the stoicism of the men who braved them to bring in the catch, the women who waited patiently for the day's end, when their labor began. The people, in few words, told him what he wished to learn.

Famous for its fierce—and frequent—storms, the seacoast here was a source of endless speculation. Even Tynemouth Pier, which had been bulit as a safeguard against shipwreck, had not been able to prevent a large storm-tossed steamer from striking the end and breaking in two like a splinter. In a single night as many as fourteen ships had gone ashore, the fishermen informed him. Still, the huge pier at Tynemouth, and one like it at South Shields, had made the approach to the river much safer than before they were put up. Now the point was called a harbor of refuge as vessels came running for safety in darkening skies and waves that seemed to be miles long, leaping as high as the clouds when they broke against the pier.

Loss of life had been lessened further by two systems of saving it, set up by the people in the headland towns. South Shields furnished the Life-Boat and North Shields the Volunteer Life Brigade, a body of stouthearted men gathered from the country around, including the Cullercoats fishermen. Winslow's nearest neighbor pointed out proudly the Life Brigade House, which stood on the cliffs near the head of Tynemouth Pier, where the

Volunteers kept vigil on stormy nights in case the disaster signal should sound, sending them out to save the lives of others.

These bearded fishermen, Nordic in feature, and their blond, sturdy wives, came in part of Scandinavian stock, hardy as gorse. Stolid, often silent, they were not unfriendly and were, in their own way, kindhearted. If they regarded Winslow a queer sort for sketching or painting all day long, they gave no sign of it and were willing in the midst of endless tasks to pose for him, particularly the women, whose duties kept them ashore, on the beach or the cliffs most of the time. Household chores were kept at a minimum; babies were tied on their mothers' backs with shawls and toted to the beach while small children toddled alongside. The squat, snub-nosed fishing boats set out at dawn, and when they put in with the day's catch in the late afternoon, it was the women who unloaded. The men, weary with hauling nets and battling the sea, trudged home to rest, while their women, filled baskets on their arms, carried the fish to market and returned to clean out the boats for the next day. The work was heavy—man's work—yet these robust women were physically capable of it and performed their tasks without complaint. During the day there were always nets to be mended, and they spent long hours, sitting in pairs on a wooden bench, bent over their tedious labor, scarcely speaking. Village gossip was soon spun out in Cullercoats, and Northumbrian fisherwomen were not given to chatter at any time.

Here was a new type of female—handsome rather than beautiful; not in the least feminine, with ruddy skin and homely dress, and not a trace of coquetry, but womanly in a classic way, Winslow Homer thought; here was a blond Athena, performing deeds of unsung heroism, and he set about portraying her as a leading figure in the drama of the British seacoast.

He was on the beach every day, doing scores of drawings and water colors. He showed the women as they waited, children at their sides, for their menfolk to return; sometimes two or three climbed up to the cliffs and stood as lookouts for the sails of the

Fisherfolk on the Beach at Tynemouth

Addison Gallery of American Art, Phillips Academy, Andover

fleet. In many pictures the women were mending nets or marching up the beach with their baskets of fish on their arms. Over and over he drew the scene or painted it, at first on the spot, then in the privacy of his walled-in garden, where he combined two or three works to compose large water colors, the size of most oils. Thinking back, he recalled that he worked very hard during the two seasons he spent at Tynemouth, perhaps harder, over a longer period, than he ever worked before in his life.

He thought about nothing but his work; his renounced love was far away, and there was nothing on this rugged coast to remind him of it, no outside distractions of exhibits, critiques, interviews, or meetings. Professional problems alone absorbed him—how to paint the diffused light, even more predominant here than in Gloucester, the soft grays and greens, the deep hues of the somber sea.

He began to experiment with different ways of securing whites, by washing out color with a wet brush and "lifting" it, or by scraping with a knife, always keeping it transparent. He learned how to suggest: when he painted the scene on the beach, the aprons of the fisherwomen were mere dots of color, yet the effect was unmistakable.

Movement in sky and air occupied him—racing clouds and winds of gale force, whirling along the coast. By the end of the first summer his technique had improved tenfold; his pictures no longer looked like colored drawings. They were full-fledged water colors.

In October the first terrible storm had risen, and he hurried to the Life Brigade House along with the fishermen and a few of the women with shawls over their heads. The scene of the Life Brigade House on stormy nights stood out in his memory, one of the unforgettable sights in his long career. There was always a roaring fire burning in the grate; the place was full of men— 'brown-bearded fishermen from Cullercoats and brave shopkeepers from Shields'—who met here on the common ground of danger, for the purpose of rescuing others. Clad in sea boots, guernseys, and sou'westers, with life belts close at hand, they lounged in groups at the great hearth or stood looking out into the storm, watching, listening for the 'guns of the *Castor*,' the signal of distress. The October storm started in the afternoon; the fishermen, who knew the signs, had come back early. There were rumors that the ship *Iron Crown* was somewhere near the mouth of the river and would be wrecked if she could not reach the pier in time. A cluster of helmeted men stood on the cliffs, straining their eyes across the churning sea; two women, wrapped in shawls, were on the pier, watching the black clouds roll along the sky, the breaking waves dash high above the cliff; a gale was blowing, and they huddled close together. Winslow, drawing the scene from the pier, wondered at the strength of women that could withstand such force.

Suddenly a shout arose from the fishermen—the *Iron Crown* had been sighted—and at the same time the distress gun boomed. The ship had gone aground.

The men rushed to the lifeboat, pushed it into the angry sea, and started the rescue of the crew of the foundering ship. Winslow had never before witnessed an actual shipwreck; some years earlier, when the *Atlantic*, bound from Liverpool to New York, was wrecked on the rocks of Mars Head, Nova Scotia, on April 1, 1873, *Harper's* had sent him to cover the tragedy, and he had done a wood engraving of one of the victims, a girl "Cast Up by the Sea"; a man, who had evidently tried to revive her, stood gazing down at her. This time, however, the misfortune took place in front of his eyes, and he tried to get the scene down as best he could . . . the confusion and excitement, the peril of the heavy sea, the heroism of the rescuers.

"The Wreck of the Iron Crown" was the first of the large water colors. Part of the work on it was done in New York, where he had spent the winter, sailing about a month after the wreck. Charlie had written that his mother was not well, and he wanted to be home by Christmas. Her age was only then beginning to show because of poor health, but she kept on painting a good deal of the time; and when he arrived she was much occupied with her Christmas present to Mattie—a bound volume of her best water colors of flowers. (She asked 'Win's' advice on the selection and then made her own choices.) Henrietta Homer, at seventy, could inscribe the gift book objectively:

> "Whose busy fingers, at three-score years,
> From Nature's forms and tints, produced
> This handiwork; that when beneath the daisies
> Those fingers are at rest:
> These flowers might yield of her joyous life
> A fragrant memory."

His mother's remarkable spirit was still inspiring Winslow to intensify his drive toward greater achievements in water color as well as in oil painting. He had returned to England in the early spring, to stay in his Cullercoats cottage again until late fall, painting constantly, as before, but this season with increased care in composing. He immersed himself in the stern, almost mystic atmosphere of the setting, epitomized in the rugged lives of the fisherfolk. Out of his self-taught knowledge came the other large water colors of "Tynemouth" (a scene of the port itself, a snub-nosed boat in the foreground). In "Mending Nets," "The Incoming Tide," "A Scotch Mist," and "A Voice From the Cliffs" he presented the unspoken drama of the life around him through the medium of water color. (The last, a replica of an oil, which he called "Hark, the Lark!" portraying three fishergirls, baskets over outstretched arms, in arrested motion, listening to the song, had the rhythmic quality of a tone poem. More luminous than the painting, it conveyed the temper of the people and the lives they led. Recently, twenty years after he completed this water color, he was able to write, "Only once in the last thirty years have I made a duplicate, and that was a water color from my oil picture, 'Hark, the Lark!' now owned by the Layton Art Gallery. It is the most important picture I ever painted, and the very best one, as the figures are large enough to have some expression in their

Charcoal Sketch for *The Wreck of the "Iron Crown"*

The Cooper Union Museum

faces.")

During the summer of 1882 he had done some traveling along the east coast of England—to Yorkshire, where he did a few drawings of Flamborough Head and a water color of Bridlington Quay, and on to Norfolk, where he found Yarmouth a picturesque subject—but he felt only the passing interest of the tourist. No place he visited stirred him as much as Tynemouth, and after he returned to his little cottage, his address had remained "Cullercoats, Newcastle-on-Tyne" for the rest of his stay in England.

He conceived the idea for a monumental work in oil, one that would represent a composite of his impressions of life in this remote corner of the globe. He began studies for a large canvas which he finally entitled "The Coming Away of the Gale." He chose a gray day in autumn, an impending storm preceded by howling winds; the central figure, a fisherwoman with her baby tied on her back, strode bravely along the beach toward the Life Brigade House, where the volunteers were preparing to launch their lifeboat into the angry waves. Her skirts flattened against her body, swept back by the gale, the woman was pushing against the tremendous force with every step, bucking it with one arm bent before her, as if to fend it off. The other arm, behind her back, supported the baby.

The painting was not completed until he returned to the Tenth Street Studios late in November. He spent most of the winter working on it as well as on the large water colors, which he exhibited in February at the American Water Color Society. They were an immediate and unqualified success. That was the only time, as far as he could remember, when the critics were unanimous in their praise. One of those who formerly considered his work "crude"—Mariana G. Van Rensselaer, writing in the *Century* —publicly reversed her opinion in positive terms: " 'The Voice From the Cliffs' and 'Inside the Bar' seem to me not only the most complete and beautiful things he has yet produced, but among the most interesting American art has yet created. . . . The dignity of these landscapes and the statuesque impressiveness and sturdy vigor of these figures, translated by the strong sincerity of his brush, prove an originality of mood, a vigor of conception, and a sort of stern poetry of feeling to which he had never reached before."

At least the critics were beginning to get an inkling of the art he sought to produce. He had little doubt that the oils, particularly "The Coming Away of the Gale," would carry his success one step further. But when it was exhibited at the National Academy's spring show two months later, the work he considered his greatest achievement to date, brought stinging lashes of disapproval from the critics, for various reasons. Prominently hung (for once) and admittedly one of the attractions of the event, the canvas seemed to offend every reviewer who set eyes on it, if not in one area, then in another. There were complaints of "its hard drawing and its theatrical arrangement of figures and accessories. . . ." This writer expanded his theme with brutal frankness: "It would be impossible for anyone not to know that there was a gale somewhere around here, but for the same reason that you know it is present on the stage. Simply, that it, because you are told so, not because you feel it." One of his colleagues, however, found that "the only element of success in it is the suggestion of the storm-laden atmosphere and the troubled aspect of the sea." Opposing views were expressed in detail, but all agreed that the picture was a "disappointment" and that, compared with the water colors, it was labored and melodramatic. The unkindest cut of all came from the *New York Sun*, which implied dismissal in a few sharp sentences: "The figures are clumsily drawn; the color is cold and ugly, but natural enough; the composition is nil. It is a picture which will not add to Mr. Homer's fame."

Although he shrugged it off with his customary indifference to the press, Winslow was stunned by the universal disfavor his aspiring work received. Bitterly disappointed, he had put the canvas away and never placed it on exhibit again. (His Yankee thriftiness, however, kept him from destroying it, and ten years later he had taken the picture out of hiding, painted over the Life Brigade House and the men launching the lifeboat, leaving only the central figure of the fisherwoman bucking the wind on the beach; he livened up the color scheme, retitled the work "A Great Gale," and sold it to the collector, Thomas B. Clarke, who sent it to the World's Fair in Chicago; there, he recalled with an ironic smile, the "new" work was highly praised and admired.)

As if to compensate for his discouragement, the English water colors sold well, at higher prices than his previous ones—the large pictures ranged from $300 to $500, and the smaller from $100 to $150; a December exhibit at Doll & Richards netted him around $2400, a tidy profit for a struggling painter.

Looking back from the vantage point of latter-day success, Winslow Homer realized that during his stay in Cullercoats he had rounded the most decisive corner of his career; he had discovered the lure of the sea as an inexhaustible source of inspiration, and in so doing he had acquired amazing technical skill; more than that, his vision had become profound. He knew that from this time on the sea would hold sway, and he also knew how he must live to attain full mastery of his art.

CHAPTER X

Prout's Neck:
The Proving Grounds

1883-1884

For some time after his return from Tynemouth, Winslow was haunted by the perils of the sea, particularly the shipwreck and the valiant rescue work, sometimes performed in vain. Although it had taken place in front of his eyes, he could not see what was happening at the ship's side, could not tell with any degree of certainty how the rescuers transferred victims to the lifeboat or saved unconscious ones.

As soon as the Academy show closed, he had gone to Atlantic City, not for a rest, or to picture the fashionable crowds along the boardwalk, as he would have done ten years before. (If he had not broken off his relationship with his girl, and they had married, he would probably still be an illustrator in order to support his family—or at best an amateur painter; and if he could not be professional, he would rather not paint at all.) While others promenaded, bathed, or idled away hours on the beach or in cafés, he singled out the lifesaving crew and made friends with them in order to find out more about the subject which held such a deep interest for him.

The crew, having hours to spend on duty without actually working, welcomed the chance to spout their experiences, and Winslow was a good listener. He asked questions which showed a real sincerity to learn about the job most vacationists took for granted, and they were perfectly willing to oblige when he asked them to show him how a breeches buoy was used. He himself handled the contraption, saw how the ropes were run through the blocks, how the buoy was strapped on the lifeguard. The men then put on a demonstration for him with a practice dummy, so he could see how a victim was brought in from the sinking ship to shore. He made notes and drawings, read reports of crew operations in past wrecks, and collected enough material for a new work on the same theme as "The Coming Away of the Gale." This time, however, he intended to depict the actual rescue rather than the preparations for it.

Before he left the resort, he saw the guards in action. It was a bright day of high winds and rough surf; few people ventured into the water, and most of those were competent swimmers. Late in the afternoon two women had decided to try taking a dip in spite of the tremendous breakers. Winslow, who had been painting the surf, had been concentrating on one wave directly in front of him and did not see them go in, but he suddenly heard half-strangled cries for help, and almost at the same moment, it seemed, the guards rushed into the sea with a life net. The women had been caught in the undertow. Inside of a few moments the two bathers, clinging to each other, were in the net and being hauled ashore by the two lifeguards, one on either side. The four figures against a background of rough sea formed a highly dramatic picture; with his artist's eye, Winslow had sketched it on his drawing pad, noting the locked bodies of the victims, their dripping suits, skintight over breast and thigh, the glistening torsos of the men in the sunlight, arm muscles bulging as they struggled against the strong current; the blue-green tones of the sunlit wave were already on his canvas, but he jotted down color notes of the blue sky and the distant stretches of ocean.

By the time the crew had brought their cargo to safety, a crowd had gathered on the beach, and Winslow waited with them in some anxiety to make sure the victims revived. After the excitement died down, and the crowd had gone up to the board-walk again, he stayed on to talk to the lifeguards, making notes of the problems the incident had posed, involving as it did two victims instead of one.

When he returned to New York, Winslow had begun prelimi-nary work on two large paintings. For the first he secured a breeches buoy, found a strapping mulatto man with a sister of statuesque proportions, who agreed to be his models, and posed them on the roof of the Tenth Street Studios. Borrowing a wooden tub from William Chase (who seemed to have everything under the sun in the big studio), he kept it filled with water and, using a dipper, started off by drenching his models to see the effect of wet skin and clinging clothes. His models seemed startled but made no protest, and every now and then he would throw another dipperful of water over one or both as he painted. This picture was to represent shipwreck and storm, an uncon-scious woman rescued by a helmeted fisherman who held the limp body of the victim in his arms as they were pulled to shore over enormous breakers. Using variations of gray, gray-greens and slate grays, to depict a stormy sky and sea, he achieved greater color harmonies than in any previous oil, and he felt both excitement and satisfaction when he stopped to view the canvas. Surely he was making progress in painting as well as water color, he was gaining as a complete artist. . . .

He decided to call the picture "The Life Line," and when the figures were well along, he began the second work, based on the lifesaving incident at Atlantic City. For this one he employed two models, telling them to bring their bathing suits when they came to pose. (He had made sufficient studies of the lifeguards before leaving Atlantic City so that he could combine the two sets of figures.) He doused them with a dipperful of water every so often, soaking the bathing suits till the models' figures were completely outlined. This was the closest he ever came to painting the nude, and he saw that he had the power to depict the human figure with the same dramatic force he gave to nature subjects; he could probably have equalled any of his colleagues who were concentrating on that genre at the time, but he had no desire to continue once he had proved to himself that he could do it. If he had been able to study in a life class years before when he was attending the Academy, his interest might have been greater. He would have had practice in drawing the nude at an early age, but since he did not, he had never grown accustomed to the idea of picturing the naked body, and the thought of hiring a model for that purpose was alien to his sense of propriety, his deep-set reserve.

He chose a simple title for this painting also—"Undertow"— but before either was completed, he had gone up to Prout's Neck, taking the canvases with him.

Arthur and Alice, who had been coming to the spot every summer since their marriage, had built a cottage there a year earlier, while Winslow was in England. They were the proud parents of two small sons—Arthur Patch and Charles Lowell Homer—and wanted their children to know and love the New England coast as they did. At the same time Charles had bought a large house still under construction close to the shore and had finished building it, not only for himself and Mattie, but as a summer place for his mother and father—and Winslow. There was plenty of room for all, and Win could have the top floor for his studio, Charlie had written.

His scheme had not worked out well. True, the house was charming and comfortable, big enough for all, and not far from Arthur's cottage. But Winslow remembered sadly that his mother was granted only one summer in the new home, for one thing. She had not come to Scarboro with the rest of the family to meet the train, and he realized when he saw her that she had faded in the few weeks he had been in Atlantic City. Her lifelong energy seemed to be spent at last; she had not even enough to paint water colors any more, with all her leisure and freedom from household responsibilities—a sure sign that she was failing physically. She was interested in everything the "young people" were doing, however, and particularly in Winslow's career, his English water colors, and the "storytelling" series he had begun. She sympathized with his disappointment over the cool reception accorded "The Coming Away of the Gale" and encouraged him to continue his present theme whether the critics found it acceptable or not.

His father and Arthur had other ideas and were not backward about expressing them. Mr. Homer still complained that "Win was an unpractical businessman" when it came to setting prices on his pictures; and Arthur, after one look at the studies for "Undertow," nicknamed it "the worms-for-bait" picture. Winslow had retaliated with two caricature drawings of his nephews, showing "Little Arthur in fear of harming a worm"; dressed as Little Lord Fauntleroy, he was squeamishly side-stepping an ordinary angleworm; in "Little Charlie's innocent amusements," the other nephew, the more mischievous of the two, was sitting on the cat, pulling the dog's tail with one hand and holding a baseball bat in the other, while in the background was a telltale broken window. The whole family joined in this kind of barbed-wire jokes; if Winslow had been inclined toward any genius complex, it would have had small chance to flourish.

As far as his work was concerned, however, he often wished he was not in such close proximity to the rest of the family. They did not actually watch him paint (most of his work was done away from the house anyhow, out of doors, sometimes on the sheltered side of the Neck, overlooking Saco Bay, but more often on the rocky coast line to the south and east, open to the sea); but they could come to his top-floor room at any time to see his work and comment on the progress he was making. His father, too, was apt to criticize his habit of painting on Sunday; every

Sunday he would ask whether Win was going to church and, when he received a negative answer, would shake his head, as if there were no hope for his wayward son. Or he would object to the 'nightcap' mug of ale Winslow usually took, occasionally with Charlie, before going to bed. At times their father's attitude struck the brothers as funny: they were men in their late forties, and he was treating them more like boys than Arthur treated little Arthur and Charlie. Then again Winslow would be keenly annoyed at his father's crochety notions, but he made no vehement protest because the unpleasantness would upset his mother and because he had a genuine fondness for his father in spite of the old man's idiosyncrasies and aphorisms.

The Maine coast was not unlike that of Northumbria; the atmosphere was less misty, the sunlight stronger here, but the views of rocks and surf resembled those at Tynemouth to the point where Winslow expected to see fishergirls standing on the cliffs or striding along the narrow strip of beach. He went so far as to include one or two of them in some of the many water colors he did during that first summer at Prout's. He wanted to extend the work he had accomplished abroad, to perfect his water-color technique, adjusting his color scale to the brighter key of the American shore. He soon began studies of pure seascape, trying out his new skill with water color long before he ever attempted the same subjects in oil. But among those initial endeavors, he recalled with a faint smile, had been the sketch on which he based the painting he had just finished; he had risen at dawn after a heavy storm and had sought to capture the pearly light over the calming sea—it had only taken twenty years for the seed to flower!

He had been coming to Prout's Neck briefly every summer from the time of Arthur's marriage, but it was not until that experimental summer of 1883 that Winslow grew to know the peninsula well; he was outdoors all day long, a bite of lunch in his knapsack (often forgotten), exploring, studying terrain, working. The loneliness of the place—only a few fishermen and farmers lived there then—appealed to him; the weather-beaten coast and the sweep of moors in back of it, the tall pines crowning the cliffs, were in harmony with the soul of the artist that was his innermost self. By the end of the season he had unconsciously reached the decision that this stony strip of land would henceforth be his home.

He still had his studio on Tenth Street in New York to dispose of before he left the city, and during the fall and following winter he had worked there, trying to find a market for the accumulated works while he was completing the large oils. One evening a dealer who came to make the rounds mentioned an absurdly low figure for the bulk of studies he had stored in the studio, but Winslow was so anxious to break up his living quarters in the city that he accepted. Then began the job of sorting, weeding out; he rarely threw anything away—no telling when the merest charcoal smudge might come in handy—but he had no idea, until he started going through them, that he had stashed away so many "notes" from early essays, as far back as the Civil War. It was days before he finally made his selections, and Alden Weir, who came to his studio to discuss the work in stained-glass windows which some of the artists had taken up, was astonished to find him sitting on the floor beside a stack of drawings and a few water colors, surrounded by portfolios from which they had been removed.

"What on earth are you doing?" his friend asked.

"I've been offered $500 for a hundred drawings and paintings, and these are the ones I've picked out," Winslow told him calmly. "When I get the money for them I'm going to leave New York for good!" And no amount of protest on the part of Alden Weir or anyone else could change his mind. When Winslow Homer made a bargain he stuck to it, whether the figures were in his favor or not. (As for his leaving New York, he claimed with a perfectly straight face that he was making the move "to avoid jury duty" and let it go at that. People could think what they liked.) He wanted to have at least $1000 before going away, however, and various small sales brought in $200 during the next few weeks. He still needed $300.

He had had dealings now and then with Gustav Reichard, who seemed to think well of his work; perhaps Reichard would give him a flat sum for a certain number of water colors and sell them later. It was worth a try, Winslow thought. Choosing about a dozen, he put them in a portfolio and took them into the dealer's store.

"Here, Reichard, I want you to give me $300 for these," he said briskly, putting the portfolio on the dealer's desk.

Reichard, evidently realizing that the pictures were worth more, had said he wouldn't care to do that, and Winslow, disappointed, had turned away, when the agent added, "But I'll tell you what I will do. I'll give you $300 and take the pictures and sell them for your account for the best prices I can get."

"Suits me," Winslow had said after a moment, hardly betraying the deep gratitude he felt. (His share of the proceeds eventually had amounted to much more than $300, and from then on, until the gallery closed, Reichard had been his New York agent.)

Before he knew it, the winter had passed, and he had completed only "The Life Line." His mother's health was so precarious that he visited her every few days, and the trips back and forth to Brooklyn alone took up a good deal of time. On April 1 the Academy's spring exhibition had opened, including among its principal offerings "The Life Line." Winslow, after arguing with the hanging committee as to placement of the canvas, had settled for a lesser position than he had hoped to receive, and on opening day he stayed in his studio, working on "Undertow," trying to keep his mind off the exhibit entirely. After the fate of "The Coming Away of the Gale," he would be satisfied if the critics didn't tear his picture to pieces and so discourage possible purchasers.

Then, late in the afternoon, the amazing news had come by special messenger that one of the country's most famous collectors, Catherine Lorillard Wolfe, who up till now had purchased only works of foreign painters, had bought "The Life Line" for $2500! It was unbelievable, yet it must be true, he thought exultantly. He wanted his mother to hear the good news as soon as possible, and when his colleagues knocked on the studio door to congratulate him—the word had hardly arrived before it had spread through the building—he was already on his way to Brooklyn in a hansom cab.

His mother was fading rapidly, but she was almost as excited as Winslow (and his father acted as if he himself had set the price). In the next few days she had even regained some of her old liveliness as she listened to the reviews read aloud to her by Winslow or his father. How much the immediate (and prominent) sale had influenced the critics was hard to tell, but almost to a man they had nothing but praise for the picture, and more than one referred to it as "a masterpiece."

The fact that "The Life Line" was the first American painting to be included in Catherine L. Wolfe's collection caused no little comment in itself. "This purchase shows that the tide is turning," the *Herald* said, "and our richer collectors are beginning to patronize American as well as foreign art. It has hitherto been—in this city at least—to the possessors of moderate means that the American artist has looked for patronage." Here Winslow, reading, nodded emphatically before going on in a satiric tone to cover up his emotion: "The Homer is well fitted to rank with the foreign paintings in Miss Wolfe's superb collection, and she deserves the thanks of all friends of American art for this spontaneous recognition of one of the strongest and most thoroughly American of the figure painters." Here was real tribute, a triumph for any painter; for the second time in his life a single painting had skyrocketed him to fame. He felt, as he had long ago about "Prisoners From the Front," that while "The Life Line" was not lauded beyond its merits, it had enjoyed a popularity he found overwhelming; but he realized that with this event his reputation had been made secure. He had reached the top ranks among American painters and this time would remain there.

To his mother the recognition seemed to bring great peace and satisfaction. Winslow had already gone far beyond the mark she had hoped her son might reach professionally, and now she thought he would surely be free of the financial struggle he had had to endure all these years. Her gift for painting as expressed in her water colors might never be known outside of her family, but through Winslow, who had been endowed with a much greater measure, it would become immortal. She was content. Scarcely three weeks later, on the twenty-seventh of April, she died.

Winslow, after anxious hours of watching over her with his father, followed by the unseemly bustle of funeral arrangements, accompanied by an avalanche of relatives, and the general turmoil of "sweeping up the heart," felt he must have the quiet of solitude. Within ten days he had arrived in Maine and that night wrote to Mattie: "I went into the house at Prout's today. Found it in good order. Thought of Mother with a certain amount of pleasure, thank the Lord. I knew that if possible she was with me. I feel quite well for the first time in two weeks." And with his return to normal came the urge to continue the "storytelling" series of sea pictures.

In the course of his daily rambles around the coast the summer before Winslow had become acquainted with some of the fishermen. Over a pipe or two, when he put his paintbrush aside, he learned that most of them dropped their seines near Newfoundland, on the Grand Banks, the three-hundred mile stretch of shoal where halibut and mackerel as well as herring abounded. It occurred to him now that this might be a good time for some studies he had wanted to make while he was in England, but in Cullercoats the men had been uncommunicative, if not actually wary of his motives when he suggested going out with the fleet, and so he had had to be satisfied with picturing their womenfolk. The Maine fishermen knew that Winslow Homer was a Yankee, "born and bred," saw that he acted like one, through and through, and this was enough for them; they did not ask his reasons for wishing to paint them at their calling.

Through Henry Lee, one of the neighbors who was a fisherman, he was able to arrange to go with the fleet when they took to the high seas. On the way out he watched the men take readings with sextant and quadrant, as regular as clockwork. At the fishing grounds they dropped anchor.

From the deck of the main schooner he made quite a number of drawings—men in carefully spaced dories 'paying out the twine,' preparing to drop pound or gill nets; baiting trawls or 'trot lines'; hauling in a huge catch of herring. At last he could observe the day-to-day life of those who depended on the sea for a living, recording the labor and the constant risk of an ancient occupation largely overlooked by an unthinking world. Fog alone was a hazard most people never considered, a fact he realized when one of the dories was lost on the Grand Banks and tossed helplessly in the gray blanket, nearly colliding with its schooner when it was finally sighted. The men feared the fog and took warning at the first sign, but they were not always successful in returning to the schooner before the heavy bank settled around them.

When the fleet returned, he could not make use of the drawings immediately, for his father and the rest of the family had arrived. If Winslow had forgotten his annoyance over Mr. Homer's eccentricities, he was rudely reminded of them when he was promptly handed paternal—and arbitrary—advice as to the value of always taking cold baths, eating nothing but certain foods (which changed from time to time), and letting his hair grow long. To 'Win,' who had nothing left but a fringe around his bald pate, this was completely ridiculous; he took delight in spoofing his father, drawing caricatures of him for Charlie and Mattie's benefit, but inwardly he rebelled against having to put up with such nonsense. His brother and sister-in-law were there only a few weeks out of the summer; and, anyway, they were not expected to accept the old man's advice as much as he, the unmarried son.

Before a month was out he had taken over the mansard-roofed stable that came with the house—and was standing empty, since Charles's only horse and buggy were kept in the barn—had it moved closer to the cliff's edge, and began remodeling it to suit his painter's needs. Living quarters were a secondary consideration; a couple of rooms at most was all he required. He spent part of the summer building the second-floor balcony on the sea side of the house, high above the coast, an architectural feature that had proved invaluable to him for many years. He saw to it that his covered porch was "braced so as to hold a complete Sunday school picknick"; it must withstand the storms and his own tramping feet.

He remembered the pleasure he felt when the job was finished, and he stood on the porch, looking up and down the coast and out over the broad ocean to Stratton and Bluff islands, more than a mile away. Here he could be in the open and yet under shelter, studying the sea like a captain on the bridge. He soon lost all count of the hours he used to put in, watching the varied aspects of the water below—the light, the colors, the waves breaking over the rocks—walking up and down, up and down, "wearing out the balcony," his brothers always said.

Arthur had helped him build the balcony; he and the boys (without whose assistance the job probably would have been finished sooner) contributed their share of work to the entire remodeling of the stable; and to return to favor. Winslow suggested sprucing up Arthur's old sloop, *The Mattie*, which dated back to his camping days before his marriage. Winslow offered to paint scenes on the three wooden panels in the cabin—two on the sides and one up forward—and his brother was so pleased he said he would act as model if necessary.

With the fishing trip fresh in his mind, Winslow painted on one side a picture of the fleet tacking into Gloucester Harbor with the day's catch, using as material one of his 1880 Gloucester water colors done in late-afternoon light. On the other side he pictured two of the schooners, spread sails against the sunset.

Then he began a black-and-white study for the forward panel, posing Arthur in his yachting cap as a ship's officer taking a noon reading with a sextant. He had just about finished it when an idea came to him: he could do a real painting of the two helmeted fishermen he had watched day after day as they stood at the rail 'shooting the sun'; one time in particular, as a gale died down, had stayed in his mind. . . . He stopped painting the final touches of Arthur's coat, saying suddenly, "I'm not going to do anything more on this panel. You can have it if you want it." Without further explanation he gathered up his palette, brushes, and paints and rushed up to the newly completed studio to start work on the picture he called eventually "Eight Bells." He had stretched several canvases, which were ready and waiting; choosing the smallest, he did an initial study and then set it aside as other concepts for paintings dealing with various aspects of a fisherman's life came to him.

After the family left he had stayed on in Maine until late in the fall, building up his idea for a series of sea epics. For one of the first, finally entitled "The Fog Warning," he had propped up the prow of a dory against a sand dune as if it was headed over a high wave; when the angle was sharp enough, he persuaded Henry Lee to put on his oilskins and sit in the rower's seat, hands on the oars. The fisherman obliged with a few shivers, as it was a raw November morning—rime on the bushes and cold gray fog rising in the sky—but this did not stop Winslow from going to the well and drawing a pail of water, which he threw over his model without warning. The fisherman was not so passive as the other models had been; besides, it was cold. Taken by surprise, he let out a stream of swear words that reached the ears of another neighbor, beaching a dory nearby ("You never heard such profanity in your life," the witness declared later.) Winslow, the ghost of a smile on his face, explained his action in a word or two and started to paint quickly, before the dousing dried.

Except when he had someone posing for him, he was by himself, but he was too busy to feel lonely. He found that the solitude was friendly to his creative powers, which needed quiet in order to expand and flourish. Toward the end of November, when snowbanks covered the huckleberry bushes and crusted the rocks below, he left Prout's Neck to spend Thanksgiving with Charles and Mattie and his father. Mr. Homer had taken a room in a Boston hotel for the winter and wanted Winslow to join him, but his son had suddenly decided he would like to paint the sea in warmer climes, and there was talk of the two taking a trip together. Finally, however, Winslow had sailed away alone in December, bound for the Bahamas.

CHAPTER XI

Interlude in the West Indies

1884-1885

TO A SEA-LOVING MAN WHO HAD NEVER BEEN SOUTH OF RICHMOND, Virginia, the tropical waters of the Gulf Stream were like noon wine. As the ship neared the harbor at Nassau, and the incredible blue was contrasted with the white limestone buildings that gleamed in the hot sunlight through the fronds of the palm trees, Winslow Homer—hopefully established as a painter at forty-eight, reserved, bald, sedate—felt a headiness and an excitement he had not sensed since his first taste of ocean travel in 1867. As he gazed at the long narrow curve of beach, bathed by the indigo waters, it seemed as if he was approaching a new world; even the air in the tropics was different from any he had ever breathed. After the two seasons among the murky grays at Tynemouth and the austere winter white of the Maine coast he had just left, the scene before him revealed whole fresh spheres of color and light.

As always when he had made a discovery for himself, he wasted no time in starting to explore it. Renting one of the little limestone houses, he had no trouble finding a Negress to cook for him, and he promptly made a water color of her as she came from the market, balancing a basket of bananas on her head. More than anything else on this enchanted island, he was fascinated by its Negro inhabitants, just as he had been in Virginia—only here they did not have to bear the stigma of being "niggers," lately released from bondage, and it was a pure joy to paint them. Carrying his water-color equipment, he roamed the island, hiking along the limestone roads, the coral beaches, the lively docks crowded with fishing boats, full of happy families. These people appeared to be on a perpetual vacation; they had a capacity for a lazy enjoyment of life that harmonized with the hot sunlight and brilliant hues of the tropics. The mood was contagious, and Winslow caught it in his rapid water-color impressions. He painted whatever he saw of note on his daily jaunts, and there was much that took his eye—the white garden walls, festooned with bougainvillea vines in various shades, and oleanders that looked over the gate as he set out (how his mother would have delighted in painting them, or the flaming red hibiscus that flourished everywhere). He observed the women in the market place, gay in their gaudy dress, stately in their walk, carrying everything from food to the week's washing in the carefully poised baskets on their heads; the half-naked bodies, burnished by salt and sun, of the men who dove for conches from the deck of a sail-boat or fished for the deadly sharks that dared to invade the harbor. The dark-skinned divers and fishermen rarely wore anything but a pair of old white "ducks," usually lopped off above the knees and held up by a tightly drawn belt around their slim waistlines. Winslow, drawing the splendid torsos with swift, sure brush strokes, felt his powers increase, not only in mastery of the figure, but in rendering movement; the pictures were full of action.

The people were friendly in an offhand fashion, carefree, given to easy laughter, indolent and industrious by turn, depending on the time of day and the circumstance. They had no objection to

Key West, Negro Cabin and Palms

In the Brooklyn Museum Collection

being painted and usually had a welcoming grin for the painter, but this did not stop their pursuits in the least, and his work reflected their attitude. These water colors had an atmosphere of gaiety beyond any he had done so far. The color alone was more varied and luminous than ever before, in direct contrast to the grays he had been using (and here, even when he used gray, it was lighter, more silvery). The whole scene was a great welcome change, and he responded to the joyful reality by returning to the naturalism and spontaneity of his early Gloucester water colors. But now his handling was freer and at the same time more firm. He knew what he was doing; his technique was no longer groping and his reawakened sense of color not nearly as tentative as it had been. Every morning, as he came out into the bright sunshine to pick an orange for his breakfast from the tree against the garden wall, he felt a surge of happiness at the thought of the new type of water color he was producing. (He painted a single branch of oranges, the fruit round, full, and shining among the deep-green foliage.)

He had stayed in Nassau nearly two months, leaving only for short trips to some of the neighboring islands like Eleuthera, Harbor, and Hog Island across the bay. The Bahamas had not yet become the resort playground of later years, so he ran into relatively few tourists—and, he thanked heaven, none of his fellow artists. (John LaFarge was bound for Tahiti, others for similar romantic spots; no one but Winslow Homer thought of picking the West Indies.) The young giants he painted were glad to give him all the information he needed, and on the flat, swampy stretches of New Providence he could find his way without a guide. As usual, the friends he made were among those who were his favorite subjects, some of whom he came to know by their descriptive nicknames like Hercules Tall-Boy and Turtle Tom. Happy-go-lucky as they were, the lives of those who lived by the sea here were as fraught with danger as those in the north; tropical storms, especially hurricanes, could be as devastating as any nor'easter, and the beguiling Gulf Stream held the extra hazards of waterspouts and man-eating sharks. He saw the mute testimony of their treachery in a deserted sailboat one day; dismasted, it was wallowing helplessly in the waves; the only sign of life was the school of hungry sharks still hovering around. He had made a sketch of the tragic sight, a theme he had embodied in one of his most dramatic paintings fourteen years afterward.

The ebony Apollos of his early Nassau water colors, however, had a kind of unconscious courage, a reckless bravery that enabled them to take the risks with heedless vigor and zest, a primitive joy of living that Winslow had been able to express in terms of tonality and movement.

He wanted to see more of the West Indies, to visit the spots his Uncle Jim's barque used to touch at; when he learned that the steamships calling at Nassau sailed southward along the cays and around the east end of Cuba, he booked passage for Santiago, where he arrived by the end of February. The great harbor of the ancient city was bustling with troopships, which detracted from the beauty of the scene, the magnificence of the mountains in the background, and the old-world Spanish fort of Morro Castle standing guard at the narrow entrance to the harbor. Trouble was brewing in Santiago and steps were being taken to prevent its fomenting into war.

"This is a red-hot place full of soldiers," he wrote to Charlie. "They have just condemned six men to be shot for landing with arms, & from all accounts they deserve it." Moved by the sight of the obsolete watchtower and cannon, he immediately made a drawing of Morro Castle as it looked in the moonlight, a record that also resulted in a painting many years later.

He took a room in a run-down hotel of fading terra cotta and rusty wrought-iron balconies, on one of the steep, narrow streets leading up the mountainside. In contrast to Nassau, the city of Santiago represented an aged civilization of bygone splendor, and although he found the hotel inconvenient and uncomfortable, especially since the climate was much hotter here, he was eager to try his hand at water colors of these picturesque streets with their seventeenth-century Spanish houses, the weathered stucco walls and red tile roofs, the intricate wrought-iron work on everything from balconies to fence railings and street lamps. He would use mellow colors, varying shades of ochre, all the way from pale gold through saffron. . . .

He set up his equipment on one of the main corners the first day and began sketching; he had had small experience in architecture, but his draftsmanship in drawing on the block stood him in good stead. He was working well, getting proper perspective on the line of buildings, when a middle-aged merchant stopped to see what he was doing. Winslow kept on with his sketch, hoping the man would soon leave, but after a few minutes two more lined up, and the three began commenting in Spanish. A Negress carrying a monkey on her shoulder came along across the street and stood directly in front of him, so he included both of them in the drawing; other passers-by, curious as to the attraction, joined the little knot of people, until it became quite a circle. The woman with the monkey crossed over and stood directly behind the campstool to get a better look; from its perch the inquisitive creature reached down and plucked at the button on Winslow's cap; he grabbed at the visor just in time to keep the little paws from snatching it off his head. The woman let out a stream of scolding, several others chiming in. A policeman, hearing the hubbhub, came to investigate. Crowds of any nature were suspicious; no meetings or gatherings were allowed at this time, even on the street.

"What's going on here?" he asked brusquely in Spanish, and a babble of voices answered him, fingers pointing at the painter. The officer scanned the sketch as if hunting for hidden meanings, then ordered sternly, "You'll have to move on; no crowds allowed."

Winslow, who spoke no Spanish, could not mistake the command and, under the circumstances, thought it wise not to object. Packing up his paraphernalia, he started to leave, while the

The Bather

The Metropolitan Museum of Art, Lazarus Fund, 1910

policeman broke up the group. After walking for several blocks, and wondering whether he should start in again, Winslow had realized that he was in front of the government buildings, including the City Hall. He went in, asked for an interpreter, and explained his case. He had come to the West Indies to paint and was determined to do so.

In his letter to Charlie a few days later he related casually, "The first day sketching I was ordered to move on until the crowds dispersed. Now I have a pass from the Mayor 'forbidding all agents to interfere with me when following my profession.' " He added, "I expect some fine things—it is certainly the richest field for an artist that I have seen." Then he went on to other matters.

"You talk very poor up North. Why do you not sell your horses and buy one from Nassau for 60 that will beat any you have for going over the road, they eat anything they can get, and have never seen an oat. Lucky Father did not go with me. No breakfast until 11, very bad smells, no drains, brick tiles and scorpions for floor & so hot that you must change your clothes every afternoon. I will be very glad to get home." (He had announced in the beginning of the letter, "Here I am fixed for a month, having taken tickets for N.Y. on 8th, leaving 27th of March.")

His Cuban water colors were more subdued than those of the Bahamas necessarily, since they reflected a different atmosphere, a sedate, if crumbling, civilization instead of the simple primitive life in Nassau. Nevertheless, his palette was brighter than it had been in some time, and he was gaining a control in his brush stroke that was to change the course of his art and, indeed, to alter the entire attitude toward water-color painting in America.

When he sailed for New York on March 27, 1885, he felt like an explorer returning with rich treasure.

CHAPTER XII

Prout's Neck:
The Ripening Years

1885-1898

HE DID NOT DISPLAY HIS WEALTH RIGHT AWAY. FOLLOWING HIS usual schedule, he planned to complete these water colors at his leisure, giving himself plenty of time to mull them over in his mind. Although the Nassau pictures needed little more than a few finishing touches, he did not want to spoil their dash by over-working. He wondered how people would take to his latest development, whether they would grasp the significance of the difference between these and his Tynemouth water colors. . . .

He stayed in New York a day or two when the ship docked on April 8. He wanted to arrange a showing at Reichard's for some time in the late fall and attend to other business affairs, as he liked to call them. One of his haunts during the Tenth Street studio days was Ritchie's print shop on West Fourteenth Street. George Ritchie was a noted etcher whose shop was frequented by a number of artists interested in etching, including Alden Weir, who had introduced Winslow to the circle. Like all print shops, Ritchie's smelled of ink and metal and acid; it was close, dark, and often noisy, but the presence of George Ritchie, who gave generously of his knowledge, made the place hospitable. Winslow, who had been reading books on etching, studying the art by himself, had begun a plate he intended to call "Saved," a reproduction of "The Life Line"; he wanted Ritchie to be his printer, and he hoped to pick up a few pointers from him or Alden or any of the others who happened to be around. As always, Ritchie was most helpful and promised to put the ground on Winslow's plates and send them to him whenever he was ready.

This settled, Winslow spent a few days with Mattie and Charlie to report on his trip and then headed straight for Maine. Prout's Neck was home now; he viewed with pride his story-and-a-half studio house, especially the balcony. That summer he had painted the place a pale green, leaving the door the natural color of the wood in order not to hide its beautiful grain; as the only decoration, he bought a handsome bronze knocker, bearing the face of a sibyl in low relief. (It was fitting, he thought with a wry smile, that a fortuneteller should adorn the front of his castle.) He planted a garden on the lee side of the house (including his mother's favorite poppies, old-fashioned pinks, verbena, and heliotrope, as well as the choice wild flowers he had found in his rambles) and he started to train the juniper trees in Japanese style, so that in a few years they would have the delicate look of oriental landscaping. He built a high board fence around the garden to insure privacy.

Charles, seeing his brother so well satisfied with the place, and realizing that their father had so little to occupy his time that he tried to supervise Winslow's projects, began to investigate the idea of buying up property for resort purposes, putting the old man in charge. He found that the Libbys, native farmers not far away, owned most of the Neck; descended from the original settlers, they were land-poor and open to selling. After a good many family conclaves it was decided that Mr. Homer, financed by Charlie, should start buying the Libbys' land, piece by piece. As soon as they had possession of a sizable tract, they would divide it into lots for sale, and with the profits they could buy more land and perhaps put up cottages to rent or sell; then they could begin to develop the place into a real summer resort, build bathhouses and lay out roads, so prospective vacationists could find their way.

Winslow took great interest in this planning. Real estate would provide the sort of part-time occupation he had been seeking—a source of income without interrupting his periods of concentrated work. He had even acquired a little land of his own through tips from Charlie with the proceeds from the sale of a "big" picture.

With that summer—1885—his life had taken on the pattern it had followed—more or less—ever since. He supervised road gangs and bossed construction crews, pitching in along with the men to dig ditches or blast, or burn brush to clear the land for cottages. From early spring until the first snow fell, he was as busy as any man of property, and as he said in a letter to Louis Prang who had spoken of Winslow's 'solitude,' "In fact, I have little time to attend to painting." He may have been exaggerating a trifle, but it was true that, except when he and Charlie went off to the Adirondacks, where he found time for a few water colors, there were months at a clip during those first ten years at Prout's when he was outwardly more occupied with worldly affairs than with his art. It was a matter of pride to him to take part in building the family income, in re-establishing his father as a business figure—no matter how much he might differ with the old man on questions of policy.

Mr. Homer lived alone in the 'big house' when Charlie and Mattie were not there; he got a colored man to look after him and a little dog named Sam to keep him company. Sam, a frisky fox terrier when he came to them, took to Winslow at once, and the artist was reminded of the appealing mongrel on the beach at Long Branch who had played a part in his ill-fated love affair. Oddly enough, the memory created a feeling of attachment to

the little dog that he would not have thought possible. Sam
accompanied him on his walks at dawn, taking the rocks at a
skittery pace, barking at the gulls that swooped overhead. The
two would start out around 4:30 on summer mornings, before
anyone was stirring, and head for Eastern Point in time to see the
sun rise. They would be back before old Mr. Homer was ready
for breakfast, when Winslow would go about his affairs, but at
sunset he and Sam would always walk over to the post office to
fetch the mail; from there they frequently went to Saco Beach,
where Winslow would watch the fading colors of the afterglow,
observing its effect on sea and sky for a long time, with Sam
settled quietly at his side. After storms they were among the
first to venture along the paths, hunting the best surf, and if they
met any neighborhood children doing the same, Winslow would
always stop so the youngsters could "speak to Sam." When Mr.
Homer decided that Sam should have a doghouse, Winslow built
it himself, letting everything else wait, even an unanswered letter
from Doll & Richards about an exhibit of the West Indian water
colors in Boston.

If he painted during the summer, it was in early morning or
late afternoon, or on rainy days when the light was right for the
canvases dealing with the Grand Banks fishermen. As soon as his
father left in September for the Boston hotel where he planned
to spend the winter (advising his son to join him before the pond
froze over), Winslow put in two months or more in concentrated
work completing "The Fog Warning" within a short time. The
hazy October weather brought with it the subtle light he needed
for the next canvas, in which he showed the muted shine of a high
sun on the herring catch just hauled in by two fishermen about to
begin, with one dextrous twist of the wrist, taking each fish out
by the gills and tossing it into the well of the dory. It was a
moment of incipient movement, done in a singular light, and his
painter's sense told him he had achieved a finer quality of painting
in "The Herring Net" than in "The Fog Warning." He began
studies for a third canvas, "Lost on the Grand Banks," based on

drawings he had made when the two fishermen were lost in the fog as they struggled to return to their schooner. This painting gave promise of being more dramatic, more indicative of man's helplessness in the face of nature's overwhelming force than either of the others; but before he had gone very far, the snows had come and the light changed. His provisions were running low, and it was so cold in the studio that his fingers were too stiff for painting anyway. He would have to get a new stove if he expected to spend the better part of the winter there another year. Mattie and Charlie wanted him to come for Thanksgiving, and Gustav Reichard had arranged to show the West Indian water colors in December. The rest of the "Grand Banks" pictures would have to be done later; he had time; he was not going to hurry his oil paintings any more; if he did only two or three a year, they would be richer, riper. He arranged to board Sam at the Libbys', locked up his studio, and left.

As always, he enjoyed his visit to West Townsend, and as always, he wrote Mattie his own brand of bread-and-butter letter when he left. (His brother's red brick house on the main street, with a back lawn stretching down to the river, had a few slight defects, and in one of his letters Winslow didn't hesitate to point them out. "Dear Mattie," he wrote, "It was a very pleasant visit to your house. I would not have anything different. There is one thing that I can tell you, knowing you better than some possible distinguished Englishman who may be put in that room to sleep. That is, if it happens to be a rainy night, the tin spout is within a foot of his head, and it's a 'ching-a-ching-link, ker, chink-a-ching link,' all night. But with one finger in each ear he can sleep until he is smoked out in the morning by the kitchen fire. But I do not wish or deserve better.")

He joined his father in Boston but did not stay at the Winthrop, where Mr. Homer had taken a room for the winter. As in Maine, Winslow took his meals with his father, making sure that the old man ate more than his latest food fad, but he thought it wiser to live in a separate—and less expensive—hotel. After a week or so he went into New York to discover more about etching from observing George Ritchie, talking over with him the problems in biting and stopping out the plates properly. He hung around the shop, absorbing knowledge of etching as the metal absorbed acid; a silent spectator, he asked few questions but let the process cut its own impression in his mind until he was fairly sure he could duplicate it.

He consulted with Reichard's about the exhibit, which was finally held around the middle of December. Subconsciously he had suspected that his latest water colors might not be fully understood; few people could be expected to feel the same excitement that he did over the Nassau pictures. Yet he had hoped that the critics would see in these water colors a new phase of his work, a firmer technique, a strength that the medium had not attained through anyone else; it still required perfecting, but surely the change must be apparent.

He was doomed to disappointment again, however. The show caused little stir, either in New York or in Boston, where he made a second attempt to display his new-found wealth the following February. The critics paid less attention to these pagan water colors than they had to the far paler pictures of his Tynemouth period. Reviews were favorable on the whole, but not one of them, including those who had praised the English water colors to the skies, could see that this might mean the dawn of a new day for an art that had heretofore been relegated to second or third place; it pained him that none of them recognized the significance of the exhibit. And the audience, the people who came to Reichard's expecting to find further examples of the composition Winslow Homer had shown in "A Voice From the Cliffs," were dismayed by the free and unstudied pictures of bare brown bodies. By this time so-called art lovers should have realized that he rarely repeated himself simply because a certain style had been successful, but few gave much thought to the intent of the painter. They came, they viewed, but were not interested. Even at modest prices of $75 apiece, the number of water colors sold netted him scarcely $1000. The Boston exhibit was not much better; it was discouraging. He wrote to Mattie in his usual droll vein: "I hope to cut short my business here; (this sounds extremely large when it means simply standing on one leg one day and on another leg some other day, looking in vain for profits.)"

Soon after the New York showing was over, Mr. Homer, who was beginning to feel rheumatic pain in cold weather, suggested a trip to Florida. Winslow would have preferred Nassau, or some islands in the Caribbean, but he deferred to his father's wishes; he could not afford another trip to Nassau just yet, anyhow, and he knew his father would be so uncomfortable in the primitive surroundings that he would make life miserable for both of them. So they had gone to Florida for a month or more, to a sleepy inland place near the west coast, where Winslow spent hours fishing in the quiet waters of an inlet, easing his irritation of the preceding weeks. But he found time to put his impressions of Florida into water color—scenes of the still, swampy surroundings —silvery water, reflecting the threads of eerie Spanish moss that hung like gray shrouds from the live oaks; the luxuriant growth of palms; the soft, damp air and limpid tropical sky. In these he continued the luminous quality of his Nassau painting; he was still experimenting with a new technique and soon would reach his stride.

In this way, almost unconsciously, he had fashioned his design for living. At least three quarters of the year, though not consecutively, he was at Prout's. In the middle of the summer he always went on a fishing trip, usually with Charlie, either in the Adirondacks or up in Canada. (They had abandoned Keene Valley for the more rugged country around Minerva and later, in search of still more remote regions, had made the trek to Lake Tourilli in Quebec.) In the middle of the winter he went to Florida with his father for a month or so; theoretically they were spending the winter in a warm climate, but Winslow never liked to be away from home that long; and one year, just before his father's death, he had stayed at the Neck later and later, until the winter was over and he had not gone away at all.

The weather was freezing cold, but he did not mind. One of the primary improvements he had made in the studio was to buy a Franklin stove with the hope that it would provide central heating, but it had fallen far short of expectation. In December of 1886 he had written to his father: "I have just put coal on the fire, which accounts for this smut. I made a mistake in not getting a larger stove. It is very comfortable within 10 feet of it. It heats the room within two feet of the floor, and water freezes anywhere within that space. I wear rubber boots and two pairs of drawers. I know very well what a mistake I am making. I should simply 'irritate my skin & take a cold bath.' But water is scarce. I take a sponge and pick out a certain portion of my body which I do at any time of tide, & always. I break four inches of ice to get at my water. I thank the Lord for this opportunity for reflection, and I am grateful for the advantages I enjoy over Sir John Franklyn. P.S. Great storm last night. Cold as the d——."

During those early years at the Neck he was far more sociable than after the influx of summer people began. Eventually his family owned three quarters of the land, but long before then, as soon as the ground had been plotted and the roads laid, people began coming as summer residents. The Homers, including Winslow, had become good friends with their next-door neighbors, the Burditts, and the others who followed them in buying lots and building nearby—the Morgans, Gilberts, Hollands, and Whittiers. With year-round residents like the Libbys and the Seaveys, Winslow was on closer terms than with anyone else in the vicinity. Mrs. Seavey still fixed roast turkey for him, or anything that was too much to handle on his little stove; and every spring, until the little dog died, he gave the Libby girls a twenty-dollar gold piece for taking care of Sam while he and his father were away.

His garden was usually well along by the time the summer people arrived, and for a number of years he had made it a custom to call on several of the families, bringing a bouquet of flowers by

way of welcome. He was never on intimate terms with anyone
outside of the family, and few people ever got inside his studio,
except on those occasions when he finished an important picture;
then he would invite the family, along with any guests Charlie
and Mattie might have, and the small group of neighbors he knew
best, to "come up" for a viewing. Even when his brother and
sister-in-law were not there, he occasionally asked a few of the
neighbors in for tea when he finished a painting or a series of
water colors, if he felt good about his work—and he usually did;
otherwise he would not consider it completed. Sometimes his
feeling of elation ran high and, if he was alone, spilled over in his
routine chores. Once he wrote to Mattie, thanking her for a
Christmas present of wine: "I have proof that there is something
fine in that wine, as I had taken a glass and was peeling vegetables
for my dinner, & thinking of the painting that I had just finished,
and singing with a very loud voice, See! The Conquering
Hero Come, & I sung it—'Sound the *Parsnip*, Beat the Drum'."
It was only on these occasions, however, that anyone was allowed
to set foot inside his studio, unless he had an infrequent visitor
from out of town, like John Beatty, and then Beatty stayed at
the Checkley House, took his meals, along with Winslow, at the
big house, and spent most of the day roaming the Neck with his
host. A knock at the studio door was seldom answered until it
was repeated several times, when Winslow would open the door
no more than a crack to see who was there before letting the
person enter or turning him away.

He made exceptions with children. His nephews were trained
not to bother 'Uncle Win' and when they were small did not often
come over from Arthur's by themselves; but the Morgan boys
might wander in to watch him paint; he did not mind, if they
were quiet. Sometimes he would give them paper and pencil and
let them draw while he painted. When the Seaveys' daughter,
Marie, was a little girl she was his favorite visitor, and he frequently took her along when he went out painting on the coast—
a privilege he would never grant an adult. His affinity for chil-

dren allowed him to enjoy their company without being annoyed by it; if they got fidgety they were free to go. As the resort grew, expanding in families each year, it was true in one sense that he 'had houses galore and no children to live in them' (he smiled ironically when he thought of it); but in another sense, all the children who lived in the Homer houses were his as much as their parents'. His love for children had always remained with him, although they did not come into his painting after he had settled in Maine. Preoccupied with nature from then on, he painted humans less and less; at first women had gradually disappeared from the canvases, then men appeared less frequently, and now he was painting pure seascape. . . .

It had taken him several years, from 1884 till 1887, to complete the series of epic pictures concerned with man's heroic struggle against the perils of the sea. Among those of the Banks fishermen, the one he had started first (when he had rushed up to his studio from Arthur's sloop) was the last to be finished and was the smallest of the series, but probably the finest, he felt. He had been in such a hurry to fix the concept of "Eight Bells" lest it elude him that it would have seemed more logical to finish up right then; but he chose to let his portrayal of two bearded fishermen in oilskins, going about the ancient task of taking latitude after a gale, grow in his mind (once the idea for it had been recorded), while he painted the action pictures. "Eight Bells" became then a summing up of the fisherman's life, of duties that existed since sextants were invented. His technique had matured in painting the other scenes so that his color was now deep and full-bodied, the two figures monumental forms against a clearing sky. He had learned to present only the bare essentials, as if he had come upon the core of truth.

All this time he had painted at intervals on "Undertow," which was completed in 1886 and shown at the Academy in 1887. Here was the boldest color he had achieved in oil so far, and the four figures, particularly the two women clinging to each other in the life net, were sculptural in form; the other pictures had been very

Etching of *Eight Bells*

Prints Division, The New York Public Library

well received, though slow to sell, and he was hoping at least as much from this. To indicate his own feelings, he put a price of $3000 on it, the highest he had ever asked. For all his insistence on the business end of his career, he never took any interest in making money, and the figure he asked was far lower than some of his contemporaries were commanding, William Chase and John Sargent received an average of five or six thousand dollars for portraits, which required much less work, he felt, than this painting or any of his sea pictures.

"Undertow" proved to be the sensation of the exhibit, exceeding his expectations, bringing almost as much praise from the critics as "The Life Line." The *New York Tribune* declared fervently: "After Mr. Homer's intense epic, one must wait a little or other paintings of the figure will seem tame. . . . The scene is 'dramatic,' the favorite word for Mr. Homer's work." Here the article compared the figures to Greek sculpture, the theme to Greek tragedy. The *Nation* proclaimed unequivocally: " 'Undertow' by its virility, its truth, its sincerity of intention, outranks every picture in the Academy exhibit." A few adverse opinions regarding the "harshness" of his color and the "hardness" of handling were still expressed, but in the main his reputation as one of the foremost among American painters seemed to be permanently established.

For all the praise lavished upon it, the "Undertow" canvas made the rounds of several exhibits, including the Pennsylvania Academy, without finding a purchaser. Some might have been interested if the price had been lower, but Winslow, strong in the knowledge that he was growing in stature as a painter all the time, inwardly as well as in the outside world, stuck to his original figure. ("Eight Bells," for which he had asked $800, was finally sold to the collector, Thomas B. Clarke, for half the amount, but that was a concession which he hoped would lead to further purchases. It did not mean that he would come down on every canvas, especially one like "Undertow," which represented so much time and effort.)

He turned to other matters, concentrating on Adirondack water colors in the summer and the etchings based on the sea pictures during the fall and winter. The process of biting the plates fascinated him, and if his first attempt, "Saved," turned out to be more amateurish than he expected, the result only spurred him to further experiment. He made use of the Tynemouth water colors, transferring "Perils of the Sea," "Mending the Tears," and "A Voice From the Cliffs" to the etcher's plate with the skill of a seasoned print maker. As soon as he finished the biting, he sent the plates to George Ritchie for proving and afterward for lettering and printing. By 1887, when he transferred "Eight Bells" to the plate, he could handle biting and stopping out as if he had been born to it; and a year later, at work on one of the last etchings he was to complete, he wrote to his friend and teacher: "It promises to be worthy of your pupil, which is more than I can say of some of my recent work. There has been altogether too much bragging for the small amount of creditable work." He left the letter unfinished until he was farther along and could estimate his success; a few days later he was able to report: "I have bitten my plate today. It took me six hours, with twenty minutes for the first line to go by. I think it is very fine. . . . If this turns out as good as I think, it is a mere echo of what I have seen you do, and I wish to assure you that I am most grateful to you."

To show his gratitude, Winslow arranged to handle the sale of the prints through Ritchie's shop, but George was more of an artist and commercial printer than a salesman and had little success in promoting the etchings for wide "distribution," even at prices the general public could afford; and although he realized fully the fine quality of Winslow's work, he could not seem to put it across at any real profit to either of them. He suggested that Winslow try C. Klackner, who had a reputation for success in the field.

Klackner, whose methods Winslow found reminiscent of Bufford's, got the idea of making photogravures of "A Voice From the Cliffs," "The Signal of Distress," and other sea pictures; it would be less expensive and they could put out much greater volume. To publicize them, he printed a circular on "Original Etchings by Winslow Homer," but he could see no necessity for making a distinction between the etchings themselves and the photogravures, a practice which was actually misrepresentation. The result was that he failed to attract either the small discriminating circle of print collectors who knew the difference or the general public, which did not realize the value of the etchings. Indeed, the framed-picture trade seemed more inclined toward the photogravures, if anything. From his studio in Prout's Neck, still with high hopes for the success of his prints, Winslow wrote to Eastman Chase in May of 1888: "I have an idea for next winter if what I am now engaged in is a success, and Mr. Klackner is agreeable. That is to exhibit an oil painting in a robbery-box" —as he preferred to call a shadow box—"with an etching from it in the end of your gallery, with a pretty girl at the desk to sell." (To him salesgirls would always be pretty, like those behind the ribbon counters in his youth.)

These fond hopes had not been realized, nor had any edition sold out, small as they were; only six prints had been made of the largest (and perhaps the finest, with the exception of "Eight Bells"), which was "A Voice from the Cliffs," the one he expected to be the best seller. (Klackner still had four very good etchings that he had never done anything with; he was probably waiting for the artist to die, Winslow thought to himself cynically.) Disgusted with the whole venture, he had done no more etchings after 1889; unless they would suddenly prove profitable, he could not take the time; there was too much he wanted to do in water color and oil painting. He wrote to Charlie: "I am very busy painting in water color, which means something that I can sell for what people will give." He made a point, especially with the family, of being as businesslike about his art as they all were about property. His strict New England conscience would not countenance the idea of his being a parasite or being regarded as such by the family. He had long ago forgiven Charlie for buying the first two paintings, but he still felt compelled to prove that he could earn his salt by being an artist as much as in any other calling.

His compulsion sometimes led to erratic behavior, partly aggravated by his father, who still handed out gratuitous advice, urging Winslow to get the highest possible price. About this time he had sent a painting to New York asking the agents to get $1500 for it. Some weeks later Reichard had written that he had had an offer of $1200 from a party who liked the picture very much; he wanted to know if he should sell. Winslow sent him a single-line answer: "Make the price $1900." This only vexed his father more; he said it was 'the most unbusinesslike thing he ever heard of,' and when Winslow reminded him that he was always advocating higher prices, the old man berated him for being 'unpractical' in not taking a bird-in-hand and scolded him hotly.

It was 1889 before he made another "big" sale, comparable to that of "The Life Line." In January, Charlie's friend, Edward Adams of New York, wrote, asking to borrow "Undertow"; he wished to hang it in his house for a time with a view of purchasing. Winslow, standing firm on the amount he had asked, sent a straightforward reply: "You have my permission to keep this picture on your wall as long as you find it agreeable within a year's limit. In regard to your making me an offer on it, I can state to you now that my price is $3,000 less what commission I should have had to pay any dealers had they sold it . . . they would have charged 20%, and that would net me $2400, *and never will I take any less.* There is no hurry, look at this a month or two before you conclude, and remember that I much prefer that this should be in your house for the winter rather than in my studio." Shortly after writing the letter he had gone to Florida and spent some time in New York and Boston on his return; when he came back to Prout's in early summer, he found Adams' check for $2400 waiting for him. He seldom had his mail forwarded while he was away.

With a sigh of relief he put the money in the bank for reserve and set about the task of cleaning out the weeds which had over-run his garden. He usually planted vegetables as well as flowers and every summer enjoyed his own cucumbers and corn. His simple life suited him to a T; he never stinted on provisions, and he made sure that his family realized the fact. One spring he had written to Charlie: "Things are looking very beautiful here today. I had my place covered with seaweed last winter, and now it is raked off just before this rain it is as green as Central Park. I have raw Bermuda onions and *young* dandelions every day. . . . Do not waste so much on appearances, you do not live well enough, you do not eat enough or drink enough. I brought down (from Boston) a Leg of Canada Mutton, 2 Spring Chickens, Bermuda onions, 6 bottles old rum, one Edam cheese, 6 bottles rare old vatted whiskey, 'good as the Bank of England,' and Boston pilot bread. You see I can afford to live better than you can, as I cut off servants that mean all these good things—each extra *one* means about 3 legs of mutton, which you go without, and eat corned beef and cabbage." Beneath this tone of banter was the wish to justify his way of living, his lack of financial success in comparison to his brothers.

So his feelings ran on a surface level. On a deeper level he cared not one jot for appearances or financial success and was solely devoted to his work. The water colors were showing a greater mastery all the time. He and Charlie had joined the North Woods Club in Minerva, and in this mountain wilderness of deep forests, lakes, and streams, he found inspiration to carry forward the technique begun in the West Indies. As at Keene, it was necessary to hire guides to penetrate the forest; and here, too, the men, old gray-bearded Rufus Wallace and young Mike "Farmer" Flynn, were Winslow's companions and models. If he came by himself (as he did a few times when Charlie couldn't make it), he did not team up with any other club member but went off by himself, or, if he wanted to probe the depths of the wilderness, he chose as his sole companions Rufus or Farmer, men close to nature and as silent as himself. One of his most daring water colors, "The Blue Boat," showed old Rufus, sitting in the bright blue canoe they paddled up and down the trout streams, his flaming red shirt in sharp contrast to the boat and the background of green shore. Painted on the spot, in full sunlight, with patches of a blue and white sky, the combination of colors, all mirrored by the water, was the boldest Winslow had attempted in the medium. With an inner glee he scribbled after his name in signing, "This will do the business."

He was drawing more freely with the brush, although he still made slight pencil sketches. Applying bold washes with a full brush, he achieved broader dimensions than ever before. He included only the bare essentials of a scene, sometimes with oriental effect. At Mink Pond, one of his favorite spots, he created a decorative and subtly beautiful scene out of one brilliant little fish, a single frog on a lily pad, and a few winged creatures in the floating pickerel weed, reflected in the calm, clear water. On another day he pictured a deer drinking, straddling a log at the edge of the pond, cooling its forelegs as it lapped up deep draughts from the spring bubbling on the shore. At Mink Pond he often painted the mountain that fascinated him more than any in the Adirondacks, Beaver, to him the most majestic of the range. These pictures possessed the tranquility of oriental art in the natural rugged setting of American wilderness, with a freedom and broad gamut of color never before found in American water color.

By 1890 the critics had grown used to his unusual style and were beginning to appreciate what he was trying to express. In February that year Reichard's exhibited thirty-two Adirondack water colors, along with two Keene Valley oils, "Camp Fire" and "The Two Guides." The reviews cited enthusiastically "those bold effects of color, extreme breadth and facility of treatment, and that science of abstraction on which this artist has based his powerful style." His works were considered "admirable examples of painting the essential and omitting the incidental." The *Sun*

admitted that they "excited an unusual share of popular attention" and in a lengthy article continued, "Mr. Homer has met
with a success, which, if pecuniary outcome is any test, could
hardly have been greater. The exhibit was a modest one, not
very loudly heralded, and occurred while others, including the
water-color show at the Academy, were open. Yet, of the two
oil paintings, the more important was sold, and of the thirty-two
water colors, only a stray example or so remains in the artist's
possession. . . . Needless to say at this late day that Mr. Homer is
a master of water color, but the simplicity and force of his brush
were never better exhibited than here. But—Mr. Homer ought to
have asked more than $125 for these admirable water colors."

It was gratifying to receive such advice in public, and Winslow
had not hesitated to accept it, raising his prices to $200 and $300;
and instead of large exhibits, he showed a few at a time at
Reichard's or at Doll & Richards in Boston. With highly favorable
reviews from William H. Downes in the *Transcript*, the Boston
shows had also been successful; Winslow reached a point where
he could sell at least half of the water colors he painted, and at
slowly increasing prices.

Between the sale of "Undertow" to Edward Adams and the
returns from the show at Reichard's, he felt he was "in business"
again, after his depressing experience with the etchings. He had
not done any oil painting since finishing "Undertow" in 1887, but
now he began with fresh vigor, choosing subjects outside his
studio door—the sea, the rocky coast, and the summer resort life
which he had been helping to develop at Prout's Neck. In a single
year he had done no fewer than five oils—more than he had done
in the medium any other year after he settled at Prout's in 1883—
but when the inspiration seized him he worked fast and hard,
lest the concept be lost, like the fleeting moments of a sunset,
before he could get it on canvas. The sight of a young girl from
the summer colony, listening to the tales of an old 'salt,' seated on
the bow of his beached boat on a day when southerly winds sent
the shadows of clouds scudding over the sand dunes, served as

the subject for "Cloud Shadows," which had the flavor of a sea chantey. Later in the season he was pacing the balcony of the studio one warm moonlit night, noting the pale light of the silver sea, when a group of resort people out for a moonlight stroll decided to rest on the rocks in front of his studio; their laughter and song drifted up to him, and after a time two of the girls came up and began waltzing on the lawn. Right then he began painting "A Summer Night," a large canvas in skillfully blended tones of soft tan, gray-brown, slate gray, and light blue that captured the sorcery of a moonlight night without sentimentalizing it or sacrificing the healthy delight the young people took in it. The only change he made was to have the girls dancing on a porch, their figures partly lit by a hurricane lamp inside the house and partly outlined by the glow of the moon, shining on the sea in a broad band. The silhouettes of the singers on the rocks just below increased the impression of wholesome activity in the picture, which was one of his most effective compositions in both color and form.

Of the other three paintings, one marked the launching of a new era in his oils born of a kind of subject he would not have thought possible for him to paint before he came here to live, and that was pure seascape. Up to now the human figure had dominated his sea pieces, necessarily, because of the story telling element present in most of them. But he was beginning to realize the drama in the forces of nature alone, and with his deeper vision nature assumed the larger role in his work. The hours he had spent watching the waves from the vantage point of the balcony had opened his eyes to the constant battle between surf and rock. For his first seascape, "Sunlight on the Coast," he chose a single wave just as it was gathering to break over the rocks. In the hard white sunlight reflected on its crest as on the broad expanse of ocean, and contrasted with a gray bank of creeping fog darkening the horizon, the glittering green wave stood out in bold relief, emphasizing the threat of its power as it prepared to hurl its huge mass of moving water against the immutable resistance of the rocks. The weather effect was one he had observed for some time before attempting to paint, and then he put it on canvas with a full brush, in spots applying the paint with a palette knife.

Another seascape marked his initial essay at painting after the snows fell; entitled "Winter Coast," it expressed the uncompromising severity of the cold in the snow-covered cliffs and soaring columns of spray from a high surf against the overcast sky, heavy with snow clouds. Here he included a solitary hunter, his kill of a wild goose over his shoulder, staring soberly at the show of brute force in the elements, the unending battle between land and sea.

Two months after completing the last, Winslow had exhibited four of the five canvases at Reichard's with unqualified critical success. The noted Alfred Trumble had written in the *Collector*: "To say that Mr. Winslow Homer exhibits the four most powerful pictures he has ever done is to do them but half justice. They are, in their way, the four most powerful pictures that any man of our generation and people has painted. Nothing of the artist's previous work touches them, and, what is better still, they are sufficient to indicate to anyone who has followed the career of this original and rarely gifted man that he has worked the problem of his art to a solution from which he will not retrogress. . . . A great American artist in the full greatness of an art as truly American as its creator; what words could mean more?" the review ended in glowing tribute.

No artist could have asked for more, yet Winslow had neither gloated over his success nor retired on it, but pushed ahead, painting as he chose. "Winter Coast" and "Sunlight on the Coast" had been bought immediately by John G. Johnson of Philadelphia. ("A Summer Night," to his mind the best of the lot, did not find a purchaser, and he finally loaned it to the Cumberland Club in Portland, where it hung for years until the French government bought it for the Luxembourg.)

The same year, 1890, stood out as the beginning of a continued promotion of his work by Thomas Benedict Clarke, famous collector—and often dealer—in contemporary American art, who had purchased "Eight Bells"; from then on he had "taken up Winslow Homer" and had done more for the artist's professional career than anyone except Charlie. It was Clarke who bought "Camp Fire" and, shortly afterward, "The Two Guides," followed by the purchase of two early canvases, "The Carnival" and "A Visit From the Old Mistress." He sold his wealthy friends the idea of buying Winslow Homers and set up a "Homer Gallery" in his house, where collectors and other painters could view them at any time. He mentioned, in writing Winslow about the gallery, that John Singer Sargent had come especially to see the Homers. Winslow, moved by the announcement, had written in answer: ". . . I am under the greatest obligation to you and will never lose an opportunity of showing it. I shall always value any suggestion that you may make. Now that you have space in your 'Homer Gallery' I can from time to time as you fancy any work, let you have it. I will be glad to have it with you in place of returning it to my studio. . . ."

Although he did not often think about it, Winslow sometimes wondered if he would have had any measure of success without these two men—Clarke as his patron, and his brother as a constant bulwark against adversity. His affection and admiration for Charlie cropped up unexpectedly, in June of 1891, when he saw his brother and sister-in-law off on a trip to Europe. Feeling rather lost afterward, he wrote to Arthur: "I thought you would be glad to hear that Charlie and Mattie have had a fine day and the best steamer in the world to start them on their journey. Considering the old tubs I have been over the ocean in, there is no doubt but they will have a fine voyage. I have never seen anyone off before, that I cared anything about, and I find it hard, and I was glad when the steamer was off, but New York seems empty to me now. They had lots of friends to say good-bye.— I bet you everything will be just as it should be in the end since Charlie has to do with it."

This was one of the times when he went to the Adirondacks alone, and he had done hardly any fishing before he began painting a water color of a trout for Charlie. When he and Farmer were on top of Beaver Mountain one day, he got the tough-skinned young woodsman to pose for him, the rangy figure outlined against the sky, far below the green valley, and in the distance the blue folded hills. His drawing with the brush alone continued to develop, building the picture as he went along, improvising with superb control . . . ever surer of his handling. If he wanted pure white for the wake of a boat, he scraped down to the bare paper now without hesitation. Later in his stay he did several water colors of the solemn, self possessed guide with his hunting dogs, from which he began two powerful oil paintings in the fall. On his brother's return in October, Winslow was still in Minerva, painting. He wrote Charlie on the fifteenth: "I am working very hard and will without doubt finish the two oil paintings that I commenced October 2nd, and great works they are. Your eye being fresh from European pictures, great care is required to make you proud of your brother. The original ideas of these paintings are in water color and will not be put on the market but will be presented to you with the one I made expressly for you."

By the time he returned to Maine, the autumn winds were causing their usual havoc of storms, and he painted two more "important" oils. "Watching the Breakers" was begun at the end of a storm, when two of the tag-end vacationers ventured to take in the thrilling sight of the still-raging surf. The other, entitled "The West Wind," was done on a dark day when an offshore gale flattened the dead grass, twisted the junipers, and sent mountainous waves charging at the shore, their spray blown backward as they broke. Winslow had found a sheltered place on the rocks and was painting the wild, lonely, splendor of the scene, when he noticed one of the year-round neighbors, Mrs. Landreth King, standing on the cliffs, her figure, in the familiar tam-o'-shanter and burly coat she always wore in rough weather, buffeted by the

The Woodcutter

Mrs. John S. Ames

wind as she watched the waves. She became part of the painting (to her great surprise when, on the day he completed it, Winslow told Alice Homer to invite her over to the studio for a viewing); and both pictures were exhibited at Reichard's with the two Adirondack oils. Thomas Clarke bought "The West Wind," the most highly praised, from the exhibit; and Reichard later sold "Huntsman and Dogs" and "Watching the Breakers." Through his agent, five pictures had been purchased in a little over a year; Winslow was able to write Mattie, on hearing of some successful business stroke Charlie had made, "You will be glad to know that I also have had great luck this past year, and as Father tells me, I am rich." From the standpoint of money, he never felt rich in his life, but he liked to talk about it.

The following year, at the World's Fair in Chicago, he had received his first gold medal, plus a diploma, for the group of fifteen Winslow Homers on display—more than any other American artist except George Inness. He had made a trip to Chicago to accept the honor, only to find that fifty-six other American painters also had been awarded medals! But he visited the fairgrounds, dazzling and garish after Prout's Neck, the display of electricity fantastic in its brilliance. He painted a small oil of MacMonnie's Fountain in the Court of Honor one night, in the full glare of electric lights, and while in Chicago arranged to have his work handled in the Middle West by O'Brien & Son, a well-known agency. He was glad to get back to Maine's lonely, rugged coastline, away from the noisy crowds gaping at the show of "civilization." Still, the trip had produced a picture, and he wrote to Reichard: "That painting in black and white I will sell for cost—that is, my expense to Chicago, $280, *net to me*. Sell it before Christmas or *I give it away*." No purchasers came in sight, so he gave the picture to Charlie for Christmas.

Seven of the paintings at the fair were loaned by Clarke, who had bought the repainted version of "The Gale" just before the opening. He had also purchased a second winter seascape that Winslow had completed late in 1892. Called simply "Coast in

Winter," it was on the order of the first, but stronger, more complex in composition. While painting it, Winslow had conceived the idea for a canvas of greater magnitude, physically, philosophically, and aesthetically, than any he had ever done. During the bitter cold weather flocks of crows, starved for food, would be driven to attack—and often kill—their ancient enemy, the fox. It was a gripping sight, if strange subject matter for an artist, but Winslow Homer had long since won a reputation for painting as he chose and was not inclined to change now. To get a feeling of starkness, he used the utmost care in his selection: against a vast white waste he presented a lone red fox, trying to escape from the two crows swooping down on his head. At the left of the fox three twigs of dried berries from a blackened bush stood out in delicate tracery against the snow. That was all. But each of these sparing choices was eloquent, meaningful in its own way.

To get the exact color of the fur, Winslow borrowed the skin of a fox one of his neighbors had shot and stretched it over a barrel in the snow. He ran into trouble painting the crows, so he asked the Scarboro station agent, who was constantly shooing the birds away from the depot, to look at the picture and tell him what was wrong. Then, on the agent's advice, he hiked over to the station every day with Sam, studying the black crows as they came flocking around, until he was able to paint them accurately. In March of 1893 he had written to Reichard: " 'The Fox Hunt' is finished, and I will send it early in the week. I shall not give a price on it until it has been seen, & I should like your advice about it. It is quite an unusual and *very beautiful picture.*" Here he drew a little sketch of a bald-headed man hiding a lamp under a big basket and captioned it, "W.H., hiding his light under a bushel." He continued the letter, "Price should be no object to anyone wishing it. When I see the prices that portraits bring— from $3,000 to $6,000—and considering the skill required in arranging and painting a scene in outdoor light, I do not see why I should not get a good price for this."

He sensed that he had created a masterpiece in a work that

was the epitome of naturalism and yet was almost abstract in its paring down of detail to the barest of essentials. However, "The Fox Hunt" found no immediate buyer in New York or in Boston, although it was highly praised in the *Transcript* by William Downes, and Winslow was for a time dispirited. He would always have a conflict between the desire to make his mark from a commercial standpoint and his love of art for its sake alone. This wish to prove his mettle practically as well as professionally made him cynical at the slightest sign of public rejection. Ready to "quit the business" once more, he wrote to O'Brien & Son, who had invited him to have an exhibit in Chicago: "In reply I would say that I am extremely obliged to you for your offer, and if I have anything in the picture line again, I will remember you. At present & for some time past I see no reason why I should paint any pictures." The recent sales, the homage paid him at the fair, were quickly forgotten. He added a crusty postscript: "I will paint for money at any time. Any subject, and size."

This was an exaggeration, he knew, and he expected others to discount a certain percentage for his passing mood. Some weeks later he was telling Charlie in a cheerful note: "It has been too cold to go to Boston and leave my water & provisions; in fact, it has been the very devil of weather, but I have been most comfortable and happy in having painted a picture, 'Below Zero,' *which is fine.*"

Not too long afterward "The Fox Hunt" had been shown at the 1894 exhibit of the esteemed Pennsylvania Academy, which bought the painting for $1200. In the same year one of his wealthy Norcross cousins (who had taken small notice of his work until he had gained a name for himself) bought "The Fog Warning" for $1500 and gave it to the Boston Museum. With the purchase he was represented in two leading public collections, but he was fifty-eight and it was about time, he told himself wryly. Up to this point no museums or public galleries had offered the recognition of purchase for permanent collections. He still had much to do.

The Fox Hunt

Pennsylvania Academy of the Fine Arts

It was then that he had the portable painting booth built, according to the plans he laid out—a rectangular cabin, 8 x 10 feet, set on runners so it could be moved wherever he wanted to work, fitted with a large plate glass 'viewing-window'—and a stove, for working in the bitter cold weather; he had frosted his fingers too many times in painting "The Fox Hunt" and "Below Zero" to risk another winter of exposure. With his portable studio he could paint in storm and high winds, when it would have been impossible to handle a canvas of any size. He could get close enough to the surf to paint the combers and still be protected from the towering spray; and he was safe from prying eyes: no one could watch him work, as an occasional stranger among the summer people, or a brash young artist, still tried to do. He never cared to take on any students or found a school of Homer disciples, though as the years went on he had many admirers among the younger artists. Now he launched into a series of pure seascapes, confident that he could execute the scene with an exactitude never before achieved. Most of the time he kept the portable studio on Eastern Point, since the fury of a stormy sea was greatest there, but now and then he moved it to vantage ground for a different aspect of the ever-changing ocean.

His work absorbed him, so that the little things of boredom, the daily routine during the summer, the care and patience he exerted with his father, the long hours of loneliness during the autumn and winter evenings did not bother him as they would have many another man. He had written to Louis Prang, who once wanted to visit him in late fall, when it would have been impossible, as the Checkley House was closed, "I deny that I am a recluse as is generally understood by that term. Neither am I an unsociable hog. I wrote you it is true, that it was not convenient to receive a visitor; that was to save you as well as myself. Since you must know it, I have never yet had a bed in my house." This was no more than the truth—he did not have a regular bed because they were all too soft. "I do my own work. No other man or woman is within half a mile, and I am 4 miles from railroad and post

office. This is the only life in which I am permitted to mind my
own business; I suppose I am today the only man in New England
who can do it. I am perfectly happy and contented. Happy New
Year."

That had been in 1893; in 1895, the day before his fifty-ninth
birthday, he repeated the same sentiments, with significant over-
tones, in a letter to Charlie. He began in a tone of calm prediction, "I am very well, with a birthday tomorrow; I suppose I
may have 14 more (that was Mother's age, 73 years) and what
is 14 years when you look back. The life I have chosen gives me
my full hours of enjoyment for the balance of my life. The sun
will not rise, or set, without my notice, and thanks.

"Only think of my absolute freedom—I have gained in one item,
a year's time, in the last 12 years, at 1 month a year (Jury Duty),
for which I am willing to pay the community in work more
agreeable to me, and *of more value to them*. Other things
(notably my being a spendthrift) are in favor of my home here."
Perhaps no one but Charlie would understand this mixture of
dry humor and solemn observation, but to no one except his elder
brother would he write such a revealing letter.

He continued, with the vigor and energy of a much younger
man, to produce the series of marine paintings—"Storm-Beaten";
"High Cliff"; "Cannon Rock"; "Maine Coast"; "Northeaster";
"A High Sea"—which burst upon an uninitiated world of art
lovers with the impact of the breakers themselves.

In 1895 Reichard decided to give up his gallery on Fifth Avenue
but wrote that he expected to remain in the field as a dealer,
implying that he wished to continue handling all the Winslow
Homers he was offered. As soon as the news of the gallery closing
was out, Winslow had a letter from Thomas Clarke, suggesting
that he act as New York agent for the artist in whose work he
already had great interest. It was an overwhelming gesture,
highly tempting, but Winslow could not take advantage of it.
With his usual straightforwardness he answered Clarke, "I must
thank you for your continued interest in my work, and for your

suggestion which I consider a great compliment. I can see that
it would be greatly to my advantage to ask you to take charge of
all my work now that Mr. Reichard has given up his gallery on
Fifth Avenue. But two years ago, and without any reason beyond
my being grateful to them for their success in selling my work
(they sold most of it to you and your friends) and my appreciation *of them all* as gentlemen, I wrote to them that '*I appointed
them my New York agents—for life.*' Since that has been said, it
must stand. Mr. Reichard has already written me that he is not
to give up the picture business."

His portable painting booth enabled him to picture small sec-
tions of the shore, close-ups of a single wave (or never more than
two) seen from different aspects of the rocky coast line with a
sense of power and tragic beauty of the sea. Observing from his
window, he could now capture the threatening forward thrust of
a mountainous wave as it broke at his feet, its spray splattering
the pane of glass with salty drops of the mighty deep. His oils
took on a measure of the direct-from-nature spontaneity of the
water colors; his technique became broader. Always using a full
brush, he applied the paint in huge slashing strokes; or, not satisfied, he put on color with the palette knife more and more. The
notes of his spectrum were higher, more resonant in tone—blues,
blue-grays, greens, blue-greens—used with greater variation, a
wider range than any of the Tynemouth oils, the sea epics, or the
early seascape. His vision became ever broader, suggesting the
whole, eliminating detail, selecting with a masterful artistry as he
went along. He never painted every ripple; it was his aim, by
means of naturalism—and the sensuous appeal of paint itself—
not to imitate or photograph the sea, but to interpret it. The
unacknowledged loneliness in his heart, the sublimated passion
and fury, were expressed in these pictures of the physical force
and violent beauty of the sea in its varying moods.

The sensation caused by the first group of these pure seascapes
at the Pennsylvania Academy's Annual Exhibition in 1895
brought forth paeons of praise from the critics. J. C. VanDyke,

Cannon Rock

The Metropolitan Museum of Art, Gift of George A. Hearn, 1906

in the *New York Evening Post*, proclaimed, "In individualism, strength, and sureness of purpose, there is no painter in America superior to Mr. Winslow Homer, and in painting the sea, it is doubtful if he has an equal here or elsewhere." *Scribner's*, citing his qualities of greatness, suggested that "one might call him the Whitman of our painters," and his latest interpretation of the sea was likened to Whitman's poetic description of "the cradle, endlessly rocking."

The exhibition closed by awarding Winslow Homer the Academy's Gold Medal of Honor—an outstanding mark of recognition which he accepted calmly, as usual. He was already at work on further paintings, one canvas of tremendous importance, which would take some months to complete. Entitled "The Wreck," it was a return to the theme of shipwrecks, but much more subtly accomplished; in it he showed the preparations for rescue—the lifeboat being hauled over a sand dune, men in oilskins rushing forward. Almost a monochrome, its harmonies were so varied that the effect was a symphony of subtle color, a dramatic and suspenseful scene of tragedy taking place off stage. Finished in the fall of 1896, it brought a second signal honor.

That year the Carnegie Institute had been founded in Pittsburgh, and John Beatty, appointed curator, assembled the first international exhibition; Winslow had promised to send two paintings, but in September he wrote to Beatty: "I have decided to send but one picture to your exhibition, but that is the best one I have painted this year." This was "The Wreck"; and while he considered it one of his finest achievements up to that time, he was not prepared for the announcement on December 5 that his work had received first prize—$5000—the picture becoming the property of the Institute. This was the only year that the prize was a purchase award, given for an American painting completed that year and first shown in the exhibit. It was the highest honor that he—or any other American artist—had received, and he was overwhelmed by the telegrams and letters of congratulation that poured in from friends.

He wondered if he could measure up to such eminence. In his letter of acknowledgment, after thanking the Institute for 'this great honor,' he had gone on to say, "Although chance may have given me this distinguished place in your permanent exhibition (by the absence of many American painters) I shall prove if possible by my future work that your opinion and this award has not been misplaced." He voiced the same sentiment in replying to Clarke's congratulations: "It is certainly a most tremendous and unprecedented honor and distinction that I have received from Pittsburgh. Let us hope that it is not too late in my case to be of value to American art in something that I may yet possibly do, from this encouragement." To Mattie and Charlie he wrote more intimately, "I have been most deeply moved by the many expressions of friendship that I have received, as well as this great distinction conferred on me." He still could hardly believe it was true, and he could not get over the feeling that he had won the award only because it so happened that very few American artists had submitted works. He scribbled on the wall of his studio: "Oh, what a friend chance can be—when it chooses!"

All this time Prout's Neck was prospering. The bathhouses had been built and had more than half paid for themselves. An aviary had been established in the pine grove on the cliff, and hunting restrictions were maintained. The resort flourished from May until the middle of September; Winslow's only complaint was that the summer people came earlier every year. The "Prout's Neck Association," composed of summer colonists, looked after the general interests, the maintenance of roads, picnic grounds, etc. The Homers gradually sold a good bit of their land (at a profit), and people began building their own homes.

One of Winslow's jobs as more property was sold was to keep his father out of trouble; the old man was constantly getting into fights about one piece of land or another; even after he sold it, he went around acting as though he owned it. He would tear down a fence if he decided it shouldn't have been put up, or, conversely, he would raise a ruckus if he heard that a new owner was planning to tear down a fence the Homers had put up. In one case Winslow offered to go and speak to a man just to keep his father from making another enemy. His approach was much milder. "I think you'd better leave that fence where it is," he said to the new owner. The man retorted evenly, "Mr. Homer, if you'll come back tomorrow morning, you won't see a single stick of that fence." Winslow's answer was, "Mister, you and I are going to get on," and they did.

"Old Father Homer," as everyone called him, was more of a known "character" in the community than his eccentric son ever would be. He scared away any children who happened to set foot on his property, roaring like a lion till they fled; but when one little girl, caught trespassing, offered him a large peppermint, he accepted the toll solemnly. Having little to do now that the resort was established and on its own, he stuck his nose into other people's affairs, trouble or no. Winslow would report to Charlie, "Father is having a good time by not agreeing to mind his own business and retire from active life"; or, "Father is hustling about, trying to get in debt by fall," and it was useless to stop him, yet he still harped about how "unpractical" Winslow was.

When the rest of the family arrived, things were always a little easier. His father had someone else to criticize. Arthur's sons, who were nearly of age, received their full share of faultfinding and familial advice from their grandfather. Winslow was fond of both of his nephews but felt closer to Arthur, who showed much of the independence of his famous uncle. Charles was set to enter the family enterprises from college and, like Charlie, had a good business head. Arthur had wanted to get away and try to make it on his own. His first attempt had not been too successful; he had worked for a time in Virginia but had fallen ill and was out of a job; he was too proud to ask for help and claimed he was getting along; Winslow, however, sent him a check for $100 to tide him over, enclosing a brief line, "No thanks for the enclosed. Uncle Winslow." Arthur often came over to have an after-dinner cigar with him on mild summer evenings (as a change from his pipe, Winslow allowed himself the luxury of a good cigar), and they would silently admire the view, without the need of words. The inspiration for one of the four oils in the 1895 show came on a bright moonlight evening when he and Arthur were sitting in front of the studio, smoking. There was a running sea but no wind, and Wood's Island Light, just off the coast, was wonderfully clear. Suddenly Winslow jumped up. "I've got an idea," he said. "Good night, Arthur." And without further ado he had dashed into the studio, gathered up his painting things, and gone down to the shore, ·where he worked until moonset, around one o'clock in the morning, nearly completing "Wood's Island Light, Moonlight." He had later told Downes that he had never touched the canvas by daylight.

Mattie's charm and tactful treatment of her father-in-law's stubborn peculiarities served as a buffer also; during the few weeks she and Charlie were at Prout's, the old man was far more peaceable than at any other time. Winslow never lost his affectionate admiration for his sister-in-law; when she was not feeling well one summer, he went over from his studio every morning to take her a little bouquet of pinks or some nosegay from his garden to cheer her. Well or sick, her presence alone seemed to soften his father, and Winslow suspected that the similarity between her and his mother brought about the change. Although he rarely mentioned it, his father missed his mother deeply (as Winslow himself did), and much of the irascibility in the old man's behavior was a cover-up for his loneliness. And since he understood, he forgave his father and looked after him as best he could.

When the doctor prescribed a little liquor as a heart stimulant for the old man, Winslow, knowing his father's pride in being a teetotaler all his life, took him an "eleven o'clocker" every morning, once for over a week. Their exchange of dialogue was always the same.

"Now, Father, don't you think you'd better take this? It will do you good." "Is there any alcoholic liquid in that, Winslow?"

(With a suspicious glance at the glass.) "Yes, Father." "Then I won't touch it." "Father, if you don't take it, I'll drink it myself." (A pause.) "Well, Winslow, rather than have you destroy the tissues of your stomach by drinking this alcoholic beverage, I'll drink it." And he downed it at a gulp, Winslow recalled with a smile.

As the old man passed his eighty-sixth birthday, he required a watchful eye more and more; he was too fragile to make the trip to Florida, so during the winter months Winslow ran down to Boston every couple of weeks to see him, but he never stayed long. "I find that living with Father for three days I grow to be so much like him I am frightened," he confessed in a letter to Mattie. "We get as much alike as two peas, in age and manners. He is very well, only he will starve himself. I shall go to Boston once in two weeks this next month to give him a dinner." Sometimes it was too cold to make the trip—12 below zero; he could not leave his water and provisions, and then he was uneasy about his father until he was able to dig out to get to Scarboro and send word.

The following year the little dog Sam, who had grown "fat as a prize white pig," died of old age; Winslow had had to slacken his pace during their daily walks to the postbox for some time because Sam was puffing so fearfully, trying to keep up with him. Yet the little dog's death was a blow—a real grief—to him and left an unbelievable void in his life. Not to have Sam accompanying him on hikes any more, or snoozing in front of the Franklin stove, or barking furiously at so much as a small field mouse was a far greater loss than he had ever imagined. He had not realized until Sam was gone that a man could have such a close companionship with a dog, and he refused to get another because he was afraid he would become just as attached to the new one. Even when prowlers broke into the studio during one of his trips to Boston, and Charlie suggested an English bull pup as a watchdog, Winslow wrote him: "On *no* account send me a dog. The only companion I want is a bobolink"—he drew a sketch of a bird "and the next time I go to Boston I shall get one. . . . As for robbers, I have no fear of them, sleeping or waking. I am a dead shot & should shoot, without asking any questions, if anyone was in my house, after 12 at night. I can do this (living alone) without chance of a mistake—you could not do this without shooting Mrs. Wilson or Mr. Welch or your wife, who might be hunting for a quiet place to sleep in. —I asked you a day or two ago if you were well—you did not reply to that—but this bulldog talk would suggest that you are all right." The prowlers had taken four pistols, two slingshots, and some old coins and other objects that he used to amuse himself with on long winter evenings; his paintings were stored in the room upstairs, but the burglars had not bothered to look for them—or if they had, he thought ironically, probably did not consider the pictures valuable enough to steal.

He did buy a pair of birds in one of the Boston shops the next time he visited his father. On these trips he spent a good part of the day hunting up props for his sea pictures in the junk shops along the water front. He had searched every one of them for an old ship's bell to use in a painting called "The Lookout—'All's Well!'" but he could not find the kind he had in mind. He finally bought some clay at the art store and modeled it himself—an ornate, old-fashioned ship's bell. This was to be another moonlight picture, and John Getshell, a Scarboro fisherman, posed for him in oilskins, as if he had just struck the hour and turned to sing out the traditional chant. Winslow had painted most of the picture on nights when the moon was bright enough. On another trip to Boston he went aboard a ship in the harbor one moonlit night, to make studies of the effect of moonlight on masts and rigging. Like "Eight Bells," "The Lookout" told the whole story of the sea and the men who spent their lives on it in simple terms of the lone seaman, the bell, the silvered mast, foam on the waves, the starry sky. He thought out the design of the picture very carefully, synchronizing it with the deep blues and soft grays of the palette he kept prepared for nights when the light was right.

Because it was a singular subject, he had sent it off to Doll & Richards with grave misgivings, priced at only $850. To his surprise "The Lookout" was hailed as a "great painting" by the most discerning of critics, Sadakichi Hartmann, and Clarke bought it soon afterward. His mind constantly filled with new ideas for paintings, Winslow was content with his life and his surroundings, except for those periods when he felt his work was not appreciated by the public, and this did not affect his feeling for Prout's Neck. In the winter his birds were cheerful company, and he wrote to Charlie, who still wanted him to get a watchdog: "My home here is *very pleasant, I do not wish a better place*, and what I wrote in my last about a dog was only that I did not wish to be bothered in providing a boarding-place for any more than *my birds*, leaving me *free* to go, and come."

For several summers, beginning in 1895, he had done numbers of water colors in Quebec, first at Lake Tourilli, where he and Charlie had a log cabin built as a base from which they would start off into the bush, led by four or five Indian guides, and carrying plenty of rum, whisky, and provisions. They would spend several weeks exploring the wilds—a network of lakes and streams noted for gleaming Tourilli trout, and traveled by canoe, with frequent portages—always returning to the log cabin on the Tourilli shore. Here Winslow kept a twelve-foot, flat-bottomed boat he had designed, built specially for fishing and painting. In 1895 he had done no less than twenty-six water colors there, and the following summers a dozen or more, including one of a leaping trout, which he presented to George vanFelsom, secretary of the Tourilli Hunting Club, with the inscription, "From Winslow Homer, Artist," as distinct from Homer, the angler.

At nearby St. Anne River he painted one of his strongest water colors—"The Portage"—in which he caught the strength and sure-footed gait of his favorite guide, Sam Picard, as he carried their canoe past the rapids. These pictures went farther than the Adirondack water colors in strong subject matter, combining the

Fisherman in the Adirondacks

The Cooper Union Museum

wild beauty of the scene with the skillful, energetic movements
of men who loved the elemental life of the north woods. As he
and Charlie pushed farther from Lake Tourilli, ending at Lake St.
John, where the landlocked salmon—ouananiche—lured many an
angler into battle, shooting the rapids and fighting the fury of the
rushing Saguenay River, if necessary, in order to catch him, the
pictures became full of action. Staying for a while at Roberval,
on the west shore, Winslow caught his share of ouananiche
(Charlie always said he used the least expensive tackle and
caught the biggest fish) and turned to painting his fellow anglers
playing the formidable salmon. At the magnificent Grande
Décharge, the point where the Saguenay issued from the lake
and swirled along for miles through gorge and crevice in rapids
so tricky that only the most skillful could navigate them, he
showed the Indian or French-Canadian woodsmen in their birch-
bark canoes, shooting the rapids or fishing in the seething pool
beneath the falls.

To get the correct motion, Winslow paid their guide ten dollars
to shoot the rapids while he stayed ashore to observe one morning. He left camp and posted himself at the best spot for viewing;
here he waited patiently, but no canoe came in sight. Worried,
he went back to camp, only to find the guide sitting calmly
against a tree, smoking a peace pipe.

"What happened? Why didn't you show up?" he demanded.

"Mr. Charles pay me ten dollars not to," the guide told him.

Winslow shook his head, smiling; Charlie was playing practical
jokes again! He would have to think up a good one to pay him
back.

Such dynamic water colors, concerned more with action than
mood, had never been painted before, and they met with small
success at first, but by 1897, when Winslow served on a jury at
Carnegie Institute, and Beatty invited him to have an exhibit of
his Canadian works there, he selected twenty-seven, which he
shipped with a letter in which he remarked confidently: "You
will find that the men of Pittsburgh will like these things and the

women will be curious to know what the men are liking and first thing you know you will have an audience." Later at a New York exhibit, and priced from $100 to $400, the Canadian works had sold quite well.

That fall—1897—he had completed the last oil in which a woman appeared—a strange angry picture of a sturdy fisher-woman, standing on the rocky beach, arms akimbo, staring at the observer aggressively, turning her back on a dark sea; sun, breaking through the clouds in one place, cast an eerie light over the threatening waves. He used odd, original tones—purple, violet, ochre, green with prevalent gray, which produced the peculiar weather effect. The woman's stance was awkward, muscular, more masculine than feminine. His last three oils of women exhibited physical strength but no feeling of sex. He had put sex down so far, for so long, that he experienced no awareness of sex in regard to women. The few that he saw (outside of Mattie and Alice) were sturdy farm or fisher women, and when he did go into 'polite society,' he paid no attention to the feminine side of it. If his paintings lacked warmth because of this, they made up for it in power and physical force. Passion emerged in pictures like "Cannon Rock" or "Northeaster" and was a unique expression of his life force.

The following summer his father, growing frailer and more cantankerous all the time, died at Prout's Neck, at the ripe old age of eighty-nine years and five months. Argumentative to the very end, he wanted communion but insisted that the Reverend admit it wasn't necessary for redemption. This the Reverend Graham could not do, although he thought a good deal of the old man, who had been a pillar of the church. Winslow, who had watched over his father as he had over his mother, and was by the bedside, marveled at the tenacity of the stubborn old man, arguing with his dying breath. . . .

After he was gone—in December—Winslow decided to take another trip to Nassau, as he had done fourteen years before, in the winter after his mother died. He had also wanted to return to the West Indies several times but changed the plans to suit his father's preference. Now there was nothing to stop him. He only hoped he would find the islands as he remembered them and that he could rediscover the treasured outlook that had so enriched his work.

CHAPTER XIII

West Indies Revisited

1898-1901

TO HIS DELIGHT, NOTHING IN NASSAU HAD CHANGED. A CERTAIN amount of tourist element had been introduced, but it was not enough to spoil the joyous primitive life of the natives, the long, narrow stretches of beach, and the brilliant tropical landscape, unhampered by hotels.

Once again he experienced a headiness, a deep sensuous pleasure in the startling colors, an immediate singing response to the pagan living—and above all, he felt a freedom that he had not known for fourteen years. And, as on his first visit, this liberation of spirit found its full expression in his water colors, which he began to paint soon after his arrival, working with the zest and raciness of the carefree black boys who were again his favorite subjects—the sponge divers, the lackadaisical fishermen, lolling on the decks of their white fishing sloops; the lively barterers of the market boats, laden with their cargo of fruit and fish, haggling over some exchange.

It was remarkable: he was in his sixties (bald, the lines deepening in his forehead), yet he gloried in painting these pictures of gladsome youth, unfettered by the bonds of civilized society, reveling in sun and sand and the tropical sea, the physical activity of outdoor living under warm southern skies. Somewhere in his staid New England ancestry, Winslow told himself, there must have been injected a barbaric strain that leaped up suddenly in him when he came face to face with the gorgeous color and uninhibited way of life on these sunny islands. He was out early every day, setting up his equipment and painting swiftly—rapid impressions of the pageantry before him.

His colors attained a brilliance that went beyond any in his previous Nassau works; those had been high in key, it was true, but, compared to these, they were not strong in color; now he let himself go, bringing out each tone to the full. During the fourteen years in between his technique had grown; he had taught himself how to achieve the maximum effect by using bold, simple combinations—a sweeping stroke of green above deep blue brought out the varied hues, the indigo splendor of the tropical sea. He put on color with new daring, building the whole picture chromatically, using a full range of tones from pure white down to the darkest. His handling was freer than ever, drawing with brush alone, swiftly, yet with absolute control. He worked with a kind of ecstasy, feeling the same surge of happiness as on his visit before. His touch was direct, forceful, the energetic stroke he applied to oils. Through him the heretofore frail medium of watercolor was at last emerging with the strength of oil painting and a much greater luminosity.

Here, he realized, was his true contribution to the world of art. His years of training as artist-reporter, working in black and white, came into full play in the medium of water color, enabling him to record swiftly, accurately, before his impressions of nature had grown stale, basing his use of color on tonal values. He felt completely at home in water color, working with a surety and ease he never attained in oil. He took full advantage of the transparency of the medium, allowing the white paper to show through wherever he chose, to achieve a luminosity far greater than in his oils. He was positive that no other American artist, including his old friend John LaFarge, for all his cultivated mind and intellectual knowledge of art, was reaching new frontiers in water color as advanced as those he, Winslow Homer, sought to establish. His belief in these works was so strong that he had not hesitated to make a prediction one day when he was in Knoedler's. (They had become his New York agent after Reichard retired altogether in 1897.) The gallery was arranging an exhibit of the series, and Winslow said to Charles R. Henschel, who was inclined to favor his oil paintings, "You will see, in the future I will live by my water colors."

He spent a month or more in Nassau and again headed south, this time stopping at several of the dots of land along the route. At Rum Cay some of his strongest water colors were inspired by the muscular boys whose livelihood was catching turtles for the market boats. He showed them in "The Turtle Pound," one looking over the top of the boarded enclosure, watching his partner grapple with an upturned terrapin as he was bringing it in. Another, in "Rum Cay," was chasing after a large loggerhead on the beach, the realistic movement of his sinewy dark body as rhythmic as a dancer. After a violent tropical storm the sight of one of these strong boys lying dead on the beach, his splintered sloop nearby at the spot where the storm had tossed them, evoked the telling, dramatic "After the Tornado."

The dismasted boat, the sharks in the storm-ridden waters, and a distant waterspout furnished material for studies Winslow intended to use in developing the theme he had begun over a decade ago.

He had the deep satisfaction of discovering all he had come back to find, and he made the most of it, working with the renewed vigor that the voyage and sojourn in Nassau had given him. Only a few months before he had written to Alden Weir, in answer to an invitation to join a group of ten prominent painters in exhibiting works "under their own direction": "You do not realize it, but I am too old for this work, and I have already decided to retire from business at the end of the season. . . . You see it would oblige me to work at this late date, when I wish to make the most of the few years I have left." Now he was painting with the energy and enthusiasm of a young artist. He had been worn out by the anxious weeks of watching over his father, but he was rejuvenated in body and spirit.

He left the West Indies for Florida around the middle of February and on the twenty-fifth, the day after his birthday, wrote to Clarke: "I have had a most successful winter in Nassau. Found what I wanted, and have many things to work up into two paintings that I have in mind. I shall not go north until it is warmer, but am through working for the winter, and desire to report myself *very well*." In the same letter he commented on the sale of the Clarke collection, which had taken place while he was gone. Though he had not benefited directly, his paintings had sold for the sixth, seventh, and eighth highest prices, an indication of the value Clarke—and the public—set on them; and the prestige of such a- sale was enormous. Right afterward Knoedler's had exhibited the Canadian water colors and sold fourteen out of the twenty-seven at prices of $200 to $250 each, including three to the Boston Museum.

"I have only just received news of the great success of your sale," he wrote now. "I owe it to you to express to you my sincere thanks for the great benefit that I have received from your encouragement of my work, and to congratulate you. . . . Only think of my being *alive* with a reputation (that you have made for me)."

The following December he had gone to Bermuda, where he rented a small bungalow beside the deep-blue sea, set off by the riotous color of a tropical flower garden—scarlet hibiscus, red and yellow cannas, small banana palms, with their plump, decorative fruit, bordered by plants of variegated foliage—and one of the first water colors he painted pictured the place where he stayed. He did a whole series of land and seascapes in the medium here, using the same free technique: washes were full, brush stroke

The Turtle Pound

In the Brooklyn Museum Collection

sweeping, colors brilliant, luminous, the white of the paper frequently showing. Here again the basis of the chromatic structure
was values. Once he said to his friend Beatty: "I have never
tried to do anything but get the true relationship of values—that
is, the values of dark and light, and the values of color." Human
figures did not appear in the Bermuda works, because he had not
found a type that interested him as much as the black boys of the
Bahamas. He found subject matter in a wide curve of beach,
lined with palms, a broad expanse of ocean beyond; the contrasting sunlight and deep shade of a limestone road, arched
trees overhead; the white sails of fishing boats against a tropical
sky.

The next winter he had returned to do more, until he had completed, with the Nassau works, more than forty water colors done
with the freedom and maturity of his new style. He prized both
series so highly that he did not want to expose them to exhibition
immediately. I have many water colors from two winters in the
West Indies," he wrote to O'Brien, the Chicago dealer, "and as
good work, with the exception of one or two etchings, as I ever
did." Some of them he hung in Marr cottage. Later he selected
twenty-one to send to the Pan-American Exposition just a year ago,
entitling the lot, "Scenes from the Bahamas and the Bermudas,"
setting a price of $4000 on the group as a whole, hoping to interest
a museum in the purchase. He felt that it would break the con-
tinuity of the series if the pictures were sold separately. They were
awarded a gold medal at the Exposition but found no buyer. He
had them returned and wrote Knoedler's: "That makes my winter's work of 1898 and 1899 *complete*. I shall leave them boxed as
they are until such time as I see fit to put them out. The price will
be $400 *each!!* for choice if I ever put them out again." He did not
know whether he should risk rejection or not. But only recently
he had picked out fourteen of the choicest (a significant number),
including "Rum Cay," "The Turtle Pound," and "Flower Garden
and Bungalow, Bermuda," and offered them to Knoedler's for
exhibition at half the price. In the daybook he kept on his

Flower Garden and Bungalow, Bermuda

The Metropolitan Museum of Art, Lazarus Fund, 1910

worktable he noted: "Murder comes now. To net me $200 each and all, good or bad, large or small."

He was angry, too, over the fate of the oil painting that had come out of his Nassau visit—"The Gulf Stream"—which he considered one of his finest, most powerful canvases, based on the water-color sketch of 1884 as well as on his recent studies. He had struggled for weeks in painting the deceptively beautiful sea to achieve the color harmonies he wanted, the startling emerald and sapphire depths of the Gulf Stream. Twice he had refused to show it at the Pennsylvania Academy, explaining that it was not ready; and he yielded only when Harrison Morris telegraphed, "The great American art exhibit cannot open without an example from the greatest American artist," but in sending it, Winslow warned, "Don't let the public poke its nose into my picture." And as soon as he got it back, he worked on it again. When he finally was satisfied, he gave it to Knoedler's, priced at $4000.

Its reception was mixed. Although most of the critics found "The Gulf Stream" a "great dramatic picture," and one of them commented that in it "Mr. Homer achieves complete color orchestration," all agreed that it was tragic to the point of being a horror picture, and a few ridiculed it as "a burlesque on a repulsive subject" and a "piece for a zoological garden." The Worcester Museum considered it for some months but finally turned it down because two women on the board found it "unpleasant." After that, Knoedler's wrote suggesting that he send them an explanation of the picture, which infuriated him. He had recently answered in scathing tones: "You ask me for a full description of my picture of the 'Gulf Stream.' I regret very much that I have painted a picture that requires any description. The subject of this picture is in *its title* and I will refer these inquisitive school ma'ams to Lieutenant Maury. I have crossed the Gulf Stream *ten* times, and I should know something about it. The boat and sharks are outside matters of very little consequence. *They have been blown out to sea by a hurricane.* You can tell these ladies that the unfortunate negro who is now so dazed and parboiled, will be rescued and returned to his friends and home, and ever after live happily."

Just thinking about it made him hot; he tugged at his mustache fiercely. For one who was supposed to be the "greatest American artist," he was certainly far from being understood by the American public!

CHAPTER XIV

Painter of the Sea

1902-1910

THE PAST TWO YEARS HAD BROUGHT HONORS AS WELL AS AGGRAVA-
tion. In 1900 he sent "A Summer Night" (along with "The Fox
Hunt," "The Coast of Maine," and "The Lookout") to the International Exposition in Paris; it was then that the canvas was
bought by the French government for the Luxembourg Gallery,
and he was awarded a gold medal for his work in the exposition.
He was getting used to receiving gold medals now; several of
them he left lying around on the worktable among the tubes of
paint. The Temple Gold Medal, which he had recently received
from the Pennsylvania Academy for "A Northeaster," he had
fished out of his pants pocket the last time he was at Doll &
Richards; he was looking for change to pay for a stamp, and it was
in with a buttonhook, his house key, a few coppers, and other
coins. The Paris medal, however, had a particular meaning for
him: it represented in a way the completion of his artistic cycle
and was the realization of the long-cherished ambition born in
1867, when he had so narrowly missed winning an award at the
onset of his career. Although he had been outwardly philosoph-
ical, he was deeply disappointed. He had not submitted work
abroad again until he had won a solid reputation at home and

was relatively sure of his ground as a painter.

He was a name now, one of twenty noted artists who served on the national jury on paintings for the American section of the exposition. He was frequently invited to judge important exhibitions, and when he accepted, he stuck strictly to the business of examining the pictures, made few comments, and did very little socializing with his fellow judges, even with old friends like John LaFarge and J. Alden Weir, who happened to be on this panel. When the international jury announced its awards, the honor he received was made doubly significant by the rejoicing among his fellow judges; as always, he was moved, and rather surprised, when his contemporaries showed pleasure at his good fortune. He carried the medal around in the outside breast pocket of his cutaway, a talisman he could touch with pride when fits of despondency took hold of him.

That fall he was spurred on to a new level of creativity as a painter of the sea. In October he completed "On a Lee Shore," an oil he had begun on a foggy day, with a heavy surf raising a commotion and turmoil on the rocks beyond any that he had observed under such weather conditions; the fierce poetry of it, and the brave fight made by a little schooner trying to keep away from the dangerous coast, inspired the picture. Finishing it within a few days, he wrote to O'Brien in high spirits on October 19, "I have a *very excellent painting*, 'On a Lee Shore.'" He drew a sketch of it, "39 x 39. The price is (with the frame) $2,000 net. I will send it to you if you desire to see it. *Good things are scarce*. The frame is not ordered yet, but I can send it by the time McKinley is elected." (The betting was so strong on McKinley, he thought of ordering two frames!) O'Brien sold the picture almost immediately to Dr. Frank Gunsaulus of Chicago for $2,850.

Shortly after news of the sale came, a tremendous northeaster hit the coast, and Winslow had the portable painting booth dragged onto the farthermost ledges of rock at Eastern Point, painting at a spot where he could not have stood up against the

gale lashing away outside. From the viewing window he saw two
great fountains of wind-driven spray as the thundering surf broke
over the ledge; he painted fast to get this effect of the wind's force
—the cold, green waves, the rocks, the sand. The hand holding
the palette was tense with excitement, but the one holding the
brush was flexible as a reed, moving swiftly with his square touch
to achieve a harmony of earthy browns, rust-red, and white. He
daubed on paint with a joyous fury matching the northeaster
outside; the precision of his brushwork had never been sharper.

Directly this canvas was completed, he had the portable moved
to West Point, for a contrasting subject—the crimson afterglow of
an autumn sunset on sky and water; he had to come here many
times to get the exact color effect he wanted. On November 13
he announced in a letter to Knoedler's: "I have got *two wonderful paintings!*—30 x 48—"Eastern Point" and "West Point, Prout's
Neck." In explaining the second, he wrote, "The picture is
painted *15 minutes after sunset*—not one minute before—as up
to that minute the clouds over the sun would have their edges
lighted with a brilliant glow of color, but now (in this picture)
the sun has got beyond their immediate range and *they are in
shadow.*" He drew a sketch, showing the globe of the earth, the
sun sinking behind it, and dark clouds floating above it. "The
light is from the sky in this picture. You can see it took many
days of careful observation to get this (with a high sea, and tide
just right)." When the work was sold for $3000 to Hugh H.
Harrison, he sent a stern warning: "I *forbid* any *glass* or 'robbery-
box' put onto the picture." He often complained when he served
on a jury that all he could see was his own bald head reflected
in the glass, and he was not going to have "West Point" suffer
such a fate.

The critics did not share his enthusiasm for the pictures he had
called "wonderful"; while opinion was generally favorable, it was
not highly laudatory, but he paid little heed, as long as it was not
devastating. He painted the sea from the topmost point, "High
Cliff"; and he had started the picture he had just now completed

—"Early Morning After a Storm at Sea," as he was going to call it —using the water-color study he had made in 1883. Then it turned so cold he decided to go south for the winter again (Bermuda first, later Florida if he could afford it), and just before leaving, he had written O'Brien, who had asked him for a painting, ". . . the picture that you refer to I promise to send to you when finished. I will look upon it in future as your particular picture.

"I do not think I can finish it before I have a crack at it out of doors in the spring. I do not like to rely on my study that I have used up to date. . . . I will notify you when I leave here."

In the next twelve months, because the light he was seeking did not appear, he worked on the canvas only once, but he was still hoping to finish it. He had sent "The Gulf Stream" to the international exhibition at Venice, and he notified O'Brien, "It is about time that I received my picture the 'Gulf Stream' back from Venice, and the beautiful frame on it will go on the O'B. Partic' picture directly I can get hold of it and finish the picture." (Until recently he always thought of it as the "O'Brien" and referred to it as such in all "business" letters.)

That week he had put it aside and started "Searchlight: Harbor Entrance, Santiago de Cuba" because he had had a sudden inspiration to make use of the studies of Morro Castle in the moonlight—a composition of cold, dark blues and slate grays, the fortress illuminated by the strong glare of the searchlight from United States picket ships in contrast to the soft glow of the moon. He knew exactly what he wanted to do and finished the canvas by January 5, working with such concentration that he did not even go to Charlie's for Christmas. He felt he had been successful in both composition and color harmonies, which were severe— striking—in keeping with the subject. He wrote Knoedler's to whom he was sending the picture, that it was *not intended to be beautiful. From this point were seen the stirring events of 1898 and 1899. I find it interesting.*"

He had stayed on at Prout's, hoping each day to find the light he sought for the "O'B." picture, though it had been the very devil of a winter, snow piled in such drifts and temperatures so low that he couldn't even go down to the painting shanty on the morning of his birthday, when he wakened to see just the effect he had been waiting for! Two weeks later, March 15, he wrote to O'Brien, "I have ordered M. Knoedler & Co. to send you the two oil paintings, 'The Gulf Stream' and 'High Cliff,'—the one just home from Venice, the other from Pittsburgh. You appear to expect three pictures. These two are the only ones. I mentioned that the frame on the large picture would fit the 'O'Brien'—but the O'B. is not finished. It will please you to know that, after waiting a full year, looking out every day for it (when I have been here), on the 24th of February, my birthday, I got the light and the sea that I wanted; but as it was very cold I had to paint out of my window, and I was a little too far away—and although making a beautiful thing"—here he inserted a rough sketch of a trumpet, marking it "own trumpet"—"it is not good enough yet, and I must have another painting from nature on it."

During the rest of the spring, and all during the summer, and through the autumn weeks, he watched and waited, looking for the light that had come today. Now the painting was complete; as it had taken shape, he had the feeling that this seascape was of deep significance, "the last thing of importance that I shall paint," he had written at one point. He was sixty-six years old, pushing sixty-seven, he amended; the way insurance companies figured, he already was a year older. How much more could he paint? he wondered. He was certain he could not do better. . . .

His pipe had long since gone out; he stuck it in his jacket pocket and stretched his arms and legs, cramped from sitting. Realizing that he was hungry all of a sudden, he got up and went into the studio. Replenishing the fire, he heated some clam chowder he had cooked the day before and drank the last pint of South Side Scarboro cider he had on hand. When he shipped the painting, he would buy some more, along with other provisions. After he had eaten, he made a place among the tubes of paint on his worktable for a sheet of paper and sat down to write his letter. Because he felt so deeply about this particular work, he took extra care to be matter-of-fact, businesslike: "October 29, 1902. M. O'Brien & Son,

"Gentlemen—When you receive the two paintings from Des Moines" (he was referring to "High Cliffs" and "The Gulf Stream," still unsold, and loaned for exhibition) "please let me know, as I wish to place them in some other locality in order that I may make room for 'the O'Brien picture.' This one will be quite enough to show, and the people who are in the clean-up of October corn may be able to buy it, but not others, as the price will be too high. This is the only picture that I have been interested in for the past year, and as I have kept you informed about it, and promised it to you to manage, I will now say that the long-looked-for day arrived, and from 6 to 8 o'clock A.M. I painted from nature on this 'O'B.,' finishing it—making the fourth painting on this canvas of two hours each.

"This is the best picture of the sea that I have painted.

"The price that you will charge is five thousand dollars—$5,000. The price net to me will be $4000.

"This may be the last as well as the best picture.

"I have rents enough to keep me out of the poorhouse.

"Now all you have to do in reply to this is to notify me when you get the two pictures back from Des Moines, and I will tell you what to do with them, and send the 'O'B.' picture." He signed his name and took another sheet of paper; he would announce the painting—and the terms—to Knoedler's, explaining that he had arranged to let O'Brien handle it, so it must go there first, but if not sold promptly, the picture would be shipped to the New York gallery.

It was two weeks before he had received the frame from "The Gulf Stream," put it on the "OB.," studied the painting from the rocks below the balcony to see if "the least thing was out," but could find nothing to correct or change, and finally wrote to

O'Brien, "The O'B. leaves here by the American Express at 3 P.M. If it is damp when you receive it, and the canvas wobbles, *do not* key it up, as the keys are glued to the stretcher and everything is in perfect order. Just put it in a warm room. There was a sleet storm yesterday, but beautiful today, so I start O'B., and glad to get it out of my sight before I finish it too highly and spoil it. I hope the original member of your firm is still alive, after all these tedious years of waiting, and that he will be on hand to greet the O'B." He was quite sure the firm would understand why it had taken so long, as soon as they saw what an extraordinary seascape "Early Morning" was. . . .

To his dismay, the Chicago gallery could not arrange to show the painting for some time, so he had it sent to Knoedler's. They wrote that there was not much interest in the subject matter, it was too obscure. Aggravated, he told them to send it to him for a few days; he wished to "paint on it about two hours." He would fix it up with a little white; he hung it on the balcony again and studied the composition a long time before deciding not to add the touches of white, but he worked on color to heighten the key and sent it back. When the newly formed Society of American Artists invited him to show in the 1903 exhibit right after the first of the year, he decided to send "Early Morning."

He waited eagerly for reviews, but when they came he wished that he had not read them: the work he had taken two years to paint, the one he considered his 'best picture of the sea so far,' was either passed over lightly (in some instances ignored) or damned by the critics. One or two hinted that he was too old, had passed the peak of his ability and now was on the downward slope. Jeering remarks about the 'pink chalk sea' and 'waves topped by bunches of wool' left him sickened, stunned to the quick. He felt as if he never wanted to paint again. On a piece of academy board in his studio was an unfinished water color of a five-masted schooner that had been wrecked on Stratton Island during a fog; he had seen her masts rising from the bank and notified the Coast Guard at Portland by telegram; then he got

Henry Lee to row him out to the scene of the wreck. He had not quite finished painting it when the tugs arrived and the crew was rescued. Winslow had brought back the bitts as a memento and put them in the yard; he could have completed the water color now, but he had no desire to pick up a brush. He spent hours staring at the sea, not observing it.

At times like this it was a comfort to look at the face of the girl in the portrait on the easel. Here was someone he loved, forever young, challenging; if they had married, she would no longer look so fresh and firm—and she would see him, growing old and wrinkled. When he came into the studio after an aimless walk along the coast line (aimless because the wellsprings of his art had gone dry) the girl's pert expression cheered him; and at night when he grew tired of the pastimes he had invented with old coins and a homemade slingshot, he would gaze at the picture on the easel and feel rested. Yet the bitterness continued; he went to Florida for a month or so to fish for red snapper, but he did not even take his water colors along.

He did practically no painting for a whole year, and when Beatty wrote, asking for a canvas for the Carnegie exhibit, he answered, "I have retired from business for good, as the last picture I painted only met with abuse, and no one understood it. I will not offer it for the next show." His friend, alarmed at his attitude, suggested visiting him at Prout's Neck in September, and Winslow was delighted, but he repeated, "I have given up the business; I have quit painting. We will do nothing but fish and have a good time."

The morning that John arrived was much like the one on which Winslow had painted the ill-fated "O'B."—still and luminous after a storm. He met his friend at the Scarboro station with an ancient horse and buggy, borrowed from the Seavey's; as they drove to the Neck, he commented on the beauty of the weather. "A painter's gray day," John said, and Winslow nodded.

"Now that I have quit painting, the term has lost its meaning," he added mournfully.

To his friend it was almost as if he had said of a mistress, "Now that she is gone." He knew full well that Winslow Homer's first and strongest love was painting. "Have you given it up for good?" he asked.

Winslow flicked the horse lightly, busy with driving, but he said after a moment, "Yes, I only painted for pleasure, and now that it has ceased to give me pleasure, there is no object left. I get lots more pleasure out of other things now; I would rather go fishing." When John gave him a look of unbelief, he added, "Oh, I suppose if there was the hope of a great financial gain, that would be an incentive." Then he shut up like a clam and was silent all the way to the Checkley House, where John had no trouble getting a room, as most of the summer visitors had gone. Charles and Mattie had come later this year and were still at the big house; John and Winslow would have dinners with them.

The first night, however, Winslow had arranged a clambake in honor of his guest. The men were all his closest friends at Prout's, John Getshell, Henry Lee, Seavey, all fishermen or farmers. The lobsters, clams, and sweet corn, steamed on a huge pile of heated boulders and consumed with the nut-brown ale Winslow brought down from the studio, made for a delicious feast and a jolly party; but there was no discussion of art with these men, nor did Winslow seem to want any.

The next day they went fishing for tautog in a power boat on the sea, had dinner at Charlie's, and spent the early evening there, so there was not much chance for conversation on art until Winslow asked his friend if he wanted to go over to the studio for a "nightcap"—a mug of ale and a mild cigar. Even then he avoided talking about his work, although he usually "opened up" with John Beatty. But he had 'quit the business' and he did not want to discuss painting. He talked at some length about the etchings and got out some old proofs of "Eight Bells" that had been rolled up in the closet for years. They wouldn't stay open, so he picked up four "weights" from among the tubes and brushes to hold them down flat. Beatty was astonished to see that the weights were four gold medals. Here was a painter who had won many honors in the six years since Carnegie Institute had bought "The Wreck," whose world-wide reputation was at its height, who was by no means poor (at Prout's the Homers were considered "rich"), and yet he was so bitter about being misunderstood that he was determined to give up painting for good—it was unaccountable. Perhaps this was only a passing phase; Winslow had been known to make such claims before.

In the morning they went on the "daily walk" along the rugged shore, Winslow in the lead, agile, sure-footed. Unconsciously he began to speak of paintings he had done, pointing out the sites of "Northeaster," "On a Lee Shore," "Maine Coast," and "Cannon Rock," mentioning the problems he had had in getting the light he needed for a certain effect. Beatty knew better than to bring up the subject of "Early Morning" just yet. He asked, "Do you ever take the liberty, in painting nature, of modifying the color of any part?"

Winslow looked startled, pausing with one foot on a higher ledge of rock. "Never! Never!" He clenched his fist and brought it down hard. "When I have selected the thing carefully, I paint it exactly as it appears." He hesitated and added, "Of course you must not paint everything you see. . . . You must wait, and wait patiently, until the exceptional, the wonderful effect, or aspect comes. Then, if you have sense enough to see it—well, that's all there is to that." He took the step up the ledge, and Beatty followed, smiling.

He pursued the subject as they continued the walk. "Do you never paint away from the scene?" he asked.

"Never!" Winslow repeated. All of the important pictures were painted direct from nature, by moonlight or in the open light of day. He added, "Of course, I go over them in the studio and put them in shape." He was prodded into talking about his work: he never underpainted with rich color as so many painters did; part of his direct approach was to start right off with the colors he wanted. Sometimes he painted over a picture, if he felt it was not successful; "The Wreck," he confessed, had been done on an old canvas. "If you ever see a three-masted schooner coming through the sky, please let me know and I will fix it," he offered, and they both smiled. He was beginning to come back to life.

In the days that followed he spoke of various problems. "It is wonderful how much depends on the relationship of black and white," he said. "Why, do you know, a black and white, if properly balanced, suggests color. The construction, the balance of the parts, is everything. When I paint one of my simple sea-scapes, the question is the truth of the values." He felt his enthusiasm return, just talking over a few ideas with a friend who understood the language. He even discussed means to make "Early Morning" comprehensible to people. "Simple white would do it!" he said.

Toward the end of the visit a storm hit the coast, gale winds driving the rain, the sound of the surf rising to an ominous pitch. This was the sort of weather Winslow loved. Putting on his oil-skins, he took a storm coat and a pair of sailor's boots for Beatty and hurried over to the Checkley House, passed the few guests huddled around the wood fire, and burst into his friend's room.

"Come!" he cried, holding out the things. "Quickly! It is perfectly grand!" His placid reserve, his apathy, was forgotten; he was in a fever of excitement. They went out into the storm and clambered over the rocks, holding fast to the wiry shrubs that grew out of every crevice, or braced themselves as best they could against the driving wind, while the spray dashed far over-head. Suddenly seized with an idea, he shouted above the roar, "We will go to my painting house." With that he rushed to the studio and searched for an extra palette and colors Beatty could use to join him in painting. They would pace the coast until the rain let up, and then they would paint the magnificent scene.

With the storm his dry spell of the past twelve months was broken at last. After his friend left, Winslow, stimulated by their talks, began two new paintings, announcing the fact gleefully in a letter to Charlie. He had promised to send "Early Morning" to

Carnegie for exhibit after all, had "lightened the scale of color to bring it within the range of the public," and he had the feeling that it would some day be redeemed, taking its rightful place among the best of his seascapes.

He painted now only when he felt like it, and every condition must be favorable, or he did not and would not work. He discovered a new setting for water colors in Florida at Homosassa, on the Gulf of Mexico, at the mouth of the Homosassa River, and now that he was in the mood again, his handling was broader than it had ever been, his washes of the greatest transparency. He pictured the anglers, fishing for speckled trout in the cold dawn, for bass in the late afternoon; at a spot where some big cabbage palms leaned over the river, he sketched an early-morning scene of a lone angler, huddled under the bank in a skiff, the mist rising to reveal a crystal-clear sky against which the palms were silhouetted; yet when the sun got too bright he stopped, refusing to finish until every condition was favorable for the effect he wanted to achieve. His latest water colors were almost improvisations of scenes, crisp and condensed; with them he found renewed pleasure in painting, and he knew in his heart that no matter how many times he might declare that he had 'quit the business,' he would never stop painting as long as his eye and his hand were steady, as long as his mind was able to bring forth fresh ideas.

He would not rush his work in any medium but would paint only as the spirit moved him. If he did two or three oils a year, that was plenty. On a night when a full moon was rising over a running sea, before the sun had quite gone down, he persuaded three of his cronies to pose for him in a dory; they were turning to admire the phenomenon as the crest of a wave in the background appeared to be "kissing the moon," and their faces, in the ruddy light of the setting sun, revealed a moment of awesome respect for nature's remarkable illusion. Just as "Early Morning" represented peacefulness after great stress, so this picture seemed to epitomize the calm, the evening of his life.

He could easily have been lionized by the ladies of Prout's

Neck, but he withdrew completely during the season now and more than once was taken for an old salt, going around in his fishing clothes—a pair of rubber sea boots and a sou'wester or battered old felt hat. He was coming up from the shore one day, carrying his fishing rod, when he saw someone wandering about the cliffs. It was a middle-aged 'city man,' who approached him as soon as he reached the top.

"I say, my man, if you can tell me where I can find Winslow Homer, I have a quarter here for you," he offered patronizingly.

"Where's your quarter?" The question came out instantly.

The man handed it over, his jaw dropping as he heard: "I am Winslow Homer." He had the grace to laugh, however, and explained that he was a collector who had come all the way from New York to meet the painter.

Having pocketed the quarter, Winslow, in one of his rare sociable moods, took the gentleman up to the studio, got out some small glasses and his best stock, and ended by selling his caller a picture.

The National Academy invited him to show in the spring exhibition for 1906, and he decided to send "The Gulf Stream," still unsold after seven years. He had written to Alden Weir that he had "been kept from the Academy's exhibitions by the fear of the corridor and the impropriety of my trying to make terms as to placement of my work," but now he hoped it was not necessary for him to try to "make terms" for a prominent placement of his work.

Shortly after the exhibition opened, he received the incredible news that "The Gulf Stream" was to be purchased by the Metropolitan Museum. After seven long years the sale was made in two days. One of his friends on the panel sent him the details: When the painting came before the jury, a murmur of admiration went up, and somebody said, "Boys, that ought to go to the Metropolitan!" A letter addressed to the director of the museum was drawn up a once, signed by all the members of the jury, sug-

Kissing the Moon

Addison Gallery of American Art, Phillips Academy, Andover

gesting that the museum purchase the picture. A messenger
delivered the letter, and the following day Mr. Roger Fry, repre-
sentative of the director (Sir Caspar Purdon Clarke), came to
the gallery and inspected the picture. Two days later the museum
sent word that it would purchase "The Gulf Stream."

The news was gratifying, to say the least; not often did an
entire jury recommend a painting to a prominent museum with
immediate success. Winslow knew he had every reason to rejoice,
and momentarily he did. Yet the fear that he might not be able
to maintain the high level of production overtook him whenever
he completed a painting, and he had fits of despondency for no
apparent reason. There were times when he did not feel well; a
pain gnawed at his stomach, but he paid no attention, and his
discomfort usually passed in a day or so.

Then, in the summer of 1908, he wakened one morning with an
alarming giddiness; he could not see well; he was a long time in
dressing; his hands were so shaky he could not manage the knot
in his tie, a simple act that was almost a reflex after so many
years. When he finally got his clothes on, he walked slowly over
to Arthur's cottage. "I don't know what's the matter with me,"
he said. "I have been two hours getting dressed and getting over
here."

His brother and sister-in-law were concerned. Alice fixed a cup
of tea for him, but when he reached for it he missed the handle
by inches—it was frightening. Arthur persuaded him to stay with
them for a while; Winslow was too shaken by the attack to do
anything but consent. He remained for two weeks, resting,
allowing himself to be waited on—a thing he would never have
thought possible. During the summers his father's old handy
man, Lewis, still came over to the studio every day to do the
chores; but when the season closed there was no one around, and,
until he went south in December, Winslow did everything for
himself, as he had always done. His general health had been
declining for some time, but he was not prepared for this strange
attack, affecting his eyesight—the vision that had been so keen—

and his hands, always so strong and controlled. Now he could hardly write his name.

He determined to get well, to overcome his difficulties; he would paint as long as he retained at least a portion of his faculties. He made his decision on a morning when he wakened very early. When Arthur came into his bedroom to see how he was feeling, the bed was empty. On the desk in the living room was a note: "I am well and have quit. Winslow." It was forty-eight hours before the family saw him again: he had gone to the studio and begun to paint.

He wanted to test his hand, to see whether he could produce a steady brush stroke, and found that he had not lost his control. He could even joke in a letter to Charlie: "I can paint as well as ever. I think my pictures better for having one eye in the pot & one in the chimney. A new departure in the art world." Little by little his hands stopped shaking altogether; he could write again; he could go fishing, but he still couldn't make the "sailor's" knot in his tie; it was puzzling. He wavered back and forth between the urge to keep on painting and the self-imposed decree to give it up out of fear of not being able to maintain the level of his peak; but the urge won out.

He created a "most surprising picture" from a brace of wild ducks he had bought for his Thanksgiving dinner. Their plumage was so handsome he was tempted to make a painting of them— an unusual one, showing them as they were shot down over the water with a double-barreled shotgun. He went out day after day in a boat with a hunter, studying the positions and movements of ducks when they were shot. He called the canvas "Right and Left!" the sportsman's cry when a fowl was brought down with each barrel in quick succession. The painting was a striking subject, rich in style, without a trace of weakened faculties, and Knoedler's sold it almost immediately to a private collector.

He was thankful that his illness had not permanently affected his keenness of vision, his firm hand. He was apparently normal,

except that he had intestinal pain, and, although he never mentioned it, he showed signs of suffering. He was beginning to look
aged, with deep lines down from his lips and many fine wrinkles
around his eyes. When he worked, it was with a kind of desperate
concentration. "I have little time for anything," he wrote to
Arthur, "many letters unanswered and work unfinished. I am
painting. I am just through work at 3:30. *Cannot give you any
more time.*"

The canvas he referred to was small in scale, but it contained
all the power of his previous seascapes. "Driftwood," he called it;
a rotting log was floating toward the shore at sundown, a man in
oilskins wading into the foamy surf with a rope to secure it. He
had a strange premonition about this painting; he wielded the
brush as if this was the last chance he would have.

The internal pain he suffered grew worse, but he endured it
silently. By the summer of 1910 he was a sick man once more,
and he knew it, but he went around his daily business at Prout's,
refusing to give in. When Charlie or the others tried to do anything for him, he insisted that he was "all right." He still looked
after the ills of his property himself, making regular calls to see
if anything needed attention. "Girt with a leather belt, in which
he carried a formidable pruning blade," he was well prepared in
case he noticed shrubbery that was affected by plant lice or other
insects and would cut out the diseased branches just as he had
always done. He and Charlie had turned over the bathhouses to
the Prout's Neck Association a few years before, not long after
they were paid for; the brothers had intended leaving the buildings to the association anyhow and saw no reason why the resort
should not have the benefit of the gift during their lifetime.

As late as August he had made no plans to go to the Adirondacks, and he noticed that Charlie did not even suggest the trip
this year. Charlie's tact and consideration were a source of great
solace to him in this nagging illness. He often thought that his
remarkable brother had never received the recognition he deserved; and one night when Charlie had taken the whole family to

The Artist (right) Outside His Studio

the Checkley House for dinner, Winslow said to some ladies who rushed up to him, full of flattery, "You must remember that my brother here is quite as distinguished in his line of work as I am in mine."

He wished others would show the same thoughtfulness that Charlie did. William Downes, who was eager to write a biography of the "greatest American painter," persisted in his requests for data, and Winslow wrote to him defiantly: "No doubt, as you say, a man is known by his works. That I have heard at many a funeral. And no doubt in your thoughts it occurred to you in thinking of me. Others are thinking the same thing. One is the Mutual Life Insurance Company, in which I have an annuity. But I will beat you both. I have all your letters, and will answer all your questions in time, *if you live long enough.*" Bold talk, but it made him feel stronger.

The pain grew sharper and too prolonged to toss off as "indigestion." Early in September, Winslow made a trip to Scarboro to see Dr. Wentworth, the family physician. There was not much the doctor could do for his condition except order him to go to bed and rest; he had been straining himself way beyond his strength. He was glad, at least, that he would be in his own "bed"; when he was away, he always complained that he was "obliged to sleep on the edge of the bedframe in order to get a nap, as all hotel beds are too soft and stale." His brothers said one or the other would come over every morning to see how he was—and make sure he didn't get up and start doing things.

Two mornings later he wakened in terrible pain and suffered a severe hemorrhage. Arthur came over in the middle of it, sent for Dr. Wentworth, stopped to summon Charlie, and came back to do what he could till the doctor arrived. Then it was all confusion; the studio seemed to fade away; he was weak, exhausted from loss of blood. The doctor was examining him. He heard "ruptured blood vessel in the stomach," but the words had no meaning. The bleeding stopped; white-aproned nurses came and moved around the studio; his brothers were talking, discussing some plan. . . .

"What are you going to do?" he asked.

Charlie explained that they thought he would be more comfortable and better cared for in the big house, or at Arthur's, in the same room he occupied during his first illness.

Winslow stopped him, his face set, his voice determined. "I will stay in my own house." He stayed. Another hemorrhage came, and after it was over, he could not see, he could not think. He was delirious for three days, helpless. He knew the nurses were taking care of him, but he was too far away to object to their handling him; the surf thundered on the rocks below, but he hardly heard it. He felt, however, as if he were being submerged by a tremendous wave—he called out his girl's name, his mother's, his brother's; he issued orders for framing the "O'B.," saw it in his mind's eye splattered with dirt and slashed with paper knives. He was on the high seas during a storm, and a voice called to him from the sky. . . .

Then suddenly his mind cleared, and he heard Charlie calling his name. He turned his head in the direction of his brother's voice, but all he could see was a vague outline of Charlie's figure. His eyesight was almost gone, but he knew he was still in his studio and he was glad.

By slow degrees he gathered strength again, until he began to believe he was going to recover. He started planning for the winter: he and Charlie would go to Florida; Charlie would enjoy the bass fishing at Homosassa. He joked with his brothers about old times. He looked forward to the day his eyesight was restored; he would paint again. No more nonsense about quitting the business. On September 17 his nephew Arthur stopped in to see him and he was sitting up. "How soon will I be allowed to have a drink and a smoke?" he asked abruptly.

Arthur, elated, reported that Uncle Winslow was convalescent, well on the way to recovery. The improvement continued for a fortnight. He was able to move around a little, and there was talk of taking him up to West Townsend; Mattie thought the dry air of the hills would be good for him.

Suddenly an alarming change occurred; his heart grew very weak, he could not catch his breath. The nurse on duty ran for his family; they were all around him. The doctor came, but could not save him; his heart had collapsed. Within a few hours, he was dead. The day was September 29, 1910.

It was as if he had gone to sleep. On one easel stood an unfinished painting of the Saguenay Rapids, chalk marks showing changes he intended to make; on the other was the portrait of the girl holding the cards of fortune in her hand. Charlie, moving his brother gently, found the gold medal from the Paris Exposition in the pocket of his nightshirt.

Photographic Credits

The photographs in this book are reproduced through the courtesy of those listed below:

Andover Art Studio 193, 287
Babcock Galleries 153
E. Irving Blomstrann 91
Brooklyn Museum 171, 173, 217, 269
Cincinnati Art Museum 157
Cleveland Museum of Art 3
Colby College 143
Cooper Union Museum 55, 65, 66, 71, 73, 75, 83, 85, 131, 185, 261
Frick Art Reference Library 77, 197
Metropolitan Museum of Art 113, 177, 221, 253, 271
Museum of Fine Arts, Boston 245
Museum of Fine Arts, Springfield 145
National Gallery of Art 121, 167
New York Public Library 7, 21, 45, 291
Prints Division, New York Public Library 69, 99, 233
Philadelphia Museum of Art 105
Phillips Studio 249
Toledo Museum of Art 187
Whitney Museum of American Art 115, 147
Wildenstein & Co., Inc. 159

INDEX

INDEX

The *italic numbers* refer to the pages where the illustrations appear.